THE FINAL ACT

THE FINAL ACT

THE DRAMATIC, REVEALING STORY OF THE MOSCOW HELSINKI WATCH GROUP

PAUL GOLDBERG

WILLIAM MORROW AND COMPANY, INC., NEW YORK

Grateful acknowledgment is made for permission to reprint from the following:
"Meatless Thursday in Moscow Cafe" used by permission of UPI. All rights reserved.
"Soviet Dissidents and the American Press" by Peter Osnos. Copyright © by *Columbia Journalism Review*. Used by permission. All rights reserved.
Quotations of Robert Toth used by permission of the *Los Angeles Times*.
Quotations from The Associated Press, used by permission.
Quotations from United Press International, used by permission.

Library of Congress Cataloging-in-Publication Data

Goldberg, Paul.
    The Final Act : the dramatic, revealing story of the Moscow
Helsinki Watch Group/Paul Goldberg.
        p.   cm.
    Bibliography: p.
    Includes index.
    ISBN 0-688-06859-6
    1. Obshchestvennaia gruppa sodeĭstviia vypolneniiu Khel sinkskikh soglasheniĭ v SSSR.   2. Human rights—Soviet Union—Societies, etc.   3. Human rights workers—Soviet Union.   4. Dissenters—Soviet Union.
I. Title.
JC599.S58G65   1988
323.4′06′047312—dc 19   87-38334
                                                                          CIP

Printed in the United States of America

First Edition

1 2 3 4 5 6 7 8 9 10

BOOK DESIGN BY JAYE ZIMET

TO THE MEMORY OF MOYSHA RABINOVICH,
MY FRIEND AND GRANDFATHER

CONTENTS

THE FINAL ACT

INTRODUCTION

When I began work on this book, I wanted to trace the curious historical forces that made a tiny group of Moscow dissidents into international celebrities.

They started out with no following, no ideology, no allies in the government, no political platform. Today, their names are getting the recognition usually reserved for world leaders: Yuri Orlov, Anatoly Shcharansky, Yelena Bonner, Aleksandr Ginzburg, Anatoly Marchenko, Vitaly Rubin, Petr Grigorenko.

From the start, I was determined to avoid writing a saga of heroism behind the Iron Curtain or a dry tract that would be of interest only to Russian scholars. Instead, I wanted to understand why these people risked their lives by openly challenging the state. I was interested in the eleven people who made up the Public Group of Assistance to Implementation of the Helsinki Agreements in the USSR. I wanted to explore their backgrounds, their thinking, and the way they dealt with each other. In short, I wanted my heroes to come to life.

I approached this project without political motivation. Though I was born in the USSR, I was fourteen when my parents emigrated, and I cannot think of any scores I would like to settle with the old country. By the same token, I am not an apologist for Soviet dissidents. Since it did not matter to me what the reader would think of my book's heroes, I had the luxury of posing my questions, then spending over two years searching for answers.

It was Ludmilla Alexeyeva, one of the group's founding members, who convinced me that a book about the group was worth doing. Alexeyeva allowed me access to her archives, gave well over a hundred hours of interviews, even acted as a "facilitator" in arranging interviews with reluctant sources. The materials, many of them never used by reporters or scholars, were abundant.

One of the highlights of doing this book was meeting Yuri Orlov. By the time of his expulsion to the West, I had spent about a year on the project.

When I started work in the summer of 1985, the Soviet human-rights movement was dead. Its leaders were in the camps, in internal exile, or in the West. Yet there were no signs that these people had had any impact on the Soviet system. If anything, it had become more oppressive as a result of their challenge.

Now that I have finished this project, the picture seems entirely different. Soviet leader Mikhail Gorbachev is releasing political prisoners, reevaluating the judicial system that had put them in jails, and, frequenty, making speeches that would not have been out of place at the dissident gatherings of a decade ago. All this is being done in the name of *glasnost,* "openness," a dissident slogan. Recently I asked Orlov what it all means, and whether he could have accomplished more by working through the system, as Gorbachev had. "Where do you think Gorbachev got his idea to release political prisoners?" Orlov asked. "Was he born with it? No."

Orlov did a great deal to keep those ideas alive.

On February 10, 1977, when he was whisked away to the KGB's Lefortovo prison, Soviet dissent was at its pinnacle. The group Orlov founded had forged a united front of dissident factions ranging from nationalists to democrats to Zionists. Similar groups had sprung up in the Ukraine, Lithuania, and Georgia.

In the United States, a commission of congressmen and administration officials was getting ready to review Soviet compliance with the 1975 Helsinki Final Act, the very issue the Orlov group was dealing with in Moscow. A newly elected president, Jimmy Carter, was challenging the Soviets on their human-rights performance. This curious interplay between U.S. officials and Soviet dissidents was more than the KGB would tolerate; it cracked down on Orlov's group.

But the crackdown failed to undo Orlov's work. The group had already given a new meaning to the nebulous international document, the Final Act of the Conference on Security and Cooperation in Europe. In 1975, when the Final Act was signed, the Soviets were widely believed to have scored a major victory, namely recognition of their post–World War II sphere of influence. To get the Final Act signed, the Soviets made some qualified promises to respect the rights of their citizens.

By the time of Orlov's arrest, European security was no longer the primary issue in the Helsinki review process. International attention had shifted to human rights, and the fate of Orlov and his comrades.

It is breathtaking that a small group of swashbuckling intellectuals could play such a role in the shaping of global politics.

In the process of altering the course of history, Orlov and Shcharansky became the last of the celebrity dissidents. And if Gorbachev's *glasnost* continues, if Soviet citizens are allowed to say what they want and leave the country if they wish to do so, no more will be produced.

I would like to express my gratitude to Orlov, Shcharansky, and Ginzburg for giving generously of their time and illuminating some matters that were unknown even to some of their comrades in the group. Ina Rubin allowed me to quote her late husband's diaries, a truly magnificent historical document spanning the entire history of the Soviet Union's human-rights movement and the movement for Jewish emigration. I would also like to thank Mikhail Bernshtam for his information about the group's creation and his forthright description of the circumstances surrounding his departure from the group.

Irene Manekofsky, one of the dynamos of the American movement to aid Soviet Jewry, allowed me to go through her personal archive and to take away a carload of papers and tapes with speeches and telephone conversations. If not for Irene, it would have taken me another year to write this.

George Krimsky, formerly a reporter with the Associated Press, who was expelled from the USSR largely for his connections with the dissidents, gave me his Moscow notebooks and copies of stories he was sending over the Teletype to AP's Foreign Desk in New York. His notes were valuable in reconstructing some crucial dates. Robert Toth, formerly Moscow reporter for the *Los Angeles Times,* offered a great deal of guidance in seeing the Helsinki group's story in a broader perspective. Harold A. Piper of *The Baltimore Sun* helped reconstruct the circumstances of Shcharansky's arrest, to which he was a witness. Peter Osnos, formerly of *The Washington Post,* was extremely helpful in explaining Western reporters' initial reluctance to write about the group.

Alfred A. Friendly, Jr., formerly of *Newsweek*'s Moscow bureau and later a staff member of the congressional Commission on Security and Cooperation in Europe, enhanced my understanding of the group and the way it was perceived in the United States.

My thanks also go to former congresswoman Millicent Fenwick, founder of the congressional Commission on Security and Cooperation in Europe, which performed virtually the same tasks as the Moscow Helsinki monitors, as well as Catherine Cosman and John Finerty of the commission for giving me access to materials in the commission's archive. Catherine A. Fitzpatrick of the New York–based Helsinki Watch Committees also steered me to a number of sources and provided photos and information. Glenn Richter of the New York–based Student Struggle for Soviet Jewry provided me with background information on the Jewish village of Ilynka. My thanks also go to Lydia Voronina, Dorothy Fosdick, Jerry Hough, Shagen Arutynyan, Yevgeny and Nina Bressenden, Yefrosinya Kulabukhova, Michael Sherbourne, Ruth Newman, Louis Rosenblum, Aleksandr and Irina Korsunsky, Valentin and Tatiana Turchin.

Jerrold L. Schecter and Stephen S. Rosenfeld made a

number of valuable suggestions, which I kept in mind throughout this project. My literary agent Leona Schecter helped me formulate the book, and Lisa Drew and David Means of William Morrow helped make it work. My parents, Sonya and Boris Goldberg, my in-laws, Julie and Jerry Boyd, as well as my friends Christie Weiss, Adrian Roe, Kate Whitmore, Maxwell Chibundu, Dudley and Lisa Hudspeth, Kate Rivers, Steve Minnig, Tom Grubisich, Michael Alexeev, Nikolai Williams, and Nathan Yu read abstracts of the book and made a number of editorial recommendations.

My wife, Kirsten, encouraged me to undertake this project. After I started writing, her brutal editing kept me on track.

Washington, D.C., 1987

CHAPTER 1

"I WOULD LIKE TO START A GROUP . . ."

Professor Yuri Orlov stood by the Bolshoi, waiting.

At 2:00 P.M., Ludmilla Alexeyeva got off the metro. Squinting in the bright afternoon sun, she looked over the small park. The diminutive redheaded Orlov was in its center, white columns of the Bolshoi to his right, the bright yellow facade of the Malyi theater behind him.

"Yura!" Alexeyeva called out.

"Ah, Lyuda, thanks for seeing me on such short notice."

The day, April 30, 1976, was unusually bright, even for late April in Moscow. The leaves were out in a delicate green one notices only in a sun-starved land. Patriotic music was blaring from the rooftop loudspeakers, a reminder of the approaching May Day.

Two hours earlier, Orlov had called Alexeyeva, a woman he hardly knew, and asked if she would mind joining him for a stroll down Moscow's streets. The place he suggested, the

Bolshoi, was halfway through town from the elite southwest neighborhood where the two lived.

"That's fine. I knew it was something important," said Alexeyeva. At five feet six, she was a couple of inches taller than Orlov, which made her feel a bit awkward around him.

Unlike Alexeyeva, a veteran of underground publishing, Orlov was a relative newcomer to the Moscow dissident circles. Yet he was acquainted with its key members, including Nobel laureate Andrei Sakharov.

Orlov seemed to be close to Andrei Amalrik, a brash self-educated historian who had written a book questioning whether the USSR would survive until 1984. The book made Amalrik a celebrity in the West and, for five years, a political prisoner back home. Orlov, a physicist, had been seen with his neighbor and college friend Valentin Turchin, head of Moscow's chapter of Amnesty International, which Orlov co-founded. He kept in touch with another neighbor, Aleksandr Ginzburg, a slight, pale, bearded man who looked like an aging hippie. Ginzburg was working for Nobel Prize laureates Sakharov and Aleksandr Solzhenitsyn. Solzhenitsyn, then living in exile, had Ginzburg run a foundation to aid families of political prisoners. Sakharov employed him as a personal secretary.

For a couple of months, at social gatherings, Orlov had been talking about something he called "forcing the authorities into a dialogue with society." That was what a small group of Moscow intellectuals had been trying to accomplish for over a decade. They had demonstrated in public places and written appeals to the Soviet leaders, to the United Nations, and simply "To the People of Good Will." Their goal was to make the authorities listen to ideas that wouldn't be voiced in the circle of Politburo yes-men.

The theater square is one of the livelier parts of Moscow.

It is a tiny park with a few small trees, benches, and walkways surfaced with brick ground to a powder. The park serves as a gathering place for Moscow's homosexuals, a market for hawking extra tickets for *Swan Lake* or *Spartacus,* and a place for lovers to enjoy bright days and engage in casual petting.

Only one bench, closest to the Children's Theater, was vacant.

"We sat down at the same time, then, by reflex, looked around for KGB tails," Alexeyeva recalled. "Then we looked at each other and broke into laughter. There we were, middle-aged people. I was forty-nine; he was fifty-two. We'd never received stolen goods; we had never sold marijuana. We are the kind of people you let into the house and don't count the silver."

The two moved closer, hip to hip, shoulder to shoulder.

"Lyuda, have you read the Helsinki Final Act?"

Orlov was referring to the thirty-thousand-word document that the United States, the USSR, and thirty-three other nations had signed eight months earlier. The Final Act was a détente-inspired blueprint for a safer world, reaffirming sanctity of existing borders, arms reduction, increased economic cooperation, freer flow of information, and greater respect for human rights. Heralding it as a landmark in the fight for peace, the Soviets published the entire document in their major newspapers.

"I haven't read it," said Alexeyeva.

"Lyu-da!"

"Yura, I've tried. It's so boring; it's so long."

"Do you know what it's about?"

"I've read everything about human rights. So what?"

"Do you realize that this is the first document in which the idea of preserving peace is directly linked to respect for human rights?" said Orlov. "I'd like to start a group, but it has to appear completely loyal. How about the Public Group of Assistance to Implementation of the Helsinki Agreements in the USSR?"

"'Assistance,' that's nice." The word had to have been meant in jest, Alexeyeva thought. The last thing the authorities wanted was "assistance" from the likes of Yuri Orlov and herself.

"Yes, assistance, what's wrong with that?" said the professor.

"So what will this Group of Assistance of yours do?" Alexeyeva asked.

"We'll gather information about specific cases of human-rights abuses, issue documents, and send them to the governments of the thirty-five countries that signed the agreement."

"Documents?"

"Documents about things we know. Mental hospitals, emigration, taking children away from religious parents, interruption of mail and telephone service." The authorities routinely intercepted the dissidents' mail and disconnected their phones.

"Why write about interference with mail and telephone service when there are political prisoners? They may be worth going to jail for, but the mail and telephone service? Really, Yura."

"We can write about political prisoners, too, but there is nothing specific about them in the Helsinki agreement. Interference with the mail and telephone service is specifically mentioned. I'd like you to consider joining."

"Assistance" was an interesting word, Alexeyeva thought. If the Soviet system decided to live up to its human-rights promises, it would have to abandon oppression and, in effect, cease to exist.

The physicist continued. The group would include the better-known dissidents. There would be no voting, no application procedures, no structure. Three signatures would be enough to issue a document, so there would be no need to worry about reaching a consensus on every issue.

Alexeyeva considered practical matters. A typewriter can produce ten pages—a hard copy and nine carbons. She divided thirty-five countries by ten copies per typewriter. To get each Helsinki signatory a copy, each letter has to be typed four times. That's work for four typists. It could be done, but what a waste. Sending letters to Bulgaria, for instance, would be like sending them directly to the Soviet KGB. It would get its copy anyway.

Alexeyeva knew she would join.

What she didn't know was that she was the first person Orlov had approached about joining the group. Nor could she have foreseen that by "assisting" the Soviets, Orlov would eventually unite the small factions of disaffected Soviet citizens including democrats, Zionists, Russian nationalists, ethnic separatists, Catholics, Baptists, Pentecostals, and Seventh Day Adventists, and that similar groups would spring up in the Ukraine, Lithuania, Georgia, Armenia, Czechoslovakia, and Poland. It was beyond her wildest dreams that the U.S. Congress would form a commission to perform virtually the same tasks as the Eastern Bloc Helsinki monitors.

Sitting on that bench by the Bolshoi, Alexeyeva certainly didn't know that the redheaded physicist who had just told her about his idea of assisting his government was about to lead Soviet dissent into its most visible and dramatic phase.

A curious cultural exchange between the United States and the USSR took place during the mid-1970s.

Thanks to some lazy translators working for shortwave radio stations, the English word *dissident* began to crop up in radio programs. The word, which the broadcasters apparently preferred to the more massive Russian word *inakomyslyashchiy* (literally, "otherwise-thinker"), began to be mentioned in the Soviet streets, at first as a linguistic novelty, and later, as if it had been in the Russian language forever. Of course, Russian doesn't just take a word. It kneads it like a glob of dough. So, two dissidents came to be referred to as *dissidenty;* a company of dissidents was called *dissidentskaya kompaniya* and the dissident movement became *dissidentskoye dvizheniye.* Soon, *Pravda,* Tass, and Soviet President Leonid Brezhnev himself started to attack the "so-called *dissidenty.*"

Around the same time, British and American Jews started to refer to would-be émigrés as *refuseniks,* slapping a Russian suffix on the English word *refuse.* (The word was coined by one of two men: Michael Sherbourne, a London schoolteacher, or Lou Rosenblum, a Soviet Jewry activist from Cleveland. Recently Rosenblum traced the word's first appearance to a bulletin he put out on February 1, 1974. "In this movement everyone talks to one another, so whether I first heard it from Michael Sherbourne or made it up myself I cannot say," Rosenblum said.) As the word migrated into newspapers, it became *refusednik,* then, after enough usage, lost the italics and the *d* in the middle— which, after all, was quite unnecessary.

The Nixon and Ford administrations' policy of détente had heightened the West's interest in the Soviet Union, which, as a side effect, heightened the interest in dissent. In terms of America's foreign policy, human rights in the USSR was widely seen as a Jewish issue, with emigration being the most important of the human rights.

In 1974, Congress passed the Jackson-Vanik Amendment to the U.S.-Soviet trade agreement. The amendment required the Soviet Union to allow more emigration before receiving most-favored-nation status in trade with the United States.

Senator Henry Jackson, a Democrat from Washington State and architect of the amendment, was offering the Soviets a simple exchange: people for trade benefits.

American Jewish extremists were harassing Soviet performers, planting explosives in Aeroflot offices and in the New York office of impresario Sol Hurok, who arranged concerts by Soviet artists. Silent vigils were held daily across the street from the Soviet Embassy in Washington. Leaflets with particulars on refuseniks were routinely handed out at Soviet art exhibits and dance performances. For a while, one Washington Jewish activist routinely dialed the numbers of Soviet prisons, misrepresenting himself as a high-ranking U.S. official and saying that he was appalled by the treatment of Jewish prisoners.

Almost every day, American activists telephoned Jewish refuseniks in Moscow. As a result, U.S. Jewish activists knew of arrests, trials, and convictions of their brethren in the USSR. They knew the refuseniks' names, addresses, even directions to their houses.

They also knew what to send to refuseniks. In 1976, the hottest items were glossy fake-fur coats, Beatles record albums, blue jeans, Hebrew textbooks, prayer books, and language audio cassettes. The jailed Jewish activists had special needs; they were asking for postcards, which, when tilted, showed women in various stages of undress, though never completely nude—that would make the cards illegal. It was said the postcards made fine bribes for prison guards.

American congressmen passing through Moscow routinely dropped by to see refuseniks and dissidents, then reported their impressions to folks back home. Several brought gifts, communications, advice. At meetings with Soviet officials, quite a few asked about specific "cases." Brezhnev accused such visitors of being "obsessed."

Few human-rights advocates in the West or in the USSR saw

the signing of the 1975 Final Act on Security and Cooperation in Europe as an event of great significance. The document was neither a treaty nor an international agreement. It had no enforcement clause, no deadlines, no criteria for judging compliance. It contained no obligations, just goals. Even its name was noncommittal: "the Final Act."

The many opponents of Henry Kissinger's détente labeled the document "a sellout," "another Yalta"—a document that, following up on the 1945 Yalta conference, recognized the Soviet domination of Eastern Europe. The West, drunk with promises of détente, had surrendered Eastern Europe to the Russians, critics said.

After the signing, a *Time* story compiled fun facts of the Final Act: The negotiations lasted twenty-two months, involved 375 diplomats, and the completed document "has four major sections known for no discernible reason as 'baskets.'"

In a last-minute compromise, the West got a concession from the Soviets, a section called Basket III that dealt with human rights. Critics didn't see it as much of a concession. The section simply referred to the 1948 United Nations Universal Declaration of Human Rights, another document containing a set of unbinding promises that have failed to alter Soviet human-rights practices.

Skepticism about the Final Act wasn't universal. "It was a weak document, weaker than the Universal Declaration of Human Rights, but it was more important," Orlov said, recalling his reaction to the signing. "If the Soviet government said [the Final Act] was important, it was, in fact, important. It was the Soviet government itself that gave us something to work with."

Orlov's idea, in essence, was to force the Western nations to demand that the Soviets cease repressions against their citizens. But, desirable as that goal may have seemed to some, could it have been too much to demand at a negotiating table? And how far could the Soviets be pushed without the results becoming devastating to détente? Most dissidents, presenting themselves as authorities on the subject, tended to say that the Soviets had to be shamed and shamed again until the glorious day when they would cave in to international pressure.

The only reliable way to find the limit of Soviet patience was to push them beyond it.

CHAPTER 2

SCIENTIFIC METHOD

I t would seem Professor Orlov had little to complain about. He spent his childhood in a Russian village, made it to the big city, entered Moscow University, his country's finest school, then earned the title of corresponding member of the Armenian Academy of Sciences. One could say that Orlov was living a scientist's dream, complete with modest—though international—recognition of his work in particle physics.

He had a job at the Institute of Earth Magnetism of the Academy of Sciences, a place denoted with the otherwordly-sounding Russian acronym IZMIRAN. It came with a stellar salary of 400 rubles a month. For that, Orlov had to come to work once a week, on Thursdays. The professor was healthy, muscular; he had an attractive young wife; he even had his hair, in its original wild curly red.

But a storm was raging in his mind. It was a professorial sort of storm, one that precipitated fundamental questions and daring plans rather than intemperate speeches. "How did Russia become so ruthless?'' was one of those questions. "How can it be changed'' was another.

In his youth, Orlov sought the answers in the "classics of Marxism.'' He read Tolstoy, too, pondering the new beginnings in which Russia's prophet saw salvation. As an undergraduate at Moscow University, Orlov read Nikolai Berdyaev, an odd Russian philosopher who at the turn of the century abandoned Marxism for mysticism, and was exiled in 1922 after an attempt to talk sense into Feliks Dzerzhinski, head of the secret police. Summoned to Dzerzhinski's office on a matter unrelated to either religion or philosophy, Berdyaev spent nearly an hour lecturing the man nicknamed the Iron Feliks about the cosmic implications of the Bolshevik Revolution's encroachment on the realm of God.

"I am not a communist; I am a socialist, perhaps,'' Orlov used to say openly, starting in 1946. "By some miracle, I didn't get killed,'' he said later.

These views notwithstanding, Orlov remained in the Communist party until 1956, when, at a party meeting devoted to discussing Premier Nikita Khrushchev's Twentieth Congress speech denouncing Stalin, Orlov and three other young scientists at the Institute of Theoretical and Experimental Physics got up to attack Stalin even more strongly than did the party leadership itself.

"In my speech, I remember voicing the idea that in their development, societies don't follow simple laws,'' Orlov said. "That contradicted Marxism, which holds that there is a unique path of development, following the laws of history that were discovered by Marx and developed by Lenin. On this basis I concluded that our society, which was built during the Stalin period, does not represent the only possible form of a socialist society. Therefore, other varieties of socialism are possible—and we must build a new, democratic socialism.''

For that Orlov and three colleagues who supported him were attacked in *Pravda,* expelled from the party, and fired. "If you knew what you were doing, you are heroes. If you didn't, you are fools,'' Abram Alikhanov, head of the Institute of Theoretical and Experimental Physics, told the four.

Orlov found work in Armenia. Yerevan, the republic's capital, wasn't a bad place for a physicist, and Orlov spent the next fifteen years making the most of his exile. He earned a doctorate, designed an accelerator, became a corresponding member of the Armenian Academy of Sciences.

The professor's curiosity was by no means limited to physics. He was just as interested in the nature of man, his biological and spiritual qualities. One thing Orlov saw clearly was the role of the individual in shaping history. An individual well placed, an individual who is heard, could change the world forever.

The one figure who seemed to captivate Orlov was Jesus Christ. Not Jesus Christ the Son of God, not Jesus Christ the Son of Man, but Jesus Christ the historical figure who changed the world—much as Orlov changed the behavior of particles in accelerators.

"Natural sciences are communication with the Lord God; nothing else," Orlov said. "When an experiment is performed in science, frequently the scientist is unaware of the colossal difficulties he will have to overcome. So, many simply refuse to experiment, in effect accepting defeat. But sometimes there are real scientists, scientists who don't want to accept defeat. In part that's because they don't fully realize what difficulties they are about to encounter; in part, because they ignore them."

Orlov believed social experiments were no different. "Under the Soviet system there is no rational way to predict anything," he said. "Largely, I had to rely on guesswork. Under those conditions, I had to act, not thinking about the results."

The one thing Orlov said he knew from the start of his Helsinki-group experiment was that it could lead to martyrdom: "When you are trying to influence a community as enormous as the Western world, a community with an enormous number of internal interests, internal passions, internal controversies, how can you affect it? How can you affect it except by ascending a cross? There is no other way. Just the cross. That's all."

In 1972, Orlov returned from Armenia and soon bought a cooperative apartment in the Moscow University–built high rise near the Belyaevo-Bogorodskoye metro station in the city's southwest. On Bus No. 226, which ran between the university co-op and the metro station, academic-looking passengers openly read the prohibited Solzhenitsyn, Osip Mandelshtam, and Boris Pasternak.

On summer nights, through open windows, passersby could hear the static of dozens of shortwave radios tuned to the Voice of America, the BBC, the Deutsche Welle, the Voice of Israel, Radio Liberty, even Radio Peking. In the next building was the apartment of Orlov's college friend Valentin Turchin. Across the courtyard, in a one-room apartment, lived Aleksandr Ginzburg, his wife, Arina, their two small children, and a teen-aged adopted son.

Every day, foreign cars with diplomatic and press license plates pulled up to the apartment complex. The cars, many of them belonging to the U.S. Embassy, ferried diplomats' wives to Arina's Russian-language lessons. This was a violation of the Soviet government regulations that prohibit foreigners from doing business with anyone outside an agency set up specifically to serve them.

Embassy officials weren't concerned, however, and neither were the Ginzburgs. That, after all, was a petty infraction compared to Aleksandr Ginzburg's primary occupation. In 1974 he became administrator of the Russian Social Fund to Aid Political Prisoners and Their Families, a private foundation that dispensed stipends to wives and children of political prisoners.

The history of Soviet dissent could be said to begin with grand events like Stalin's death in 1953, or with Khrushchev's denouncing "the cult of [Stalin's] personality" three years later. But there was another key moment:

In 1959, Ginzburg, a Moscow University journalism student, was using a dormitory bathroom. He rifled through a box of paper (toilet paper was nonexistent in Moscow at the time) and found rough drafts of poetry and literature and history papers. There, Ginzburg claims, he got the idea of organizing a group of friends, young poets and writers, and publishing an uncensored journal which he called *Sintaksis*. It was the first known unofficial periodical. Filling *Sintaksis* wasn't difficult since Moscow was beginning to accommodate a freewheeling, vodka-guzzling subculture of unofficial artists and literati, a sort of Greenwich Village East.

Poets gathered under the statue of Vladimir Mayakovsky, a hooligan-poet of the 1920s and the guru of American "beat" poets of the 1950s. Under the statue, Moscow's progressive poets threatened to "pop the cherry of Socialist Realism," rhapsodized about the symbols of Christianity, and called for "throwing hand grenades into the machine of government."

These young poets gravitated toward young artists who had abandoned the official Socialist Realism art form, and painted scraggly black cats, television antennas, cubes, spheres, and phalluses instead of rosy-cheeked milkmaids in Ukrainian folk costumes. Some of it was art, some of it was hooliganism, some of it was inspired, but nearly all of it was energetic.

Sintaksis was one of the first journals in what became known as *samizdat,* a word formed out of *sam,* "self," and the abbreviation of *izdatelstvo,* "publishing house." Self-publishing led to Ginzburg's expulsion from the university. Then he was charged with forgery as a result of taking an exam for another student. The offense was basically cheating, but the court meted out an unusually harsh sentence: two years in the camps.

Despite his problems, Ginzburg retained his ties with the university. One of his acquaintances was Andrei Sinyavsky, an ethnic Russian who at the time published books in the West under the Jewish name Abram Tertz. In 1965, Sinyavsky and another covertly published writer, Yuli Daniel, whose pen name was Nikolai Arzhak, were arrested and charged with slandering the state. Sinyavsky's wife asked Ginzburg to compile the unofficial transcript of the trial.

The Sinyavsky and Daniel trial was a landmark in Soviet dissent, and the controversy it triggered is alive more than two decades later. In February 1987, Soviet poet Yevgeny Yevtushenko offered a new version of the causes of the Sinyavsky and Daniel trial. Yevtushenko said that shortly after the 1966 trial, as he was visiting the United States, he was invited to Senator Robert F. Kennedy's Manhattan apartment. According to Yevtushenko's story, Kennedy asked the poet to follow him to the bathroom. The senator turned on the shower, lowered his voice, and asked Yevtushenko to tell the Soviet government that it was "our agents" who supplied Soviet agents with the names behind Sinyavsky's and Daniel's pseudonyms. "Because of Vietnam, our [U.S.] standing has begun to diminish both at home and abroad," Kennedy said, according to Yevtushenko. "We needed a propaganda counterweight."

If Yevtushenko's story is true, it could have staggering implications. Virtually all key characteristics of Soviet dissent—from aid to prisoners to *glasnost* to the emergence of Andrei Sakharov on the political scene—can be traced to the Sinyavsky and Daniel trial. The whole truth may never be known, but Yevtushenko's story has a number of holes. "If our agents told their agents about Sinyavsky and Daniel, then their agents would have told their employers, the Soviet government, that the Americans had fingered the writers," Donald Jameson, a former CIA official who had directed the agency's operations in the USSR, wrote in *The New Republic*. "Why should Kennedy have bothered to pass on information the Soviets would have had already?"

Yevtushenko's story has another apparent weakness: Sinyavsky's and Daniel's pen names were among the worst-kept secrets in Moscow. Alexeyeva, a friend of Sinyavsky, Daniel, and their wives, said she knew the pen names for about three years before the writers' arrest. She got the story from neither Daniel nor his wife, Larisa Bogoraz, but from several mutual friends. "I'd guess there were one hundred or so people in our circle of friends, and at least half of them knew," Alexeyeva said later. "If the CIA gave out their names, they didn't tell the KGB anything it didn't already know."

Nearly two years after the writers' trial, Ginzburg was accused of slandering the Soviet system by having compiled the unofficial trial record.

The trial inspired an underground journal, called *Khronika tekushchikh sobytiy,* translated as "Chronicle of Current Events" and commonly referred to simply as *Khronika.* It was named after a BBC Russian news show. *Khronika* was a characteristic invention of Soviet dissent. Instead of calling for a revolution or printing recipes for Molotov cocktails, it did nothing more than compile the history of all forms of dissent in the USSR. With phone-book precision—and about as much verve—*Khronika* covered instances of persecution of Baptists, Adventists, and Pentecostals; trials of nationalists in the Ukraine, Lithuania, Latvia, Estonia, Georgia, Armenia, and Russia proper. It reported deaths in the camps and, on happier occasions, the releases of prisoners. Frequently *Khronika* covered the trials of its editors.

In 1972, shortly after he was released from the camps, Ginzburg received a visit from Aleksandr Solzhenitsyn, the husband of his friend Natalya Svetlova. Solzhenitsyn had just received the Nobel Prize for Literature, and he wanted Ginzburg to distribute a quarter of the money to families of political prisoners.

The same year, Orlov moved into Ginzburg's Moscow neighborhood.

Those were extraordinary times, the height of what the participants called the Human Rights Movement. The movement's participants, who referred to themselves as *pravozashchitniki,* rights-defenders, had an unwritten code of ethics and something loosely resembling an ideology.

In essence, rights-defenders disregarded Soviet legal and social traditions and demanded that the government respect its own legal principles and do its business openly. At interrogations and at trials, they claimed that if one were to follow the letter of Soviet law, it would be legal to publish books abroad, collect materials from open trials, openly criticize the state, and hire Western attorneys after getting in trouble with the authorities.

At virtually every gathering, they raised glasses "to those who aren't with us" (a reference to political prisoners), then "to the success of our hopeless cause." Orlov wasn't too wild about the latter toast. "If I thought our cause was hopeless, I would have busied myself with something else," he used to protest.

After particularly bad searches or attacks in newspapers, dissidents were known to sue the KGB. It became standard among them to argue that Articles 70 and 190-1 of the Russian Republic's Criminal Code, which prohibit anti-Soviet propaganda and slandering the state, are unconstitutional since the law of the land guarantees freedom of expression. Orlov's friends never pretended to represent anyone but themselves. They never formulated a political platform or, for that matter, political goals. Their opposition was ethical, they said, and political goals would simply trivialize it. They fought like gentlemen, openly. Their manuscripts and appeals were signed, their demonstrations were in the most conspicuous places (including Red Square and Pushkin Square), and the quotes they gave Western reporters were for attribution. They also believed that the more they were quoted in the Western press, the less likely the authorities would be to arrest them.

"I've decided to devote the next five years to pacifying my social conscience," Orlov started saying to his friends almost immediately after returning to Moscow in 1973.

The opportunity presented itself in September 1973, when Soviet newspapers started an offensive against Andrei Sakharov, calling him a traitor and an "agent of reaction dancing to the flute of imperialism." Orlov, who by then had met Sakharov, disapproved of the newspaper campaign so strongly, he wrote a letter to Leonid Brezhnev about it.

Orlov invited the General Secretary to answer thirteen questions about such matters as the lagging of Soviet science, the stagnation of the economy, and the destruction of the environment. Or course, Orlov informed the party leader that he was not a revolutionary but a believer in slow democratization of the Soviet society.

The professor invited Russia's First Communist to consider the basics of Marxism. "The most significant oversight in Marxist theory of social development is that it doesn't encompass the natural spiritual needs and qualities of a human being," the physicist wrote. "In fact, Marxism denies their very presence in human nature. Yet, this supposition isn't proven scientifically, that is by means of experimental biology, biochemistry or biophysics."

This led Orlov to the following question: "Don't you think that our approach to man and his place in the society is primitive and out of balance with the existing human needs and qualities?" Orlov's question number 13 wasn't a question at all: "Of course, you do understand that putting members of the opposition into psychiatric hospitals and maiming them with medication is a lot like sterilization of political opponents by the Nazi Reich. Here, I guess, I have nothing to ask." No Communist, least of all the CPSU boss, cherished being compared to the Nazis.

Shortly after mailing the letter to Brezhnev, Orlov was notified that in a financial austerity measure, his job had been eliminated. Finding another job wasn't easy. After the dismissal,

Orlov thought of accepting a standing job offer he'd had from the Armenian Academy member V. A. Ambartsumyan. When he returned to Yerevan to accept, Ambartsumyan refused to meet with him, saying through a subordinate that "there are situations when even an Academy member is helpless."

To make ends meet, the internationally acclaimed physicist had to make a living tutoring high-school and college students.

Among his students was the son of a high-level prosecutor. In 1974, one of the people Orlov had met at the prosecutor's apartment approached him with a message. "The prosecutor likes you," the man said. "So he asked me to tell you that the authorities will tolerate your writing and signing letters of protest, but they will not tolerate your getting involved with organizations."

"I heard him out, then went about my business as if nothing happened," Orlov recalled later. "In this, I had no fear. I may have fear of wild beasts, heights, water, but not men, except bandits, perhaps. If work had to be done, it had to be done, and if I didn't do it, who would?"

Orlov interpreted the warning as more than just a friendly gesture from the prosecutor. It also told Orlov that the KGB took him seriously. "I think, partly, it was the memory of my speech in 1956, partly it was a bow to my titles: a Corresponding Member of the Armenian Academy, a Ph.D., a professor," he said.

In 1975, Orlov and Turchin formed the USSR chapter of Amnesty International. The purpose of that experiment was to see what would happen if a group of private citizens attempted to bring the USSR into the international human-rights community. Amnesty officials, following the organization's rules, cautioned Turchin against getting involved in politics. In accordance with Amnesty's policy, the chapter was forbidden to sound off on political prisoners in the USSR, limiting itself to letter writing on behalf of prisoners of conscience in Yugoslavia, Spain, and Sri Lanka.

In March 1975, Orlov wrote his only *samizdat* essay, called "Is Nontotalitarian Socialism Possible?"

"As is well known, serious discussion of such questions isn't encouraged," Orlov wrote. "It can lead to up to seven years in the concentration camps or treatment in a psychiatric institution." The system punishes its critics because it has to; a totalitarian socialist state isn't equipped to deal with anyone who deviates from its norms.

On the surface, those norms may seem odd: "An individual isn't encouraged to work hard, and is forgiven for little transgressions. As a result, peasants do virtually nothing, scientists systematically produce worthless work and don't show up in their offices for months at a time, and, every morning, a large number of workers report to their plants drunk. Yet, these slacking workers are assured continuing wages, free medical care and relatively secure retirement. Unconditional loyalty is the only thing the state demands in return.

"Dictatorship thrives when an average citizen has a guilt complex and feels gratitude to the state for its forgiveness of his transgressions," Orlov wrote.

That perverse social contract, one where demonstrations of loyalty absolve incompetence and laziness, lies at the core of socialism, he wrote. And it's a stable core; stable because it is inert. "All the aspects of totalitarian socialism are tied in a tight knot," Orlov wrote. It was a knot that couldn't have been tied had the state not owned the means of production, thereby acquiring control over its work force. The greater the state's involvement in production, the more it has to worry about maintaining discipline in the workplace, the more likely it is to move toward controlling all aspects of its employees' lives, the more likely it would be to squelch all criticism while turning workers, peasants, and the intelligentsia into lazy but loyal drunks.

CHAPTER 3

"WHOM ARE YOU ASSISTING?"

Being fired or being denied an exit visa had some hidden benefits.

Many dissidents received clothes from the West, instantly becoming some of the best-dressed people in Moscow. Many more received money from Jewish groups in the West, entitling them to shop in Russia's hard-currency stores, called Beryozka, "birch tree." On any given day at Beryozka, a visitor could see a refusenik buy the same off-brand Italian overcoat a KGB operative had tried on minutes earlier.

At such exclusive social events as openings of foreign exhibits, the invited Soviet officials were furious to find dissidents and refuseniks among VIP guests.

In this atmosphere of increasing contacts with the West, Orlov decided to improve his English. He could read scientific literature, but couldn't understand the newspapers and spoken English. Early in 1976 he chose a class taught by Anatoly

Shcharansky. Short, puffy, prematurely balding, with Elvis side-burns, the twenty-eight-year-old Shcharansky spent his days running around Moscow. Shcharansky's closest friends called him "the Bubble" because, one friend explained, "He was little, round, and always on the surface."

On cold days, he was easily recognized by his Ecuadoran llama sweater, quite likely the only one of its kind in Moscow. The sweater was a bit small for Shcharansky. It was a gift from an American tourist, a woman who was so touched by meeting a live refusenik, she gave him the sweater off her back.

Shcharansky first applied for an exit visa in 1973, but was unsuccessful. Later he married the tall, statuesque Natalya Shtiglitz. She was allowed to emigrate to Israel, where she changed her first name to Avital. Shcharansky's subsequent attempts to join Avital in Israel were unsuccessful.

By the time he met Orlov, Shcharansky had made himself thoroughly obnoxious to the Soviets. He had spoken openly to the Western press; he acted as a translator for Jewish activists at press conferences; he made connections with foreign reporters, often agreeing to help out on stories that had nothing to do with Jewish emigration. This aid built up the reporters' goodwill.

Shcharansky had some unconventional ways of making English grammar less tedious. Instead of building diagrams of such innocuous sentences as "Jane is going home," he dissected phrases including "If I were Brezhnev, I would let all Soviet Jews go to Israel." Later, secret police confiscated several of his students' notebooks.

The study group also included Orlov's old friend Vitaly Rubin, a gaunt fifty-two-year-old man with an intense gaze. For nearly four years, Rubin, a scholar of twelfth-century Chinese philosophy, pondered the reason the authorities gave for denying him permission to emigrate: possession of state secrets.

"The only secrets I know are those of Confucius," he said frequently to friends. Whenever officials asked him where he worked, Rubin answered, "Hebrew University in Jerusalem." That was true. The university had, in fact, appointed him to its faculty. In his apartment in Moscow, Rubin ran seminars on Jewish culture, spending much of his time reading the smuggled works of Martin Buber, Abraham J. Heschel, Gershom Scholem,

Franz Rosenzweig, and other titans of twentieth-century Jewish thought.

Another of Shcharansky's students was Orlov's and Rubin's friend Andrei Amalrik, who had just returned after serving nearly five years in the camps and internal exile, partly for writing "Will the Soviet Union Survive Until 1984?" in which he voiced the strong opinion that it would not. (It was Rubin who suggested the title.) Because of the essay and the great number of people who wanted to believe it, Amalrik became world famous.

Amalrik liked the name he was given in the Soviet press: "provocateur." He disregarded more than just political norms. Frequently, in public, he chastised his artist wife for spending too much money. Once, shortly after the Ginzburgs got married, he said to Arina, "How could you have married him? He is so dim-witted." And, shortly after getting out of the camps, Amalrik said to Alexeyeva, "Lyuda, you've gotten so much older and so much fatter." Alexeyeva, after some reflection, agreed. Her husband took offense.

Amalrik was anything but a diligent language student. Lydia Voronina, a friend of Shcharansky's who also took the class, remembers Amalrik's consistent attempts to make English grammar more rational. *"Davay narisuyu—Let me draw it for you,"* he used to say whenever his classmates were dumbfounded by his sentences.

Apart from language study, by the spring of 1976, Orlov, Rubin, Amalrik, and Shcharansky spent much of their time discussing politics. Once, in early March, Shcharansky suggested a scheme for influencing the Soviet leaders:

First, the Soviet intelligentsia would invite Western counterparts to hold seminars and discussions of human-rights issues.

Then, after these discussion groups were formed in the West, Soviet citizens who had spearheaded the movement would start a similar group of their own. Quickly, a series of international seminars would be called by the group in Moscow. The goal of that movement would be to take the questions of human rights—and living up to the promises in the Helsinki Final Act—out of the hands of their governments and make them a public issue.

"Where the governments cannot find common criteria, the citizens' groups would," Shcharansky said later. "Where the governments fail, the people would succeed."

The plan had several safeguards built into it. The Soviet intelligentsia would organize into a "seminar" rather than an "organization," a "party," or a "group." That name would put it into a gray area of Soviet law, which says nothing of public seminars. In addition, the seminar would be part of an international network, a consideration that could make the KGB hesitant to crack down.

Amalrik seemed to like the idea, Shcharansky recalled in an interview later. The "provocateur" drafted a declaration calling for the formation of seminars in the West. Amalrik suggested that the letter contain twenty-five signatures. He even named it "the Letter of 25." Shcharansky was to get five Jewish refuseniks to sign the appeal. Orlov was to get five scientists, and Amalrik five writers and artists. The other ten signatures were to be reserved for activists representing a broad spectrum of political views.

Shcharansky signed the petition, and got four others to sign. The Jewish part of the Letter of 25 was completed in a matter of days. But Amalrik hadn't brought back any signatures, and Orlov seemed to be hesitating. A month passed, with Shcharansky periodically asking Orlov whether he had had a chance to proceed with the letter.

"Oh, yes, yes, I am thinking about it," Shcharansky later recalled Orlov's replies.

Meanwhile, the KGB began to pressure Amalrik to emigrate, so he borrowed some money from sculptor Ernst Neizvestny and set out on a journey around Russia. (Since the sculptor, too, was planning to leave, the debt was to be repaid in foreign currency.)

April went by, and Orlov's response to Shcharansky's inquiries hadn't changed. He was thinking about it.

"I was thinking, 'What the hell, no matter whom we get to sign our declaration, nobody in Europe will care,'" Orlov recalled. "We would get no response. All they care about in Europe is disarmament, and they think nothing else is in any way related to that. And now I know I was right to think this of the

Europeans. So I decided that if we wanted compliance with the Helsinki Final Act, it was up to us to monitor it. If we wanted a group started, we were the ones who had to start it. Nobody would do it for us."

The group, Orlov decided, had to be formed in Moscow. It had to focus on the Helsinki Final Act, and it had to include the better-known Soviet dissidents.

Early in May, Orlov approached Shcharansky with a handwritten draft of a document announcing the formation of the Public Group of Assistance to Implementation of the Helsinki Agreements in the USSR.

The idea was different from Shcharansky's.

"Yura said, 'This is the way it should be done,'" recalled Shcharansky later. "I said, 'This is far more risky than what I had suggested, but since I am the one who got you thinking about it, there is nothing I can do but join.'"

The relationship between Jewish activists and rights-defenders was generally cordial, but the two groups tended to avoid any hint of a United Front strategy. In his diary, China scholar Vitaly Rubin described the differences between the two groups:

"I have never been a Russian democrat. With all my respect, even reverence, for those people, I have never felt any desire to join them, because from childhood I saw this as the country of slavery, I understood that from top to bottom it is permeated with anti-Semitism, and felt no desire to sacrifice myself for the enemies of my people. . . ." he wrote on July 27, 1975.

"Last time I saw a gathering of Russian democrats, it was at some going-away party. I was amazed by their trait which, in the past, had somehow escaped me—their blabbering. It was obvious that their cause had lost all sense. Nobody in this country needs it; that is nobody but the democrats. It can't help anyone; it can't make anyone happy.

"Even if it is possible to keep oneself morally clean, even if it is possible not to take part in the lie, even if an individual is prepared to sacrifice himself for the cause, it is still impossible to obtain for the Russian people what they do not want, to obtain

that for which the people themselves aren't willing to struggle. . . .

"Recently I wondered, what would have happened had I not
been a Jew, but had my political views regarding everything Soviet? I would have had to do what many ethnic Russians are
doing now: I would have had to ask for an Israeli visa, to grab
the coattails of the Jewish people. For a man of my self-esteem,
this would have been torturous. Thank God I am a Jew!"

Nearly a year later, when Russian democrat Orlov invited
Jewish patriot Rubin to join his Helsinki-monitoring group,
Rubin accepted. No, he hadn't all of a sudden become a Russian
democrat; he was joining to represent the cause of Jewish emi-
gration. And since that cause was within the framework of the
Helsinki Final Act, Orlov and Rubin had a common platform.

No, said Malva Landa. She would certainly not join anything
called Public Group of Assistance to Implementation of the
Helsinki Agreements in the USSR. The name, she said, implied
nothing less than dissidents working with the state to implement
an international document the Soviets regarded as central to
their foreign and domestic policies.

"Your group will advance the Soviet goals!" declared Landa,
a fifty-six-year-old retired geologist who had been running politi-
cal-prisoner aid efforts long before the infusion of Solzhenitsyn's
money. "The Helsinki Agreement is nothing but a Soviet ploy
aimed at deceiving the West into recognizing its postwar domination of Eastern Europe."

"Malva, it doesn't matter what the group is called," Orlov
tried to object. "What matters is who's in it."

Still, Landa's response was an emphatic no. The prospect of
"assisting" the Soviet government in anything, even if the word
"assistance" was used in jest, appalled her, Landa said. "Assistance" contradicted her dream of seeing the "Bolsheviks" go
on trial for crimes against humanity. Once, at a KGB interrogation, she refused to answer questions. "Not until Nuremberg,"
she said.

For similar reasons, Tatiana Khodorovich, a dissident and
Orlov's friend, refused to join the group. But Orlov stood by the

name. "I didn't want the name to imply a challenge to the government," he said later. "We weren't looking for confrontation a priori. We were simply a monitoring group. If they were violating the Final Act, we reported that. If they made progress, we wrote they had made progress.

"Landa and Khodorovich didn't like my game playing when I was naming the group. They thought anything that has the appearance of politics had to be deplored and avoided, but I thought the element of political game playing was essential."

Valentin Turchin also declined to join the group. Amnesty International had cautioned him against getting into politics.

Ginzburg, too, was a tough man to recruit.

He was simply too busy, he said. Two years earlier, Solzhenitsyn in Zurich and Ginzburg in Moscow had announced that Ginzburg had been named chief administrator for the Russian Social Fund. Ginzburg would distribute the proceeds of Solzhenitsyn's *Gulag Archipelago* to families of convicts.

Ginzburg had other obligations, too. After serving his term for completing the record of the Sinyavsky and Daniel trial, he lost his Moscow residency permit. That meant he could stay in the capital no more than seventy-two hours at a time. Usually, he stayed seventy-one hours, then took a four-hour train ride to his official residence in Tarusa, remaining there long enough for one of his rehabilitation officers to see that he was there. Then he would return to Moscow.

Ginzburg said it was his wife, Arina, who finally talked him into joining. "You say you don't have the time, but when it comes to prisoners, you won't be able to stay out of it," Arina said. "You might as well join. You'll wind up in jail whether you're in it formally or informally. Do it formally."

Orlov's other recruit, Mikhail Bernshtam, wanted to go beyond a public tribunal. The red-bearded, bespectacled thirty-two-year-old self-educated demographer was hoping for a military coup, followed by a prompt execution of twenty thousand people. He derived that figure by estimating the number of key officials in the party apparatus. After the liquidation, Bernshtam argued, Russia would be ready for democratic governance. When challenged—and that happened at many a dissident gathering—Bernshtam said that while a Nuremberg-style tribunal would make some dissidents happy, it wouldn't be expedient. It would delay the necessary bloodshed.

Bernshtam and Orlov became acquainted shortly after Bernshtam was released from a mental institution where he was placed after attempting to estimate of the number of people killed after the Bolshevik revolution. He submitted the work for peer review by Soviet demographers, but men with a straitjacket showed up instead. After his release, Bernshtam tried to organize a compendium of essays he called *Through the Swamp,* which he envisioned as a scathing attack on the intelligentsia and which he modeled on *From Under the Rubble,* a collection edited by Solzhenitsyn. One of the works he wanted to include was Orlov's "Is Nontotalitarian Socialism Possible?"

When Bernshtam told Landa he had decided to join Orlov's group, she seemed appalled. "You want to hang Bolsheviks on lampposts. So why are you so hot to 'assist' them in anything?!" she screamed.

Orlov also received a go-ahead from Anatoly Marchenko, a thirty-six-year-old worker who was first railroaded into the camps for a fight at age nineteen, served a two-year term, then made an unsuccessful attempt to cross the Soviet border and wound up back in the camps. One of his camp buddies was writer Yuli Daniel. After serving the second term, Marchenko wrote *My Testimony,* a brilliantly unassuming account of life in Khrushchev-era camps. Marchenko also wound up marrying Daniel's ex-wife, Larisa Bogoraz.

Another group recruit was Anatoly Korchak, a physicist who had never been associated with dissidents. Orlov also wanted to recruit former Major General Petr Grigorenko, whose military career ended in 1964, shortly after he started an underground organization that, using old Bolshevik tactics, printed leaflets demanding that the USSR return to the revolutionary principles of Leninism. Leninist activities got Grigorenko committed to a psychiatric hospital. He was released, only to be demoted to private for having protested the 1968 Soviet invasion of Czechoslovakia. In 1974, when Grigorenko was in a mental institution, an unofficial poet called him "a lucky man born in a straitjacket."

In April 1976, soon after the general got out of the hospital, he and Orlov met in Sakharov's apartment. Orlov gave his sales pitch. The general listened, showing no excitement. "I felt sick, and that may be why I saw nothing new in Yura's reasoning," Grigorenko recalled in the 850-page memoir he composed after being expelled to the West.

"I said to Orlov, 'Of course, the organization would introduce a new stream, but it would be doing the same human-rights defense that was being done before it.'

"It didn't occur to me that in that conversation Yura was inviting me to take part in the new organization," Grigorenko remembered.

CHAPTER 4

THE EXPERIMENT

I n 1975, soon after the Swedish Academy awarded him the Nobel Peace Prize, Andrei Sakharov found himself inundated with visitors bearing grievances, requests, and suggestions.

Up to three dozen people a day showed up at his cramped apartment on Chkalov Street, asking the academic-turned-fighter-for-justice to step in on their behalf, write letters to bureaucrats, arrange meetings with foreign reporters, offer blessings, or, sometimes, procure medication. Sakharov looked kindly on some requests, but for the most part, he had Ginzburg meet the supplicants outside the apartment door and say that Sakharov wasn't available. Typically, Ginzburg said, he invited Sakharov's visitors for chats at his place in Belyaevo-Bogorodskoye.

By 1976, Sakharov had spent eight years speaking out for human rights. He had written dozens of epistles to world leaders, and, along with other scientists, had taken part in a dissident experiment—the Committee of Human Rights. After severe internal disagreements, the committee had ground to a halt, failing to produce any results.

Since that experience, Sakharov developed an aversion to working within organizations, and with it, a stock response to anyone suggesting that he join or head any dissident group. It was an aversion that survived the Helsinki-group era. It survived even his years of exile in Gorky. "Because of my psychological makeup and aspirations, I am not and cannot be leader of any movement," Sakharov said in an interview with *The Washington Post* in 1986.

Orlov and Amalrik, too, had contributed to the barrage of suggestions that had descended on Sakharov. Early in 1976, months before the Helsinki-group idea, Orlov and Amalrik came to Sakharov with a proposed petition inviting the Politburo to begin a "dialogue" with society. The invitation was to be addressed to the new Politburo "elected" at the Twenty-fifth Congress of the party that was slated to begin in June 1976.

"In many countries, the Communist parties are moving from confrontation to dialogue with other societal groups," the invitation read. "The time has come to put an end to intolerance and listen to the voices of dissidents. Realizing this, we are extending our hand and inviting the representatives of CPSU to meet with the representatives of the Democratic Movement."

Sakharov said he didn't want to sign. When Orlov and Amalrik returned with another, more straightforward, invitation to the Politburo to get involved in a "dialogue" with society, Sakharov repeated that he wasn't interested in signing collective letters.

Now Orlov was about to ask Sakharov to head the Public Group of Assistance to Implementation of Helsinki Agreements in the USSR.

"By that time I knew Sakharov quite well, and I knew how he felt about groups and group documents, so I knew he wouldn't accept," Orlov said later. "But it would have been impolite of me not to ask him to head the group. The offer was just a matter of courtesy, but, of course, if he had agreed, it would have been wonderful, too."

On the morning of May 12, 1976, Orlov was served a summons to appear later that day at the KGB Cheremushki regional office.

The word of his attempt to start the group had reached the secret police, Orlov decided. Complying with the summons would have allowed the KGB to warn him about the legal consequences of this act. The physicist knew the agency's options. He could have been charged with willful and malicious slander against the USSR under Article 190-1, punishable by up to three years in the camps or five in internal exile. He could also have been charged with a similar offense under Article 70, which carries the punishment of up to seven years in prison and five in internal exile. The third option was the worst by far—treason. Here, the maximum penalty was death.

Orlov decided to ignore the summons and stayed home, weighing the options of starting the group ahead of schedule.

The announcement was to be made on May 15, and in the remaining three days, Orlov had to contact virtually all his prospective recruits. Orlov wanted Sakharov to host the group's first press conference, largely because reporters would be more likely to show up for a press conference held by an international celebrity. If the announcement were to be moved up to May 12, Western reporters would have to be invited on short notice, perhaps even late at night.

After 3:00 P.M., another summons arrived. The KGB was serious, Orlov concluded. Its next step would be to bring him to the interrogation by force, and that meant the formation of the group had to be announced immediately.

Orlov began to call prospective group members. He was able to reach demographer Bernshtam.

"Would you be able to come to my apartment?" Orlov asked.

"Right now?"

"Yes."

Bernshtam had spent the night and the better part of the day writing. He was tired and badly needed a shower. "I haven't even had a chance to wash up."

"It's important."

"If it's very important, I will come," said Bernshtam.

When Bernshtam got to Orlov's, the professor met him at the door. "Let's go outside," he said. His apartment was bugged.

"I have been summoned to the KGB," Orlov said.

"Does it mean we will announce today?"

"I am against it for strategic reasons. But for political reasons it's better to announce," said Orlov.

The group hadn't had a chance to plan out its future documents. To announce now would mean having to learn on the job, but not announcing would be at least as perilous, Orlov said. That way the KGB would be able to spend the next few days issuing warnings to his recruits, threatening them with prosecution or offering deals. Without the announcement, some prospective members might not feel ashamed to tell Orlov that they had reconsidered.

"I want them to deal with us as a group, not one by one," Orlov said.

"What do you want me to say?" asked Bernshtam. "I can see you've decided, and I agree."

Bernshtam went to take a bath at Ginzburg's. Then, from a telephone booth, he called Sakharov to ask the Nobel laureate if Orlov and he could come over later.

Late that evening, Bernshtam and Orlov met again. Orlov suggested taking a cab to Sakharov's, an idea that struck Bernshtam as extravagant.

As they got to Sakharov's apartment building, a minor dispute erupted over who would pay the 4-ruble fare. "I just made some money on lessons. Besides, it was my idea to take a cab," Orlov said, insisting on paying. "I just got paid for a dissertation I ghost-wrote," said Bernshtam. Both rejected the idea of splitting the fare, and, after a brief debate, the more emphatic Bernshtam paid the driver.

It was around 10:00 P.M. by the time Bernshtam and Orlov appeared at Sakharov's. The evening of rushing around had been only a limited success. Orlov and Bernshtam had yet to reach Grigorenko, and they had been unable to reach Shcharansky, who was visiting his parents in Istra, a town just outside Moscow.

At Sakharov's, Orlov made a few changes in the group's announcement: The name sounded loyal indeed. Public Group (there are thousands of those) of Assistance (very positive) to Implementation of the Helsinki Agreements in the USSR (why shouldn't citizens assist their country?). What followed was anything but loyal:

"The group will accept written complaints about violations of said articles directly from the citizens and concerning them personally as well as others, and—in a short form—would readdress those complaints to all the heads of governments who signed the Final Act as well as to their constituents. The group will retain the originals of complaints signed by their authors. . . .

"In some cases, when the group encounters specific examples of especially inhumane actions such as:

* Taking children away from parents intent on bringing them up in their faith,
* Forced psychiatric treatment of individuals aimed at changing their thoughts, conscience, religion, or beliefs,
* Especially dramatic cases of separation of families,
* Cases of especially inhumane treatment of prisoners of conscience,

the group plans to petition heads of government and their constituents with requests to form international commissions for checking the information on site, because the group will not always have the capability to conduct direct investigation of such important and responsible information. . . .

"The group hopes that all of its information would be considered at all official meetings planned under the Final Act."

The final passage came straight out of the declaration Shcharansky had suggested earlier:

"In their work, members of the Group of Assistance are guided by conviction that problems of humaneness and unrestricted flow of information are directly related to problems of international security and are calling upon people of all the countries-signatories of the Helsinki Agreement to form their own national Groups of Assistance to aid the process of complete implementation by their countries.

"We hope also that there would soon be formed the International Committee for Assistance."

"This is a serious document," said Sakharov after reading Orlov's handwritten announcement.

But, the Nobel laureate added, he still wasn't interested in joining, let alone heading any group. Working in groups contradicted his psychological makeup, Sakharov said once again. Groups meant meetings, debates, tempers, details.

Finally, Orlov and Sakharov hammered out a compromise: Sakharov would not join the group, but would host the first press conference and would announce that he fully supported the group. Sakharov's wife, Yelena Bonner, would join, but under no circumstances would she be expected to do any work.

"I have to say, I joined the group only formally," Bonner recalled a decade later. "I even said right at the outset that I wouldn't do any work. But I gave my name so that people would not think that Sakharov was against the group."

Orlov apparently didn't attach quite so much significance to Bonner's joining the group. "I was happy there was one more person joining, but I couldn't see Yelena Georgievna [Bonner] as a substitute for Andrei Dmitrievich [Sakharov]," Orlov said. "I respect her a great deal, but she is a person like the rest of us, an ordinary dissident, so to speak."

With the understanding that this would be the first and last time she would do any work for the group, Bonner sat down to type up Orlov's announcement.

But before the press could be called, Orlov needed to phone another illustrious figurehead, Grigorenko.

"'Petr Grigorievich, I want to announce the group. And I am counting on you,'" Orlov said in a conversation Grigorenko later recounted in his memoirs.

"'Yura, why do you need me, with my diseases? It's unlikely that I can be of any use to you now.'

"'We need your name.'

"'Well, if it's really so valuable, then let's continue this conversation tomorrow.'

"'No, it's impossible. I am calling from Andrei Dmitrievich's apartment. Foreign correspondents are already here. If I don't announce it today, then it seems I'll never announce it. For a week I have been followed by "our best friends."'

"'Well, then go ahead and include me.'"

Sakharov picked up the phone to call his usual contacts in the Western press corps.

The phones at most news bureaus weren't being answered;

11:00 P.M. was too late for a press conference. Only one reporter, from Reuters, showed up. It seems that when Orlov had told Grigorenko that "foreign correspondents are already here" he was hoping for a better turnout. There is also a chance that Grigorenko made an error in reconstructing the conversation.

The press conference began around 11:00 P.M., May 12. By morning, the Voice of America, BBC, Radio Liberty, and Deutsche Welle had picked up the Reuters wire story and broadcast reports of the formation of the Public Group of Assistance to Implementation of the Helsinki Agreements in the USSR.

Two physicists, three historians, a pediatrician, a journalist, a laborer-turned-writer and a general-turned-dissident took on the task of documenting their government's violations of the human-rights provisions of the Final Act.

"It's dangerous," a Jewish acquaintance warned Shcharansky. "They don't treat Jews as being as dangerous as people who want to change the system."

By joining the Orlov group, Shcharansky and Rubin had, in effect, become dissidents rather than merely Jews trying to emigrate.

Shortly after the news of the group reached the West, Ginzburg recalled, he received a note from Solzhenitsyn's wife, Natalya. "You are crazy," the note said.

CHAPTER 5

"WARNING TO PROVOCATEUR"

Orlov had some definite ideas about the way he wanted the Western press to cover his group's formation:

Day One stories would be straightforward nuts-and-bolts stories about the new group. On Day Two, Orlov wanted a hiatus, which would allow the news to sink in. On Day Three he wanted stories with headlines like: DISSIDENT STARTS GROUP, IS DETAINED, WARNED.

Orlov realized he had received two summonses, and the KGB wasn't about to issue a third. The agency would have him plucked off the street and brought to an investigator for the "official warning," then would release him. During the Stalin era, a man with a plan such as Orlov's would have simply disappeared, but in 1976 the KGB was bound by procedure. The new KGB had to wait for crimes to be committed before starting to prosecute—and it had to issue warnings.

To make sure a full day would elapse between Story One and Story Two in the Western press, Orlov decided to disappear

from Moscow for a day, making it impossible for the KGB operatives to find him. So, at 4:00 A.M., May 13, as the KGB agents
stationed around his first-floor apartment took a break or fell
asleep in expectation of the changing shift, Orlov opened the
window and disappeared into the night.

"It was a tactical move," he said.

But was the world clamoring for news about his group?

"Have you heard about this new group of assistance to something or other?" a friend asked Alexeyeva on May 13.

"Oh, my God, it's been announced. And I haven't told my
mother or husband," thought Alexeyeva, who hadn't had a
chance to listen to the radio the day before. "Who's in it?"

Her friend could list Ginzburg, Marchenko, Grigorenko,
Bonner, and Orlov. It appeared that Alexeyeva's name didn't
make the news item broadcast over the radio, an understandable
omission since she was unknown in the West. "Thank God for
that," she thought.

Shcharansky, listening to the radio at his parents' house in
Istra, assumed he was among the group members.

"When I heard the news on the radio, I was sure I was in the
group," Shcharansky said. However, the following day, in Moscow, he was surprised to hear his friend Rubin ask, "Tolya, have
you changed your mind at the last moment?"

That day, Shcharansky's name was added to the list, bringing
group membership to ten.

The morning after the announcement, Grigorenko began to
grumble about not having had a chance to think the matter
through. After all, the general had a lot to lose. He had gone
through treatment in psychiatric institutions, so the authorities
could easily dispatch men in white coats to his door and announce that his condition had suddenly taken a turn for the
worse. "I wish we had had a chance to do more planning," he
said to Orlov, then launched into a counterproposal to disband
the group and start a "producer cooperative" that would "produce" documents. Technically, producer cooperatives are
permitted under Soviet law; a "group" could be defined as an
anti-Soviet organization.

Reading between the lines of Grigorenko's suggestion, Orlov

and Alexeyeva concluded the general believed he had been pressured into joining the group. Almost immediately, another recruitment error came to the surface. It turned out writer Anatoly Marchenko had never agreed to join the group. Earlier, Alexeyeva conveyed the invitation with a friend who was about to visit Marchenko near the Siberian city of Irkutsk. But the message apparently got garbled in transmission, as did the response. Nonetheless, Marchenko agreed to stay on.

The story of the group's formation didn't excite editors in the United States. On May 14, *The New York Times* and the *Los Angeles Times* picked up a Reuters story that said nine dissidents on May 13 founded a "monitoring unit" to review their country's performance under the Helsinki Final Act. The "unit," Reuters reported, included Major General Petr Grigorenko and Mrs. Andrei Sakharov. *The New York Times* ran the story on page 8; the *Los Angeles Times* on page 19. *The Washington Post* ran no story at all.

That day, on page 1, the Los Angeles paper published another Moscow dateline story, one that the editors had judged to have greater appeal:

IT'S MEATLESS THURSDAY IN MOSCOW CAFES

MOSCOW (UPI)—The Soviet Union has banned the eating of meat in most Moscow restaurants on Thursdays.

Accentuating the positive, a sign outside a restaurant on a Moscow side street advertised: "Fish Every Thursday."

It was confirmation of a fact that has not been announced but which Soviet citizens have learned by word of mouth—meat is off the menu on Thursdays at the majority of restaurants in Moscow.

Western analysts said it was an effect of last year's poor grain harvest.

An official of Moscow's public catering department confirmed the ban. She said it applied to all Moscow restaurants with the exception of those that cater to foreign tourists and restaurants which serve regional specialties.

There was no lack of meat in the shops.

The meatless-Thursday story was quick and clean, a little zinger to add crunch to high-fiber breakfasts throughout the greater Los Angeles area. The Helsinki-group story was cumbersome. A group of the same old dissidents form a "unit," give it an unwieldy Soviet-style name, and set out to monitor a thirty-thousand-word wishy-washy document that doesn't even have an enforcement clause.

To cover the Helsinki group adequately, newspapers would have had to treat Soviet dissent as a political story, explore its alignments and subtle undercurrents. But did a tiny group of Moscow intellectuals warrant such coverage? To cover the group—or even to see it as a story—would have required reporters to read between the lines of a language most of them couldn't read at all.

"I thought there would be intensive coverage of the announcement," Orlov said later. "Now I know we were on page twenty."

On the morning of May 15, Orlov returned to his apartment to wait for the KGB to pick him up. But before he heard from the KGB, he got a visit from Bernshtam and Malva Landa.

Landa said she had heard a foreign radio broadcast about the group, and had given the invitation some thought. She said she still disliked Orlov's name for the group, and the idea of "assisting" the Soviets still revolted her. Nonetheless, she said she would be willing to join under the condition that she be allowed to outline her reservations in a letter that would be passed along to Western reporters.

"I feel the humanitarian articles of the Helsinki Agreement are insufficiently exact and sometimes unacceptable," she said in the letter. "I am joining the group, the name and the purposes of which I find unsatisfactory, hoping to take a more active and more effective role in collecting and transmitting information, unmasking inhumane actions of the Soviet administration."

By now the group had eleven members, most of whom planned to meet to plot strategy at Alexeyeva's apartment later that morning.

Orlov, Bernshtam, and Landa decided to walk there together. The three had barely left Orlov's apartment building when a dark Volga pulled up behind them. Quickly, before hot-tempered Landa got a chance to scream or strike the car's occupants with her backpack, plainclothesmen jumped out of the car, grabbed diminutive Orlov from behind, threw him in the backseat, and sped off. "Malva, who definitely would have started to scream had she had a chance, didn't get that chance," Orlov said later.

The plainclothesmen took Orlov to the Cheremushki regional KGB office.

"So you went ahead and announced the formation of the group before you came to see us," said an official who didn't identify himself, referring to the two summonses Orlov had ignored May 12.

"I didn't know what you wished to discuss," said Orlov.

Nobody has the right to question the Soviet government's sincerity in signing and implementing the Helsinki Final Act, the KGB official said. For that reason, he continued, the authorities considered the group illegal and unconstitutional.

Legality is something the courts, not the KGB, should decide, Orlov replied.

Orlov was released, but even before he left the KGB building, Tass moved this dispatch:

WARNING TO PROVOCATEUR

As it has become known to a Tass correspondent, the organs of state security have issued a warning to one Yuri Orlov about the unconstitutional nature of his activities.

Orlov, who once performed scientific work and was elected a corresponding member of the Academy of Sciences of the Armenian SSR, has in recent years dedicated himself exclusively to anti-Soviet activities.

Seeking to gain popularity among opponents of relaxation of international tensions as well as among the enemies of the USSR, Orlov, among others, began to hammer together a group of dissidents, calling it pretentiously and provocatively an organization of control over Soviet implementation of the Final Act of the Conference on Security and Cooperation in Europe.

It is difficult to classify Orlov's actions as anything but an attempt to cast doubt in the eyes of the world community about the sincerity of the Soviet efforts aimed at uncompromising realization of the undertaken international responsibilities, or as just another provocation aimed at erecting a barrier to relaxation of international tensions.

On May 15, Orlov was summoned to the organs of state security, where he, in accordance with Soviet jurisprudence, was officially warned about the unacceptibility of his actions. Such an action has a dual purpose: to put an end to Orlov's activity, and to prevent Orlov and other parties connected with him from committing acts punishable by law.

Now Orlov and others knew the KGB didn't regard monitoring of the Final Act as just another dissident exercise of tilting at windmills. "That Tass story helped us. It told [Western] reporters that we were important," Orlov said later. "First, they [the KGB] were bowing to my titles: Corresponding Member of the Armenian SSR Academy of Sciences, a Ph.D., a professor, well known in scientific circles. Second, I was well known to them. I wasn't that well known among dissidents, but thanks to my 1956 speech, which was denounced in *Pravda,* no less, I was highly regarded by the KGB."

The following day *The New York Times* reported that on May 15 three plainclothesmen had picked up the group leader, Yuri Orlov, and taken him to the KGB, after which Tass announced that Orlov had been warned to end his dissident activity.

"The Kremlin has denounced Western efforts to monitor Soviet compliance as interference in Soviet internal affairs," the story continued. "However, the prospect of having Soviet citizens, even dissidents, watching its actions in a formal manner poses a more awkward problem for Moscow. Today's incident suggested that the authorities planned to head off such a threat by treating it purely as anti-Soviet activity, which is a criminal offense under Soviet law."

The Helsinki group story had moved up to page 3, and it was longer than the Reuters May 13 piece. Thanks to the KGB, the story was becoming simpler—and thus more salable: GOOD DISSIDENTS VS. BAD KGB. To make page 3 of the *Times,* dissidents had to be warned. To make page 1, they would have

to be accused of treason, terrorism, and foreign-currency manipulations, arrested, and threatened with execution.

In the course of a year, all of the above would occur.

After leaving the KGB building, Orlov headed for Alexeyeva's apartment, where the group held a meeting to plan future documents.

Shcharansky was ready to write about "reunification of families," code for emigration. Ginzburg and Landa were prepared
to write about political prisoners. Orlov was ready to write
about interruptions of mail and telephone service.

"We have political prisoners, some of them women, and we
are going to lament about some dissidents who had their phones
cut off," Bernshtam objected to Orlov's priorities.

"But that's straight out of the Final Act," said Orlov.

"I won't sign it," said Bernshtam.

Bernshtam suggested a document, too. The historian and demographer wasn't happy with Orlov's decision to limit Helsinki-
group issues to human-rights abuses. Bernshtam wanted to deal
with military and trade issues too, a task he planned to accomplish by sounding off on the Soviet military maneuvers near the
Finnish border. Bernshtam interpreted this as the Soviet expression of support for Urho Kaleva Kekkonen, a candidate for the
presidency of Finland. The maneuvers constituted interference
in the internal affairs of a sovereign state, Bernshtam said.

"What is the Helsinki group? Are we a political opposition?
If we are, we shouldn't limit ourselves to Basket Three of the
Helsinki Final Act!" Bernshtam said.

"We are not a political organization," said Orlov. "We are a
human-rights organization."

When the conversation shifted to U.S. presidential elections,
Bernshtam, once again, was in the minority, he recalled.

"I am a Reagan supporter," he announced. "I wish Reagan
would beat Ford and Carter."

"But Reagan is not an intellectual," said Ginzburg. "I don't
want an actor-cowboy to run a great nation."

"How's an actor worse than a lawyer or a college professor?" retorted Bernshtam.

Everyone else in the group favored either Senator Henry

Jackson, author of an amendment that derailed the U.S.-Soviet trade agreement, or Jimmy Carter, who, despite being a mere Georgia peanut farmer, pledged to make the pursuit of human rights the centerpiece of America's foreign policy.

"I look at you, I listen to you, and I don't believe it. This is a meeting of a shadow government of Russia," said Galina Sokolova, Bernshtam's girlfriend.

"Yes, that's precisely what it is," said Rubin.

Five days later, Rubin wrote in his diary: "Yesterday Yura Orlov said quite correctly that the formation of the group raises the dissident movement to a new level. So far, the official reaction reveals extreme aggravation, which, in the final analysis, serves as advertisement for the group."

One of the group's more urgent goals was to appease Grigorenko. The general was making it clear that he was unhappy about having been rushed into the decision to join, but he was also making it clear that there was something he wanted.

That something was a document about Mustafa Dzhemiliev, a Crimean Tatar activist who had been sentenced three weeks earlier to a second prison term for anti-Soviet propaganda. The thirty-three-year-old Dzhemiliev meant a lot to the Moscow human-rights crowd. The young man was pleasant, correct-thinking, nonviolent, brave. Grigorenko used to call him affectionately *synok,* "my little son."

But what did the Dzhemiliev conviction have to do with the Helsinki Final Act? After all, the young man was convicted in accordance with Soviet law, and the Helsinki Final Act recognizes the sanctity of laws of signatory nations. That was not a simple problem, and Orlov asked Grigorenko to collaborate with Bernshtam in drafting the group's Document 1.

The document, which was presented at a press conference May 18, six days after the group was formed, argued that Dzhemiliev's conviction was illegal under Soviet law. And since the prosecution violated Soviet law, the conviction also contradicted the Final Act. "The violation of Soviet laws makes it impossible to apply the Final Act provision of noninterference in internal affairs, for that article calls for respect for *laws* of signatory countries, rather than respect for *lawlessness* covered up by falsifications."

The 1,200-word document failed to cause an international

stir. It had no news value; it was an intricate knot of legal theories juxtaposing Soviet laws with an unenforceable international declaration. Besides, the events surrounding the Dzhemiliev trial had been covered by the Western press.

If the Dzhemiliev trial was remembered at all, it was because on its opening day, Sakharov hit a uniformed guard in the face while being dragged from a courthouse hallway. In the same melee, Bonner struck two policemen. Sakharov and Bonner were arrested and held for a couple of hours. Later, at a press conference in his apartment, Sakharov appeared embarrassed by the incident, which constituted a crime punishable by up to five years' imprisonment. "I cannot deny it happened," he said to reporters, then added, "In my opinion, the militiamen should have stood on the side of the law and not on the side of the law violators."

For the dissidents, the Dzhemiliev conviction was a fresh wound; for newsmen it was a stale story. The document didn't make any of the major newspapers in the United States.

Orlov didn't think the Soviet postal service would deliver envelopes addressed to heads of thirty-five states. So he set out to find a roundabout way to make the group's findings known. Once, at a party, he approached a West German diplomat.

The diplomat said he would not be able to accept documents from the group.

"Why not?" Orlov asked.

"Your group has been pronounced unlawful by the Soviet government. We have no right to be in contact with such groups," Orlov later recounted the diplomat's reply.

"Does anyone in your country have the responsibility of watching over the Soviet Union's compliance with the Helsinki Final Act?" Orlov persisted.

"No. Nobody does."

"So why can't you accept documents from us?"

"Because you are not an official group, and since you are an unofficial group, we have no right to be in contact with you."

The American diplomats were more sympathetic to Orlov's cause. A midlevel official with whom Orlov had been acquainted said regulations prevented the embassy from accepting documents from Soviet citizens. But he suggested a way around the rule: Orlov would hand his group's documents to U.S. citizens— say, reporters—who would pass them along to the embassy. The U.S. officials would then distribute the documents to the embassies of Britain and Canada.

"They didn't say they wouldn't accept our documents," Orlov said. "They said they couldn't accept our documents *officially*."

CHAPTER 6

KISSINGER'S TORMENTOR

On May 17, 1976, three days after the KGB "officially warned" Orlov, a tall patrician lady rose to address her fellow members of the U.S. Congress.

"Mr. Speaker, we are coming now to the moment of decision on the question of [forming] a commission on security and cooperation in Europe to monitor the accords that were written into an international agreement in Helsinki," Representative Millicent Fenwick, a Republican from New Jersey, said in her husky voice.

The House was about to act on Fenwick's bill which would create a bipartisan commission consisting of six senators and six House members, joined by the representatives of the Commerce, State, and Defense departments. It was a political hybrid of the legislative and the executive branches; a mix that, critics said, made it a political eunuch.

Once, at a breakfast meeting, Secretary of State Henry Kissinger told Fenwick she was setting a "dangerous precedent." Dangerous because Congress would in effect be given a say in the carrying out of foreign policy, which Kissinger considered the exclusive domain of the executive. But Fenwick's idea didn't go away, and Kissinger began to jokingly call the New Jersey congresswoman his "tormentor."

Fenwick had first introduced the bill nine months earlier, but the administration's opposition contributed to keeping it moored in the Senate and the House Committee on International Relations. Late in April, eight months after introduction, the bill cleared the Senate and got out of the committee.

It seemed fitting for such a bill to come from Fenwick. She referred to the downtrodden as "poor dears," spoke proper English, smoked a pipe, and generally stood out enough to inspire the Lacey Davenport character in the *Doonesbury* comic strip. Over the years, Fenwick advocated the most exquisite of causes, including human and civil rights.

In the summer of 1975, Fenwick traveled to the USSR, where she met with dozens of dissidents and refuseniks. This bill was something she was doing for them—and the cause of civil liberties everywhere.

"I think we should take note that at this moment there is a small group of dissidents, Jews, Catholics, and others, maybe only nine people in all, who have formed a group in the Soviet Union to do the same thing," said Fenwick. "We in this country are free, but in that country, one of the group, Dr. Yuri Orlov, was picked up on the street and questioned for many hours concerning his activity in this regard. Dr. Vitaly Rubin, a distinguished sinologist, is also in the group.

"They and we are hoping that these international accords will not be just another empty piece of paper.

"Here today we have a chance to take a first step in the direction of true compliance. Mr. Speaker, in enacting this legislation, I think we would be speaking to those principles that have distinguished this country for many years. There is nothing new about America's concern for other people. When I was a child, there was a terrible flood in the Yellow, or Yangtze, River in China, and many small churches in Ohio and in New Jersey and in Colorado sent aid to the Chinese. This is the kind of nation we have always been.

"Respect for the dignity of the individual has been one of

our principles, and the rights of the individual, and the right of dissent as proclaimed so eloquently by Thomas Jefferson in his inaugural address.

"Mr. Speaker, this kind of concern is native to America. This ought to be the basis of our international relations. These ought to be the things of which we speak to the world: a concern for our fellow human beings, knowing that we are all one family, regardless of distance and descent or any other kind of barrier; concern for their right to freedom of religion, for their right to travel and be unified with their families. This is what this bill is about."

In August 1975, Fenwick was in a congressional delegation on a junket to the USSR.

On that trip Fenwick met some of the most desperate people she had ever seen. They were Jewish refuseniks. They were out of work, and desperate enough to seek help from representatives of a foreign power. Those visits inspired a speech, which she later repeated in the House, at meetings with her constituents, and to the press:

"We would meet them at nights at hotels in Moscow and Leningrad. I would ask them, 'How do you dare to come see us here?'

" 'Don't you understand?' they would say. 'That's our only hope. We've seen you. Now the KGB knows you've seen us.' "

At least once the "we-met-them-at-nights" speech was accompanied with: "I felt, my God, it's like being on a transatlantic steamer in the middle of a terrible storm, and seeing people go by in rafts, and we are trying to pick them up, but can't. But at least we have our searchlights on them."

During meetings with refuseniks, Fenwick took notes. Later, several of the refuseniks she met said they had assumed she was a congressional secretary rather than a member of Congress. In Moscow, Fenwick got a visit from Lilia Roytburd, an Odessa woman. Eleven months earlier, Lilia and her husband, Lev, had applied for an exit visa to Israel. The application was denied. Lev was fired from his engineering job, called "an imperialist puppet" by the local newspaper, then apprehended at the Odessa airport as he carried an appeal he wanted to present to

Senators Edward Kennedy and Jacob Javits. He was arrested and charged with striking a militia officer.

"She took out of her wallet a picture of herself and her son and her husband, and there was a young healthy woman with thick, black, bushy hair," Fenwick recalled. "I asked, 'When was this picture taken?' I thought it was five or ten years ago.

"She said, 'Six months ago,' and I looked up at her tiny ravaged face with hair slicked close to the skull, and tears came to my eyes. I still have nightmares about it." The two images of Lilia Roytburd kept haunting Fenwick long after her return to the United States.

On her last day in Moscow, Fenwick strayed from the delegation to stop by at Belyaevo-Bogorodskoye. *New York Times* reporter Christopher Wren had given her the address of his source Valentin Turchin, head of the Moscow chapter of Amnesty International. "I had never seen an American congressman, especially a woman American congressman," recalled Turchin. His wife, Tatiana, had half an hour to make tea. Then, the Turchins remember, they dispatched one of their sons to get Orlov.

Appearing to have stepped out of the pages of *Vogue* of the 1940s (where she had been an editor), Fenwick settled down for a cup of Indian tea, lit up her pipe, and asked Tatiana Turchin how many children she had. Tatiana said she had two sons. Fenwick said she had eight grandchildren.

"What marvelous tea," Tatiana remembered Fenwick saying. Tatiana wrapped her a pack to take home. No major political issues were discussed.

Fenwick didn't retain much of a memory of meeting Orlov. She remembered the Turchins and their "humble little apartment" in the newer section of Moscow. She remembered the tea. ("They made such an effort. Strawberry jam and such, you know.") And she remembered that "there was someone else there." In Fenwick's mind, the memory of Yuri Orlov was displaced by the image of grief-stricken Lilia Roytburd.

On the last day of the trip, in Yalta, Fenwick asked General Secretary Brezhnev to look into some of the humanitarian cases she had found. The Soviet leader told her she was "obsessed."

In Fenwick's case, the General Secretary may not have been too far off the mark. The way Fenwick tells it, she was haunted by Lilia's image. "I kept thinking, 'We've got to do something for Lilia. We've got to do something.'" On the trip, Fenwick also became a believer in the dissident theory of Soviet susceptibility to international pressure: The harder you push, the more you will get.

On September 5, 1975, days after her return, Fenwick introduced her bill proposing the creation of the Commission on Security and Cooperation in Europe.

The commission would, in effect, systematically monitor fulfillment of promises made in the Final Act. This was far more ambitious an undertaking than the Jackson-Vanik Amendment, which simply tied emigration to trade benefits, avoiding the question of what happens to the rights of those who aren't trying to leave the USSR.

On November 17, Senator Clifford Case (R-N.J.) introduced his version, taking eight months to shepherd it through the Senate. Fenwick had to make some compromises along the way. Representative Dante B. Fascell (D-Fla.) allowed the bill out of his Subcommittee on International Operations after he and Fenwick agreed that Fascell would chair the commission. "I always say, 'Get the cash, let the credit go,'" Fenwick later said of that deal.

On April 23, 1976, the bill was reported out of the Committee on Foreign Relations. On May 5 it sailed through the Senate. On May 17, the day Fenwick informed her colleagues about the Orlov group, the bill passed the full House.

On June 3, when President Ford signed the bill, only he, Fenwick, and Case were present.

The commission's formation came as a pleasant surprise to Orlov. It seemed like an incredible coincidence. A congresswoman he had met had formed a commission that would have similar aims as his Moscow Helsinki Watch group.

In September, while the Helsinki Commission was hiring staff, Orlov wrote to Fenwick that the Moscow group would now send its findings to the commission. He also offered Fenwick a glimpse at his motivation for starting the group:

"[Dissidents] can be compared with people who openly throw themselves on barbed wire, hoping that there will be others who will step on their bodies to cross that wire," Orlov wrote on September 5. In late November, Orlov received a reply from Helsinki Commission chairman Dante Fascell. "We look forward very much to receiving more of the [Moscow group] reports in the months to come," Fascell wrote.

Later, the KGB seized the Fascell letter and used it to demonstrate that Orlov was receiving instructions from the United States. In their criminal case files, Orlov and Shcharansky saw the secret police asserting that Fenwick's Helsinki Commission had organized the Moscow Helsinki Watch group.

In their quest for an international conspiracy, the KGB detectives had apparently dismissed the possibility that when the future founder of the Helsinki monitoring commission in the United States met the future founder of the Moscow Helsinki Watch group, neither said anything the other considered worthy of remembering.

CHAPTER 7

THE BOYS FROM
SAD-SAM

I n May 1976, as the Public Group of Assistance to Implementation of the Helsinki Agreements in the USSR announced
its formation, Western reporters reacted skeptically.

"It didn't seem important. There was simply too much other
noise," recalled Robert Toth, a *Los Angeles Times* reporter.
Contributing to that noise were hundreds of dissidents of all
shades who were coming out in the open, holding press conferences, issuing statements, demanding, demanding, demanding.

"It's not enough to organize a new group of the same people," recalled Peter Osnos, *Washington Post* Moscow bureau reporter from 1974 to 1977. In Moscow, Osnos had earned the
animosity of several dissidents by trying to explain to them that
their story had been blown out of proportion by the Western
press. Sometimes, the dissidents' chats with Osnos deteriorated
into shouting. Amalrik, for instance, could make an evening's
conversation of Osnos-bashing.

"Behind our backs, it turns out, the journalists were reasoning, 'What are dissidents? They are a small group. But what about the grass roots? Do dissidents have any support there?'" Orlov said after his release. "It was true, we were a small group. But it was wrong for some of them to conclude that small groups are unimportant. Some of them seemed to think that only national leaders play important roles in history. This seems to be a very popular approach to history in the West."

The relationship between Soviet dissidents and Western reporters was never simple. It began in 1966, on the courthouse steps, when reporters were waiting for news from the Sinyavsky and Daniel trial.

Over the years, reporters and dissidents grew closer. Reporters needed stories; dissidents needed to let the world know about their causes. Frequently, reporters and dissidents broke bread (and drank vodka) together, but neither group seemed to truly understand the other.

There has hardly been a reporter who can't recall a dissident contact saying, "You must do this story because it will help so-and-so." Generally, it was pointless to argue that helping so-and-so is not the reason Western journalists are sent to the USSR.

On many occasions, dissidents accused reporters of insensitivity and lack of knowledge of Russian language and history. A number of reporters were also accused of having forgotten they were free men and bowing to the Soviet authorities.

Yet Western reporters were the Soviet dissidents' most important connections. Minutes after being written, news stories from Moscow came off the Teletypes at the Voice of America in Washington or Radio Liberty in Munich. Then, within minutes, they could be translated into Russian and transmitted back to the USSR. It was common for refuseniks and dissidents to make a statement to the press, then to hear it over shortwave radio. A mere two-hour lapse between a news event in Moscow and its coverage by the Voice was common. Fewer of these stories made the papers and television and radio broadcasts inside the United States. Most dissident stories were considered too specialized. The stories would rattle off the foreign wire, then wind up slashed to three graphs or simply spiked by editors.

In 1965, Amalrik contemplated writing a Gogol parody about a Western reporter who is called to the Ministry of Foreign Affairs, accused of being systematically anti-Soviet, and given a lashing. The reporter contemplates his dilemma: On the one hand, it is unpleasant to have been whipped, but one has to consider Russia's long-standing traditions. Besides, should he protest, the Russians could take offense; they are, after all, so sensitive to interference in internal affairs. Legal implications aren't clear cut, either, the journalist thinks. Reporters don't have diplomatic immunity. It could also be embarrassing to present a naked rear end as an exhibit. One shouldn't be guided by emotions that stem from a hot-whipped rear end. Instead, one should clearly and impartially consider the positive as well as the negative. The journalist understands this; he even understood it while he was being lashed.

The parody was never written, except as a brief synopsis in Amalrik's memoirs. Instead, Amalrik wrote an essay describing one day in the life of a foreign reporter in Moscow. The reporter starts off by having his translator, whom he knows to be a KGB spy, read to him from *Pravda* or *Krasnaya zvezda* (*The Red Star,* the armed-forces newspaper). He takes that as "the official comment." Then he walks down the hall of the foreigners' compound where he lives to discuss the story with his neighbor, a man just like himself. He quotes the neighbor as "observers." Under extraordinary circumstances, he also turns to his maid or his chauffeur for a "man in the street" quote. "Then the reporter has to decide whether the story fits into the context of 'liberalization' or 'return to Stalinism.'"

Amalrik wasn't happy with Western newspaper editors, either. When *The New York Times* paid him $150 for an essay, he called the honorarium "symbolic" and told the *Times* to give it to its "pensioners." Later, in the West, he found out that he had been paid no less than other free-lance contributors. Presumably he also learned that by and large the *Times* retirees are a comfortable lot.

By 1976, the relationship between dissidents and reporters was becoming more complicated: Editors in the United States were getting fed up with tales of human desperation behind the Iron Curtain. To be salable, a story had to have a new twist, a new angle.

*   *   *

The Moscow assignment came as a relief to *Los Angeles Times* reporter Robert Toth.

For two years, Toth had what may have been the worst beat next to those of night cops. He covered the White House, an assignment that, during the Watergate era, meant picking up official reactions to allegations of misconduct by the president and administration officials and fashioning them into stories with leads that went something like "The White House Tuesday denied . . ."

For a year after the White House, Toth recuperated at Harvard, with a Nieman Fellowship for journalists. That year, he took a course in genetics, learning once again the tragicomic saga of the Soviet Academy member Trofim Lysenko, who, in the 1930s, claimed to have disproved genetics as a bourgeois pseudoscience. Genetics is non-Marxian, Lysenko claimed, since Marxism holds that development of plant and animal life forms is determined by environmental rather than hereditary factors. This scientific discovery led to the extermination of Soviet geneticists.

At Harvard Toth had refreshed his interest in engineering, a field in which he had an undergraduate degree. He sharpened his science writer's instincts, once again picking up the specialization he had dropped when he joined the *Los Angeles Times*'s Washington bureau.

Toth was the last-minute replacement for the Moscow job after Joe Alex Morris, the reporter who had been picked for the bureau, developed cancer. Toth had less than a summer to prepare for the assignment—not enough time to learn Russian. Still, he had a daring plan for his three years in Moscow. Instead of focusing on the Soviet economy or Kremlin watching, he wanted to break stories about Soviet science, medicine, technology, areas that had rarely been probed by Western reporters. This was an ambitious plan, considering that the Soviets have had a tradition of making an arbitrary distinction between "secret" and "open."

Toth knew that the Soviet scientific community was in upheaval. Hundreds of Jewish scientists, doctors, engineers, and mathematicians were petitioning to emigrate to Israel. Many had been denied emigration and hence had become non-citizens—not trusted enough to continue their work at home, yet considered too knowledgeable to be allowed to leave.

Non-Jewish scientists were also coming out into the open, challenging the state. They, too, were losing jobs, becoming political pariahs and, therefore, potential sources. A large number of Soviet citizens had lost all reluctance to talk to Western journalists. Jews and Gentiles alike were calling press conferences, issuing statements, holding demonstrations. Some of their *press-konferentsii* were legitimate news events, and nearly all were places to make contacts that could produce stories having nothing to do with emigration and dissent.

Soon after Toth arrived in Moscow, word got around that the new *Los Angeles Times* bureau chief was an *"intelligentnyy chelovek,"* a refined man rather than a pushy American newshound. He could sit and listen through stories without trying to fit them into the "inverted pyramid" format taught in journalism schools. His interests and engineering background made him easily accepted in the intelligentsia circles.

In July 1974, Toth came to a press conference at the apartment of Aleksandr Luntz, a mathematician who had been denied emigration and who had become the leading spokesman for Soviet Jews. Toth exchanged a few words with a balding young man, the translator. On a later occasion, Toth wound up using the translator's name in a story. Just after that story appeared in the Los Angeles paper and the *International Herald Tribune,* Toth and the translator had another, more memorable, meeting.

"If you are going to use my name, spell it right," the young man said to Toth, "spell it correctly. S-h-c-h, not S-h, as you had it." Then, as if trying to avoid coming through as yet another nitpicking dissident, Shcharansky added, "It will never become a household name."

To make inroads into Soviet science Toth needed a translator, a dissident who would agree to strike an informal, or better yet unspoken, reporter-source deal: a little publicity for a little translating and a little guidance.

Soon after their second meeting, Shcharansky started to call Toth at his apartment in the foreign reporters' compound at 12/24 Sadovo-Samotechnaya Street, a place nicknamed "Sad-Sam" by its residents. Since the phones were bugged, Toth typically came out of his apartment, crossed the four-lane Garden Ring Road, and waited under the clock of the Obraztsov puppet theater. Frequently Toth brought his three children, and the four Toths and Shcharansky strolled in the nearby square, passing the *Literaturnaya gazeta*, a farmers' market, the Mir movie theater, and the old circus.

On some such walks, Toth told Shcharansky about the limitations he faced back home. Dissidents, Toth said, weren't the reason the *Los Angeles Times* had sent him to Moscow. His editors wanted stories about all of Russia, its science, culture, and people.

Shcharansky listened. After a few such meetings, he surprised Toth by bringing stories that had nothing to do with dissent or emigration. Those were pieces about science, medicine, politics, academics, humor. Once, Shcharansky and Toth drove to the Sakharovs' dacha. Since the physicist spoke no English, Shcharansky translated.

"He realized that for helping me get stories that interested me, I would be more receptive to his ideas on dissident stories," Toth said in an interview later. "It was an unspoken quid pro quo."

As a result, on March 26, 1976, the *Los Angeles Times* readers who got as far as page 7 of Section VII found a piece about the emigration problems faced by Lydia Voronina, a Russian woman seeking emigration to Israel. At the time, Shcharansky and Voronina were roommates. It was a Kafkaesque Eastern European story with a fresh (if slightly forced) American spin:

Soviet Woman's Exceptional Case

HER MOTHER WON'T LET HER EMIGRATE

MOSCOW—Lydia Voronina's is an exceptional case. Soviet officials using precisely those words told her so.

"Yours is an exceptional case for which the law has no provisions," one said in refusing her permission—without citing a legal reason—to emigrate and join her husband in Israel. "Only if your mother approves can you go," she quoted the official as saying.

Her mother is a senior influential official in the Soviet Justice Ministry. Even the daughter doesn't know her precise title. A dedicated lifelong Communist, "she is the personification of 'Soviet Power,'" Lydia said, "and will never agree to let me go because that would be to deny her entire life."

The case shows that a high Soviet bureaucrat can use extralegal methods 20 years after Stalin's death. . . .

Toth said he was never given the more bizarre aspects of the story. He was never told that Voronina and her husband had been divorced and that in her exit application she said she sought "reunification with a former husband."

When Shcharansky tried to peddle stories Toth believed weren't unusual enough to sell to the foreign desk in L.A., he said, "Hey, didn't I do something like that two weeks ago?" Inevitably, Shcharansky backed off. "He understood that, and he sought ways to get around it," Toth said. "Maybe that was one of his great traits."

This relationship went beyond journalism. Toth generally agreed to use his embassy contacts to send the refuseniks' appeals, letters, and manuscripts to the West. On one occasion, Toth went out of his way to buy a pair of snow tires for a young man who served as the refuseniks' courier. The tires were obtained through a U.S. Embassy official.

In May 1976, Shcharansky told Toth about a human-rights group that was about to be formed, the Public Group of Assistance to Implementation of the Helsinki Agreements in the USSR. This news didn't strike Toth as significant; protocol stories were usually handled by the wires, then run in the back of the paper, if at all. Toth was in Moscow for the more exciting stuff.

The Soviets seemed to have ended their practice of expelling reporters they found particularly offensive. The last such expulsion had taken place in 1972, before Nixon's visit to Moscow. So, by 1976, reporters began to lose their fear of the KGB.

Early in 1976 Associated Press reporter George Krimsky decided to try to put together a story about a typical day in the life of a Soviet soldier. Krimsky, thirty-four, told his refusenik and dissident contacts that he wanted to be introduced to a recently discharged recruit. The source would be guaranteed anonymity, and the questions Krimsky would ask would deal strictly with the life-style. What's it like in basic training? Does some sergeant make them bounce a kopek on the just-made bunk? Is there leave? Do they drink? Smoke? Get laid off post?

In retrospect, Krimsky said, the attempt to do the Soviet GI story was a big mistake.

Unlike Toth, Krimsky spoke enough Russian to get around.

He wasn't a Russian scholar, just a guy with an intuitive feel for the language. As soon as he arrived in the USSR, Krimsky's notebooks began to fill with little expressions he picked up along the way. They were curiosity items, the especially hideous forms of bureaucratese and the especially light street slang and intelligentsia argot.

The Russian expression for "new types of weapons of mass destruction" appealed to him during a Brezhnev speech. "Please rid me of your presence" he scribbled on a less formal occasion. "Long live the Great October [revolution] which opened the new era of revolutionary renewal of the world, the transition from capitalism to socialism," he scribbled while at Moscow's Lenin Museum. *"Besovshchina,"* "demonism," he jotted down at some press conference. "Live forever, learn forever, still you'll die a fool," he wrote on another occasion.

Unlike most of his colleagues in the Moscow press corps, Krimsky had no stellar academic credentials. In Moscow, the boot camp for future news executives, he was a maverick—a massive, rumpled, lumbering chain smoker, the kind of man who runs on adrenaline, nicotine, enthusiasm, and caffeine. Krimsky's Russian name was the legacy of his grandfather, a Russian Jew. The name means "from the Crimea."

George grew up on Long Island and the West Coast, went to Middlebury to study political science and psychology, flunked out after two years, and never went back. To avoid being drafted for less cushy duty, he volunteered to the Defense Language School in Monterey. He got the language he cared to know least—Russian.

After two years of listening to Soviet cables from a monitoring station on a hill in West Berlin, disheveled, unshaven, and with no experience, Krimsky wandered into the newsroom of the *Republican and American,* in Waterbury, Connecticut.

At that stage, Krimsky's career ambition was to report from the USSR. After two years of covering Waterbury's suburbs, Krimsky sent his résumé to AP. On top of the résumé was his picture, taken in front of the Crimean Bridge, *Krimsky most,* during his tourist trip to Moscow. There he was, an American named George Krimsky in front of *Krimsky most,* smiling. He was hired for AP's Los Angeles bureau—just in time to cover the Manson slayings.

In 1975, on his arrival in Moscow, two unexpected guests showed up at the bon-voyage party for the man Krimsky was to replace. The guests were Andrei Sakharov and wife, Yelena Bonner. Foreigners were amazed to see the two walk through the militia checkpoint at the entrance to Sad-Sam. Sakharov had been writing appeals, running an unofficial think tank, standing outside the courthouses where political trials were held, but up to that day he had never done anything quite as demonstrative as appearing at a party put on by Western journalists.

Dissidents seemed to be losing what little fear they had to begin with, Krimsky concluded. That meant they would make fine background sources.

Within weeks after first tapping his dissident network on the Soviet GI story, Krimsky got a call from a refusenik named Leonid Tsypin. Tsypin said he had the perfect subject, and he was ready to set up a meeting. The former Soviet soldier, in his mid-twenties, wore Levi's blue jeans with a matching jacket and spoke English fluently. He introduced himself as Igor Glebov. "He was as smooth as straight Stolichnaya," Krimsky recalled.

To check the GI out, Krimsky invited him to dinner at his apartment. The young man accepted, a move that signified that he didn't mind being seen by the militia guard. Krimsky's wife, Paula, made dinner; Krimsky put vodka on ice. By the time Krimsky got to the first question, he was mellow, as, presumably, was his guest.

There is no telling how much vodka was consumed that night—"Enough. I couldn't make a fist the next morning," Krimsky said later. Also the next morning, he recalled a few puzzling bits of information his guest had fed him:

"All Soviet soldiers wear uniforms saturated with chemical-weapon repellents" was one. "Ninety percent of all noncommissioned officers in the Soviet Army are Ukrainian" was another. What was that, wondered Krimsky; all he wanted to know about was bouncing coins on the beds, going on leave, and getting laid. Later, Krimsky recalled, he drove the young man to the metro station. As the two sat in Krimsky's car, the young man said something like "I'd like to meet with you again, but my work is sensitive. . . ."

Krimsky suggested a way out: a code. Call me at the AP office, say you are "John," then set up a meeting. If the meeting is set up for Wednesday at 4:00 P.M., it means Thursday at 3:00 P.M. Krimsky even scribbled a note to that effect.

A week or so later, while having a hamburger at the U.S. Embassy, Krimsky ran into an official from the military attaché's office. "Is it true that ninety percent of all noncommissioned officers are Ukrainian?" Krimsky asked. "Hell, no," the official replied.

The Soviets had to have been aware of the strengthening of ties between dissidents and the press. They also knew of the emergence of the new breed of dissident this relationship seemed to foster—the networking rebel. Shcharansky was a good example of that new variety. He was at the heart of the Jewish emigration and human-rights movements. His circle of acquaintances stretched from Minsk to Washington, and he could produce instant contacts for anyone within his network.

He was receiving foreign visitors, taking them around town, and he didn't object to being photographed or quoted. He was hobnobbing with embassy officials, helping reporters develop stories. Prominent U.S. visitors frequently tried to intervene on his behalf, as when Senator Patrick J. Leahy, a Vermont Democrat, brought Shcharansky a letter from Avital.

With détente still a buzzword in Washington, this was not the time for Moscow to crack down on the few networking activists and their friends in the press. Not ready to cut their ties with the West, the Soviets exercised restraint. In May 1976, it still wasn't clear which administration would take over in Washington. Would it be Ford and Kissinger? Or would a Democratic front-runner, most likely Carter, become president? In this atmosphere of uncertainty, a crackdown on dissidents and the expulsion of reporters seemed too drastic. So the Soviets decided on a halfway measure—a threat.

It was delivered on page 9 of the May 27, 1976, issue of *Literaturnaya gazeta.* In an article titled THE CIA AMENDMENT TO THE USA CONSTITUTION, three U.S. reporters were accused of espionage. It was the first such accusation in more than five years. "The First Amendment to the U.S. Constitution is being violated by Krimsky, a correspondent of Associated Press, [Christopher] Wren, a representative of *The New York Times,* and [Alfred] Friendly [Jr.], a journalist from *Newsweek.* Their loyalty to their true master, the CIA, in a remarkable way coincides with their responsibility to the free press."

As evidence of this "espionage," *Literaturnaya gazeta* reported only that it had received letters from Soviet citizens in Moscow, Tbilisi, and Tallin. Those letters "concretely and convincingly describe the hostile work of these gentlemen 'correspondents in plainclothes' in the Soviet Union, including their heightened, and more than journalistic, interest in several military-related materials and military sites."

All three reporters and their publications promptly denied the charges. Friendly, whose Moscow stint with *Newsweek* was ending, barely had enough time to file a suit against *Literaturnaya gazeta* in a Soviet court. (The suit was later dropped because *Newsweek* wasn't interested in pursuing it.) AP and *The New York Times* didn't join Friendly's suit.

When he read the *Literaturnaya gazeta* story, Krimsky began to suspect that he might have been framed with the help of his "GI" source. A month later, *Literaturnaya gazeta* published another attack on the Western press:

> The Editors of *Literaturnaya gazeta* have received a letter signed by 14 American journalists accredited in Moscow. In its content, it is a protest; in its tone, it is an ultimatum. Objecting to our publication of the article "The CIA Amendment to the U.S. Constitution," the authors of the letter "strongly protest," are "appalled" and "deny."
>
> They demand "satisfaction": the newspaper must apologize. Or . . . God only knows what will happen. In any case, while reading the letter, our imagination portrayed 14 in-

sulted . . . musketeers, who, holding their half-drawn rapiers, froze in threatening anticipation of a reply. . . .

We don't mean to repeat ourselves, but we remember the teaching of Voltaire that every letter merits a response. . . .

The newspaper's response included a list of questions Wren had asked during his trips around the USSR, questions that *Literaturnaya gazeta* claimed were aimed at finding out the way a Yakutia hydroelectric station supplies electric power to the military and the number of troops in the city of Aldan; Wren even took pictures of "objects prohibited for photography" in Ust-Ilimsk. *Newsweek*'s Friendly, who by then had filed a libel suit, was accused of asking about "the presence of troops" in Khorezmskaya oblast (region). Krimsky was the star of the story:

> Apparently feeling that the pose of "insulted innocence" is inappropriate for the occasion, another member of the "holy trinity," Associated Press correspondent George Krimsky, decided it would be better not to apply to the newspaper with his grievances. At the time, the newspaper already had a copy of this letter:

Dear Comrade Editor,

Should you decide to publish my letter, I request that you not state my name, address, and place of work. I shall describe these events to the appropriate authorities, and will ask them to consider my appeal as a . . . wholehearted confession. Besides, my name is very well known by the Associated Press reporter in Moscow, George Krimsky.

I met him a month and a half ago. After learning that I had served in the Soviet Army and work at a Soviet military installation, he expressed an interest in the life of "simple soldiers" in the Soviet Army. We met several times since, and every meeting was followed by my being treated to alcoholic beverages to which, I must say, George himself isn't impartial.

At first I was attracted by his attention, and by what I thought to be his attempts to obtain objective information about the life of our country. He did a lot of talking about the role of the "free press" and its influence on politics in the countries of the West. I thought George was a sincere and honest man, and that we could be friends. That is, until his behavior made me suspicious.

At one of the meetings, which took place in George's apartment, after plying me with liquor, he offered to take me home in his car. Then, having stopped in Lyalin Street, he, for the duration of an hour and a half, questioned me about service in the army, about the moral-political condition of the troops, the discipline, the relations between officers and subordinates, and many other things. Then, after a long and incomprehensible ride around town which lasted for about two hours, he scribbled on a sheet of paper the code that I must use in my telephone conversations with him. George said that from now on he would call me "John," and asked me to use that name in my conversations with him. Then there were other questions about the army, then, insistent follow-up questions.

We agreed that I would call George every Monday, but on May 24, I didn't do so, and wrote two letters instead. One was a letter to the official organs, since I have now understood what sort of use the representative of a foreign news agency, who called himself my friend, had for me. Why am I writing to you? Because your newspaper devotes a lot of attention to propaganda of the Helsinki decisions to develop contacts and exchange of spiritual values.

May 24, 1976.

P.S. So you would not have any doubts about the sincerity of my story, I am sending you the note (or, more correctly, the instruction) which was written to me by the Associated Press correspondent George Krimsky.

Later, reflecting on his error, Krimsky said, "All reporters had some kind of a system to protect their sources, but it was stupid of me to write it down."

The story ran on Tuesday, June 22. For the next seven days, Krimsky kept a chronology of the KGB assault on his reputation. Abbreviations, lower case, and all, it was Krimsky's report to himself:

wednesday, june 23—the day was hectic, full of fone calls from various asundry russians . . . several russians, all shady, said they wanted to protest to litgaz [*Literaturnaya gazeta*] on my behalf. i told them that would do neither of us any good but they could do what they wanted.

that night, i meet L. [Leonid Tsypin], the source who introduced me to the legendary "john." he told me that john asked me to arrange a meeting, that john told him that he had been questioned by the kgb at the defense ministry and gave them a false confession, saying the relationship was based on his desire to buy a western tape recorder. i told L that was bullshit, that the guy was a complete stooge for the kgb—the proof being that he enclosed in his so-called letter of repentance a note on our "arrangement" (time and date) which i had written. L seemed genuinely shocked by this and said he had learned a good lesson.

thursday, june 24—while working night, soviet man called in english and asked, "is this the spy?" i wearily replied that it was, and i then recognized the voice as that of "john." i asked what he wanted. he said he wanted to meet. i said i thought that was very funny. what did he want to meet me for? "i want to join the cia," he replied. i told him i wasn't a recruiter for the cia and he'd have to talk to the agency directly. i told him he was a "bad actor" and asked him not to call again. then i hung up. this conversation proved to me that this guy was hardly the ashamed, repentant citizen he claimed to be in the letter, but an "agent provocateur" for the kgb who couldn't resist a needle.

By late spring, the dissidents and the press had been warned to stay away from each other. It was a double-edged warning: Soviet citizens were told not to trust Western reporters, even those who seemed "sincere" and weren't "impartial to alcoholic beverages." Reporters were warned to stay away from Soviet citizens since they were likely to report on them to the KGB.

Shortly after the *Literaturnaya gazeta* story, Tsypin, the re-fusenik who had set up Krimsky with the "GI," was virtually cut off by other refuseniks. On May 17, 1977, *Vechernyaya Moskva,* Moscow's evening newspaper, published Tsypin's letter inform-ing the Moscow visa office that he was withdrawing his applica-tion for emigration to Israel.

CHAPTER 8

DISCORD IN
THE NOBLE FAMILY
OF DISSIDENTS

"Who is this Bernshtam?" Yelena Bonner boomed into the phone.

"I don't know him very well," said Alexeyeva. "I think he is a friend of Ginzburg's."

"He is an anti-Semite! I have his letter!"

That day, Mark Azbel, editor of a *samizdat* journal called *Jews in the USSR,* had brought Bonner the letter to the editor written by Bernshtam.

Among other things, Bernshtam accused the journal of carrying out an "anti-Russian pogrom," "defaming the great classical Russian literature," and launching an "ideological war against the Russian people, against the history of the fatherland, and, most importantly, against Russian Orthodoxy, which is called upon to save the world. . . ." More specifically, Bernshtam was angry at the editing and change of title of his article "A Christian Tract," which had appeared in the journal, and he accused the journal of defaming his character to his wife.

It was a complicated story, which was made all the more complicated because in several places in the eleven-page double-spaced letter, Bernshtam, disregarding the dictums of Russian grammar, did not use quotation marks around "Jews in the USSR." Bonner and other readers concluded the omission meant Bernshtam was blasting all Jewish people in the USSR, not just the magazine. In another sentence, Bernshtam used the quotations around "Jews in the USSR," but made the verb that followed the journal's name plural. Had the sentence referred to the journal rather than the Jewish people, the verb would have been singular. Bonner was outraged.

"Something must be done!" she screamed into the phone. "I don't want to be in a group with this kind of person!"

Alexeyeva, who made it a policy to stay out of what she called "Jewish issues," suggested that Bonner get Orlov to deal with the matter. Bonner said she had already tried, but Orlov wasn't available.

Later that day, Sakharov asked Ginzburg how well he knew Bernshtam. "Do you think he could be an anti-Semite?"

"No, he is not an idiot," said Ginzburg.

That evening Ginzburg dropped by Bernshtam's apartment to get more detail on the letter, Bernshtam recalled.

Earlier that year, via the dissident grapevine, Bernshtam learned that a woman who worked for *Jews in the USSR* was badmouthing him to his friends. He wanted her to stop, so he went to one of the editors. "Look, she's got a big mouth," Bernshtam recalled saying to the editor. "You are a man, she's a woman. You're in charge. Stop her."

When the editor told Bernshtam he didn't want to get involved, Bernshtam got incensed and drafted the letter.

No, Bernshtam assured Ginzburg, he didn't mean to accuse all Soviet Jews of having wronged him when he aimed his accusations at Jews in the USSR instead of "Jews in the USSR." (Bernshtam, who was born of Jewish parents, had been baptized as a Christian at birth.)

"You are an idiot," Ginzburg shot back. "You know, to me, the most disgusting figure in *For Whom the Bell Tolls* is André

Marty. You know why? Because during a civil war he is looking for enemies on his side."

"Alik, you are right," Bernshtam replied. "It's idiocy and it's disgusting. I am ashamed."

"What he said was like a cold shower," said Bernshtam later. "It made me return from a crazy state to normal."

To correct the misunderstanding, Bernshtam drafted another open letter, sending copies to *Jews in the USSR* and to Bonner. The original letter was not meant to be understood as an attack on "persons of Jewish nationality residing in the USSR," he wrote.

"Persons of Jewish nationality residing in the USSR" was a phrase that grew out of Stalin's anti-Semitic purges. It implied that Jews are not full-fledged Soviet citizens but mere residents of the USSR. Bernshtam said he used the phrase deliberately, to show just how crazy Bonner's original accusation was. He had attacked the Jewish journal, not Jews collectively, he said. "In my clarification, I used the Stalinist cliché on purpose," he said. "To show that I am not an idiot, I gave the letter a sarcastic undertone."

After seeing the Stalin-era term in Bernshtam's apology, Bonner became even more livid, demanding that Bernshtam be publicly expelled from the group. This wasn't a matter that could be handled quietly: She wanted Orlov to issue a public statement decrying anti-Semitism, and she wanted the Western press to be informed.

"I had no feelings about it one way or the other," Orlov recalled. "I could understand Yelena Georgievna's disgust, but I didn't want to satisfy her demand for the public drumming out of Bernshtam. I thought what she was suggesting was bad strategy. I didn't want to start the group's work with a fight over questions raised by Bernshtam when I was actually interested in other matters. The best thing, I thought, would be to cover it up with cotton. We had other goals."

But the Bernshtam question refused to go away. Bonner had called at least one reporter, AP's Krimsky, screaming about the Bernshtam affair. "It was inside baseball," said Krimsky later. "It was certainly not a news story, but, hell, these people were my friends, so I went up to Orlov and asked him about it."

That horrified Orlov. "The journalists wanted a scandal,"

Orlov recalled. "They sniffed out a juicy story: 'Discord in No-ble Family of Dissidents.'"

Orlov realized that something had to be done about Bernshtam; it had to be done quietly and, if possible, politely. It was Bernshtam himself who eased Orlov's quandary.

While controversy raged over his allegedly anti-Semitic let-ters, Bernshtam drafted a prototype document decrying Soviet maneuvers on the Finnish border as an attempt to threaten Finland and influence the forthcoming elections. These maneu-vers, therefore, constituted interference in internal affairs of a sovereign state, and as a result were a violation of the Helsinki Final Act. Bernshtam learned through what he said were his sources in the Leningrad military district, that sixty thousand troops were involved. "I thought that was a matter the group should address," Bernshtam said. "Orlov still had not convinced me that we were strictly a human-rights organization, and I con-tinued to view the group as a political organization. That was my position, and I continued to defend it."

Orlov found that position unacceptable. "It was completely contradictory to our declaration, and it was simply dangerous," he said. "He actually had numbers of troops! Where he got those numbers, I don't know. I thought that we didn't have the luxury of getting into Basket One [arms control provisions of the Final Act]. Doing so would have meant opening ourselves to espionage charges. It would have been equivalent to planting a bomb under ourselves."

The schism between Bernshtam and the group was so great, Orlov decided, that there was no need for an expulsion. The controversies Bernshtam had started should be allowed to play themselves out. That would lead Bernshtam to the conclusion that he should leave the group. In the end there would be a courteous conversation and, perhaps, a letter.

Meanwhile, Bernshtam continued to stand his ground. "Don't we sometimes publish documents with two or three sig-natures?" he asked Orlov.

"Yes."

"So why don't all of us sign?"

"We shouldn't."

"So why not release it as a Helsinki-group document under my name alone?" Bernshtam suggested.

"That would look like opposition, a minority opinion within the group."

"If this can't be published as a group document, it would be a standard dissident 'appeal,' and I don't want to write that," said Bernshtam, moving closer to the decision that the differences between him and the group were irreconcilable. At another meeting, a few days later, Orlov handed Bernshtam a folded sheet of paper.

"CLOSED LETTER TO MIKHAIL BERNSHTAM FROM YURI ORLOV," Bernshtam read unfolding the sheet. He smiled at a light-handed allusion to the two "open letters" that had got him into a battle with Bonner.

Don't write any more open letters, Orlov's closed letter said. Stick with scholarly work, Orlov advised, because when you get into political commentary, you get misunderstood, then all of us get misunderstood, and we all wind up looking like idiots.

"Yura, I think there has already been enough harm done," said Bernshtam after reading the letter. "I can't understand Yelena Georgievna's Russian and she can't understand mine. I want to resign."

"No," said Orlov. "Don't resign. If you want to, just stop working with the group."

CHAPTER 9

SENSATION NO. 1

On May 27, about a dozen reporters gathered at Alexeyeva's apartment to hear the group's Document 2.

"Orlov was about half an hour late when Krimsky said, 'If Orlov has been arrested, that's sensation No. 1,'" Helsinki-group member Rubin wrote in his diary.

"Soon Orlov showed up, and Tolya [Shcharansky] said, 'The sensation didn't take place.'"

Reporters were handed a document that was anything but a sensation: It attacked the Soviet practice of interrupting the dissidents' telephone service.

"According to the Final Act of the Conference on Security and Cooperation in Europe, participating states strive to ease free movement and contacts between people," the document began. "In the conditions that prevail in the USSR, 'free movement' of people to other countries and back is *impossible. . . .* Therefore, mail and telephone communications play an exceptionally important role in establishing contacts between people and in free flow of information of humanitarian nature. . . .

"On August 31, 1972, the Council of Ministers of the USSR amended Article 74 of the USSR Code of Communications to 'prohibit the use of telephone lines (including intercity, urban and rural lines) for purposes contradictory to state interests and public order.' In reality, this law is applied in such a way that after several conversations with parties outside the Soviet borders during which there is an exchange of information *that does not coincide with the officially approved information* (such as the conditions of prisoners of conscience, persecution of dissidents, the texts of appeals in defense of the persecuted, as well as receipt of information from abroad pertaining to the reaction of the world community to the events in the USSR) the phone is disconnected, without even a warning.

"Generally, the phone is disconnected for six months, then turned back on with a warning not to use it again for conversations with parties outside the USSR, though there are frequent occurrences when the telephone is turned off permanently and the number transferred to another phone-system user."

Below, the document presented a list of eleven "parties whose phones were turned off *after* the signing of the Final Act of the Conference on Security and Cooperation in Europe" and thirty-two "parties whose phones were disconnected before the signing of the Final Act, but were not reconnected pursuant to the signing and remain unconnected till present." The list included Orlov, Turchin, Vladimir Voinovich, a dissident writer; Nina Bukovskaya, mother of imprisoned dissident Vladimir Bukovsky; and the names of virtually every Jewish refusenik activist then known in the West. Also listed was Lydia Voronina, the subject of Toth's *Los Angeles Times* story about the Communist mother who was blocking her daughter's emigration. It was, in fact, Voronina's mother who had written the law used to disconnect the dissidents' telephones.

For reporters, it made a fine document to file away, a kind of master list of Soviet dissidents. But it wasn't a news story.

On Friday, May 29, Rubin wrote in his diary: "In the evening, I received a postcard to call [the visa office] immediately. What could it mean? If it hadn't said 'immediately,' there could have been no question about it, they are denying my application once more. We'll find out Monday."

"Well, it seems the postcard meant something," he wrote three days later. "It seems the Great Day is coming. They asked me for documents and photographs. It seems they are ready to allow me to leave, though they haven't said so yet. It seems the new life is about to start, though I can't feel it yet. Still, this is the right time to reflect.

"I remember what a shock it was to be denied emigration. At the time I still thought that, given that I had done no secret work, they wouldn't say no. After that, I frequently recalled an episode in 'The Wall' where a man going to his own birthday party is grabbed by the Nazis and forced to take part in some meeting of the [Warsaw] ghetto government. He tries to convince everyone that it's unjust, but someone tells him, 'What makes you think there can even be talk of justice?' That's what happened to me. At first, I felt something heinous is being done to me, a total and unbelievable injustice. Then I became convinced (even I needed convincing!) that there can't even be talk of justice. After that, I calmed down, accepted my fate and did my best to make the most of my time here. Perhaps I hadn't succeeded at making the best of the situation. Be that as it may, I understood that the situation is completely out of my control, so I tried to go on with my life here, not even thinking about emigration."

The visa office, indeed, was prepared to let the Rubins go. In conversations that week, Rubin frequently repeated that the Soviets had finally caved in to international pressure. But the final straw, he said to friends, was that the Soviets simply couldn't afford to have a man as well known as Rubin taking part in Orlov's Helsinki monitoring group.

Before leaving, Rubin recommended a successor: Dr. Sanya Lipavsky, the refuseniks' miracle worker. Lipavsky could arrange telephone conversations from the apartments of his patients. He could obtain rare Western medication, arrange abortions, give a life-saving second opinion in medical emergencies. Lipavsky was always ready to help, even when it involved taking time off from work.

Later, in his diary, Rubin wrote that he and his wife, Ina,

knew that since the summer of 1975 Lipavsky had been supplying information to the Americans. Rubin also knew that
Lipavsky's initial contact had been with Melvyn Levitsky, the
U.S. Embassy's designated liaison with the dissidents, and a personal acquaintance of the Rubins.

Rubin wrote in his diary that he considered Lipavsky's deal-
ings with the Americans dangerous. But throughout 1976
Rubin's diary brimmed with admiring references to Lipavsky as
a Jewish hero.

Before recommending Lipavsky to Orlov, Rubin bounced
the suggestion off Shcharansky and Dina Beilina, a Jewish activist who wasn't in the Helsinki group. "Dina Beilina and I said,
'Who's Lipavsky? He is a doctor and a chauffeur, nothing else.'
And the idea was forgotten," Shcharansky said later.

Orlov recalls that Rubin, just before his departure, introduced him to Lipavsky. Rubin said the doctor was knowledgeable about Jewish affairs in Moscow and had a car that Orlov,
no doubt, would be able to use.

"I didn't like him [Lipavsky] from the start," Orlov said. "I
judge people by their faces, and his was not a good face. I never
called him, never asked him for anything."

Rubin was replaced by Vladimir Slepak, a bearded electrical
engineer who at the time had been denied emigration for six
years. As for Lipavsky, his dark secret was yet to be revealed.

The Helsinki group's Document 2 was almost twice as long as
Document 1. Fearing the trend, Alexeyeva began to complain.
It seemed her original calculation of thirty-five copies per document was incorrect. She had to produce forty-five copies—
thirty-five for the Helsinki signatories, nine for the press, and
one for the archive she kept in her apartment. Since copying
machines were a rarity in the USSR, and the ones that were
available were guarded by official censors who determined
whether copying given materials "coincides with state interests,"
Alexeyeva had to rely on her staff of *samizdat* typists to produce
the forty-five copies. With each typewriter taking nine sheets of
onionskin paper and eight sheets of carbon paper, this meant
five complete retyping jobs per document.

Knowing her comrades' tendency to write at great length,

Alexeyeva had to cope with the fear of documents reaching or even surpassing the twenty-page level. "Even an enthusiast loses enthusiasm after typing the same thing twice," Alexeyeva said. Her worst fears materialized with Document 3.

Its twenty-eight single-spaced pages included a four-page summary of the conditions of political prisoners, a bibliography, a detailed description of the nutritional characteristics of penal-institution food, a list of thirty-one Vladimir prison inmates who had been living on "lowered food rations" and a list of eighty-seven witnesses, complete with the witnesses' names, dates of birth, current whereabouts, year of arrest, and the number of years served in penal institution or exile. The document's authors—Ginzburg and Landa—also quoted from an internal penal-system memo that mandated lower rations for prisoners who didn't fill work quotas.

There were footnotes and a table that presented the nutritional analysis of one day on the "lowered nutrition regimen":

rye bread	450 grams
wheat flour	10
miscellaneous grains	50
fish	60
meat	0
fat (or vegetable oil)	6
potatoes	250
cabbage	200
tomato paste	5
Total calorie count	1,400 calories
Total protein content	38 grams

A footnote quoted a World Health Organization report that estimated that a man engaged in physical labor expends between 3,100 and 3,900 calories a day and a man at rest expends about 2,200 calories. The daily protein requirement is generally defined at one gram per kilogram of body weight, assuming an adequate calorie intake.

"Article VII, Section 1(a) of the Final Act states that the participating states 'will promote and encourage the effective exercise of civil, political, economic, social, cultural and other rights all of which derive from the inherent dignity of the human person,'" the document said. "The Group's information on the Soviet penal system . . . indicates that the Soviet administration has committed gross violations of Article VII, Section 1(a) of the Final Act. The Group does not believe that torture and cruel or inhuman punishment fall within the category of 'rights inherent in a state's sovereignty,' thereby rendering Article VI, Section 1(a) of the Final Act (nonintervention in internal affairs of signatory states) inapplicable.

"The Group believes it is necessary to form an international commission to study these alleged violations, beginning with torture by hunger and torture by confinement in punishment cells. . . . The Group is prepared to turn over all relevant documents to such a commission."

In the first thirty-eight days of its existence, the Moscow Group of Assistance to Implementation of the Helsinki Agreement in the USSR had churned out nearly two thousand single-spaced typewritten pages addressed to thirty-five heads of state, received a warning from the KGB, demanded the release of a just-convicted political prisoner, called for reconnection of the dissidents' telephones, and exposed the conditions of Soviet prisoners. It had also called for the formation of two international commissions—one to monitor compliance with the Helsinki Final Act, and another to monitor the conditions of Soviet prisoners.

"The documents weren't written in a declarative style; they weren't wordy; they were factual," Orlov said later. "It was easy to sign such documents. They weren't emotional; they didn't contain stylistic differences between people. For instance, my style is dry, and another person, say Malva Landa, is more emotional, and if she puts together a document, I may not be comfortable signing it because it's got a different temperament, and, of course, vice versa. She would think my style is dry. But our documents didn't leave room for these stylistic differences between people. With a factual, scientific document, the question becomes simpler: If you agree with the facts, you go ahead and sign it. If you don't agree with the facts, you don't sign."

With a dozen or so reporters attending each of the group's

press conferences, group members were the last to suspect that their efforts went virtually unnoticed in the West and that, for the most part, the reporters showed up at group press conferences to gather materials for other stories. If any stories were filed, only shortwave radio stations broadcasting to the USSR considered them newsworthy.

CHAPTER 10

THE SNAKEPIT AND OTHER CONNECTIONS

When foreign radio stations broadcast a news item about the formation of a group monitoring the Soviet compliance with the Helsinki Final Act, millions of Soviet citizens listened.

Among the listeners was Mykola Rudenko, then fifty-six, a writer and poet. Within six months, Rudenko announced the formation of the Ukrainian Public Group of Assistance to Implementation of the Helsinki Agreements in the USSR.

In Vilnius, Viktoras Petkus, a Lithuanian literary historian employed as a hospital orderly and a Catholic church sexton, heard the announcement. At forty-seven, he had served two prison terms totaling thirteen years. Six months later he started the Lithuanian Helsinki group.

Zviad Gamsakhurdia, then thirty-seven, heard the broadcast in Tbilisi. Gamsakhurdia had just lost his position as professor of American literature and English at the Tbilisi State Univer-

sity. On January 14, 1977, Gamsakhurdia started the Georg
Helsinki group.

In Yerevan, Eduard Arutyunyan, forty-seven, an economist,
heard the news. In April 1977, he started the Armenian Helsinki
group. Thousands of Crimean Tatars, an ethnic group Stalin had
pronounced guilty of disloyalty during World War II and de-
ported them from the strategically sensitive Crimean peninsula
to the more secure Central Asia, listened to the report. Also in
Central Asia, the news of the group was heard by a tribe of
Meskhetians who, like the Crimean Tatars, had been suspected
of treason and resettled. Meskhetians suffered from more than
just persecution—they were struck by a case of cultural schizo-
phrenia. One group of Meskhetians called themselves Georgians; another called themselves Turks. The Georgians wanted
to return to their homeland in the Caucasus mountains; meanwhile, the more radical among the Turks wanted to return to
Meskhetia and have it annexed by Turkey. Both factions dispatched emissaries to Orlov.

The Volga Germans, Stalin's other World War II deportee
nation, also heard the news. The Germans, most of them descendants of post-Reformation Anabaptists, took the spirit of
the Reformation beyond the Lutherans. Anabaptists were pacifists, a belief for which they were routinely tortured and ex-
ecuted by their fellow Germans. In the seventeenth century, a
large number of the Anabaptists' descendants, the Mennonites,
settled on Russia's steppes. By the start of World War II, the
Volga Germans fell under Stalin's suspicion. The descendants of
Mennonite pacifists, many of them also pacifists, were loaded
into freight cars and sent to the deserts of Central Asia.

By the 1970s many Volga Germans were trying to return to
Germany.

Listening to their shortwave radios were Baptists, Pentecostals, and Seventh-day Adventists, some of whom had spent
decades defying the authorities by proselytizing, refusing to register with the state, even running elaborately hidden underground publishing operations. For the most part, the Baptists,
Seventh-day Adventists, and Pentecostals were ethnic Russians
whose forebears were converted by American preachers at the
turn of the century.

Sitting by her shortwave radio was Irina McLellan, Russian wife of University of Virginia professor Woodford McLellan. The McLellans had been married for two years, but the Soviets denied Irina an exit visa to join her husband in the United States. Within days after hearing about the group, Irina sought out Alexeyeva to offer her services as a typist and to submit a complaint.

Also listening was Aleksandr Lyapin, a photographer. In later months, Lyapin, who lived outside Leningrad, made two visits to Orlov. After the physicist's trial, he went to the Red Square, doused himself with gasoline, and lit a match. He survived and was committed to a psychiatric hospital.

One day in June, Valentina Afanasievna Yefimenko, Alexeyeva's seventy-one-year-old mother, went to the Beryozka hard-currency store and, with foreign royalties from a mathematics workbook she had co-authored, bought a small brown Sony shortwave transistor radio. That was the first time Yefimenko had spent her modest foreign royalties on herself rather than her grandsons.

In the past, Alexeyeva had taken great pains to keep her mother from learning about her politics. It was only by accident in 1971 that her mother learned that three years earlier Alexeyeva had signed a number of "open letters" and, as a consequence, had been expelled from the Communist party and fired from her editing job at a publishing house.

But in the summer of 1976 Yefimenko developed a curious habit. Just before Helsinki group press conferences were about to begin, she would walk through the apartment, glance at the reporters, then return to her room. She would emerge three hours later, just after news items about the press conference her daughter had hosted were broadcast from Washington, London, or Munich.

Still, staying true to family tradition, Yefimenko and Alexeyeva never talked politics.

Also that summer, as the Moscow Helsinki group became well known, Alexeyeva and her husband, Nikolai Williams, were suddenly deluged with invitations to parties. People seemed to have lost their fear of associating with her. Alexeyeva started referring to herself as a "wedding general," after a pre-revolutionary merchant-class tradition of inviting generals to weddings to lend grandeur to the affair. Alexeyeva was certain that some hosts lured their other guests by saying something like: "Oh, why don't you come. Lyuda Alexeyeva will be there. She is a member of the Helsinki group."

At one of those parties, the hostess led her into a quiet corner to confide: "I am an aristocrat, you know."

Alexeyeva nodded, restraining herself from saying, "Congratulations."

"I believe all Bolsheviks should be shot," the hostess continued.

"And then what?" asked Alexeyeva, horrified by the prospect of the annihilation of over fifteen million people including her elderly mother.

"Then we will live by the laws of Christ."

Some of the Moscow Helsinki group's more important connections can be traced to a brisk Mordovian morning in May 1968, when two young men, thin and worn out by the long journey, were led to the showers of Camp 17a, called *Gadyushnik,* the "Snakepit," by its administrators.

Their hair cropped, the young men looked more like army recruits than especially dangerous state criminals who, as the readers of Soviet newspapers knew, were convicted for anti-Soviet propaganda under Article 70 of the RSFSR Criminal Code and taken to 17a.

"They've brought some children," an elderly inmate said to writer Yuli Daniel. The "children" were Aleksandr Ginzburg, then thirty-two, and Yuri Galanskov, twenty-nine.

Ginzburg was serving a five-year sentence for having covered the Sinyavsky and Daniel trial. Galanskov, a mediocre poet, was serving seven years for having produced a *samizdat* journal as well as receiving foreign currency from a right-wing émigré group in the West. He tried to exchange the dollars on the black market and use the rubles to buy a printing press, but the transaction went awry when Galanskov accepted a stack of mustard plasters for his dollars.

As a result of both official and unofficial publicity surround-

trial, Ginzburg and Galanskov became celebrities. By ¬me of their arrival at the Snakepit, other inmates had ¬ned of their deeds from *Izvestia, Literaturnaya gazeta, Komsomolskaya pravda,* and *Vechernyaya Moskva,* which called them "lackeys of imperialism" and published a number of letters from readers calling for harsh punishment. At the Snakepit, such publicity guaranteed respect from other convicts.

It was a small camp, just over 180 inmates, all of them political. Among them were war criminals finishing up their Stalin-era twenty-five-year sentences, religious leaders and nationalists doing three- to seven-year terms; there were also returned defectors doing the typical twelve to fifteen years. Generally these would be former soldiers and sailors who either jumped ship or crossed the Soviet border and then, after a while, began to miss Russia's birch trees and returned. In the camp, these people were called *podberezoviki,* after the red-capped mushrooms that grow under birch trees. Many *podberezovik* inmates collaborated with the KGB to get two years or so knocked off their sentences.

Altogether, every third Snakepit inmate worked with the administration, writing reports on their bunkmates in exchange for some lenience from the administration. So obsessed was the Snakepit's administration with security, that inmates and guards were periodically ordered to dig up patches of grass to make sure nobody had temporarily hidden forbidden literature, communications from the outside—or a bottle of vodka.

On walks, Ginzburg was frequently approached by the Pentecostals, Baptists, and Seventh-day Adventists with suggestions that he convert. Ginzburg always declined, saying he was Russian Orthodox.

The day he was taken to his barracks, Ginzburg started to chat with a half-blind plumber named Fyodor "Fedya" Sidenko, who was serving five years for an attempt to trigger the exodus of Pentecostals from the USSR. In 1965, at the seaport of Nakhodka in the extreme southeast of the USSR, Sidenko handed his own and a friend's passports to a Japanese guest at the hotel where he worked. Sidenko didn't know who the Japanese guest was. In a note, written in Russian, he instructed the hotel guest to pass the documents over to the United Nations.

The UN, he hoped, would take the necessary steps to assure his release from the USSR.

Later, at the trial, Sidenko learned that his Japanese connection, a trade representative, was so dumbfounded by the passport-bearing plumber, he handed the papers to the desk clerk, who handed them over to the militia, which forwarded them to the KGB. Crusty and massive, Sidenko struck Ginzburg as a likable, though comical, character. Every time he saw an inmate talk to a guard, Sidenko would come between the two and, addressing the inmate, mumble, "What are you doing? What are you doing? Can't you see he's got horns?"

In his talks with Ginzburg, Sidenko described the reason he wanted to leave. No, he said, he wasn't out to emigrate to ease the hardship of living. His emigration was mandated by the Lord. Shortly after World War II, the Holy Spirit revealed Himself to a woman from Sidenko's sect. I shall pour out my wrath upon this land of sinners, the Holy Spirit said, just as I poured out my wrath upon the sinful Rome. Plague upon plague will come upon this Russian land, punishing the godless with death and destruction. But before I pour out my wrath, I will send my hunters to bring out the Jews, my Chosen People, and all the righteous ones who have suffered in my name.

The time seemed to be ripe for deliverance. The Pentecostals had suffered enough by any reasonable measure. Their religion was brought into Russia by a preacher named Ivan Voronayev. He was a Russian who, near the turn of the century, left for America, "got religion," then, in 1921, came back to preach in Odessa. By 1928, two hundred thousand Russians, mostly in the south of the country, became Voronayev's followers.

They believed in the spiritual symbol of the Pentecost, a feast fifty days after the resurrection of Christ when the Holy Spirit entered the apostles, making them speak in tongues. That was taken as a sign that the Lord wanted his Word spread to all nations in all tongues. That meant proselytizing, which, in the Soviet case, also meant breaking the law. When the Soviet authorities demanded that the churches register with the state-approved Council of Churches, a large number of Pentecostals refused. Preacher Voronayev, who refused to register, was first arrested in 1930. He died in the camps.

By the time of Sidenko's desperate attempt to contact the UN, three generations of Pentecostals had gone through repressions by the Bolsheviks and the Orthodox Church alike. Most Pentecostals of Sidenko's generation hadn't been allowed to enter universities as a result of refusing to join the Young Pioneers and the Young Communist League. Most hadn't known their grandparents, who perished in Stalin's camps. Quite a few didn't know their parents, either. What they did know was that the country in which they lived was trying to build heaven on earth, while the Righteous were aiming to get to the real heaven. That was an irreconcilable difference.

Ginsburg's natural curiosity made him notice a tall, bearded, robust old man with a stately, measured walk and low-key manners. The old man talked calmly, a manner that set him off from other convicts, who tended to be nervous and emphatic. There always seemed to be a line to see him. As soon as he would finish walking with one convict, another would come by.

Ginzburg was so intrigued by the old man, he asked writer Daniel about him. "That's Vladimir Andreyevich Shelkov," Daniel said. Shelkov, head of a Russian offshoot of the Seventh-day Adventist Church, had a few months to go of his ten-year term. Once, on a walk, Ginzburg caught Shelkov walking alone. "Vladimir Andreyevich, when can we meet?" Shelkov set up a time.

As the two walked, Ginzburg told a few stories of Christians he had met. It was the manner of obtaining information Ginzburg had picked up in the camps. Instead of questioning directly, like a KGB interrogator, he told stories. If the other convict trusted him, he would answer with stories of his own.

Shelkov responded with a short history of his church. It was started in America of the 1840s, based on the visions and teachings of Ellen G. White, whose name Shelkov Russified to Yelena. Russia's Seventh-day Adventists believed it was wrong to take a life, be it killing a human for a cause or an animal for dinner. He talked about the church, he talked about the state, he talked about the problems that occur when the two get into each other's realm.

"What can I read, Vladimir Andreyevich?" Ginzburg asked. "I've got three years to serve; as soon as I get out, I'll read it." The reading list Shelkov suggested consisted of Ellen White's books published before the revolution, a few books typed up clandestinely in the Adventist underground and a few that were smuggled in from the West. For the time being, Shelkov didn't suggest ways for Ginzburg to get those books.

The Russians have learned to romanticize their prisons.

The same twisted history that makes the Russians expect their writers and poets to suffer—or, better yet, die violently—has spread prison slang beyond the barbed-wire fences and given rise to a curious *samizdat* genre of prison nostalgia. Shortly after his release, the gulag's premier writer, Aleksandr Solzhenitsyn, contributed to this incarceration romanticism by putting on an old camp uniform, attaching to it his old camp number, *Shch*-262, and posing for a photograph. The Russian word *zek,* slang for "prisoner," acquired additional meaning and now serves as a root for an adjective that means "superb," *zekonskiy.* On top of that, the Russians coined a diminutive abbreviation for "capital punishment," *vysshaya mera naka-zaniya,* commonly referring to it simply as *vyshka,* and a diminutive form of "psychiatric institution," *psikhushka.*

The Soviet *zeki,* Ginzburg included, have a hard time stopping once they launch into prison stories. It is as common for an unofficial Soviet author to write about prisons as it is for an American author to write about growing up Jewish in Brooklyn or WASP in a New England prep school.

Ginzburg's was an extraordinary incarceration. By tuning in to the Voice of America, Radio Liberty, or the BBC, the Soviet radio listener was able to hear that Ginzburg and the authorities had locked horns over the issue of Ginzburg's marriage. He insisted that his fiancée, Arina Zholkovskaya, was his common-law wife, and, as such, should be allowed two conjugal visits a year with him in the camps. The authorities said the burden of proof of the relationship between Ginzburg and Zholkovskaya was on them, and the only admissible evidence of their relationship would be a child. They had none.

Ginzburg wrote long, sarcastic appeals; Zholkovskaya wrote shorter, but angrier ones. Finally, Ginzburg announced a hunger strike, in which he was joined by ten of his camp buddies including writer Daniel. Later, radio listeners throughout the USSR were informed that the authorities had backed down, allowing Ginzburg and Zholkovskaya to get married in the camp. Later still, shortwave-radio listeners were able to hear a tape recording of Ginzburg's voice. It was a part of a twelve-minute message Ginzburg had made in the camp and sent to Moscow. It wound up on *CBS News*. Later, it was learned that Ginzburg had been transferred to the Vladimir prison.

The sad story of Ginzburg's friend Galanskov was also reported. Even before his arrest, Galanskov suffered from an acute stomach ulcer. Over the yearlong pretrial detention the ulcer went untreated, leaving Galanskov doubled over in pain during conferences with his attorney. He received almost no care in the camp either. The doctors frequently refused to release him from work, and when the ulcer finally ruptured, a doctor's assistant attempted to perform the surgery. Galanskov, thirty-three, died on the operating table on November 4, 1972.

The news of his death made the Western papers—and the foreign broadcasts—as did the saga of his family demanding to put up a cross on his grave at the camp cemetery. Such a demand was unprecedented; the inmates' graves normally are marked with planks bearing the identification number of the deceased. After several foreign broadcasts, however, the authorities backed down, and Galanskov's mother, his widow, and a group of relatives and friends were told they could put up a cross on Galanskov's grave. They put up a big one.

Frequently, the guards at the Snakepit told celebrity inmates that their names were mentioned over the foreign radio stations. "Hey, they talked about you over the Voice again," they would say.

Smuggling information out of the camps took considerable ingenuity. Consider the recording of Ginzburg's voice that was played over CBS: One of the camp guards, hearing that Ginzburg knew how to fix radio equipment, asked him to repair a tape recorder. He gave Ginzburg a tape reel, but, as a precaution, kept the microphone.

Ginzburg fixed the tape recorder, then rigged the wiring to bypass the microphone, which allowed him to use the speaker as a recording device. Then he cut about twelve minutes' worth of tape off the reel and called a recording session formated as a radio broadcast. The "broadcast" was emceed in English by a

Latvian named Gunars Astra, who introduced the "g[...]
cluding Ginzburg, Stepan Soroka, a Ukrainian; Balys Ga-
jauskas, a Lithuanian; and Viktor Kaenins, a Latvian.

Then Ginzburg wound the tape around a match and sealed it
in a condom. From that point on, it was dispatched through
what was called the "eat-then-shit-eat-then-shit" mail. The condom was swallowed by an inmate who was to get a conjugal
visit. During the visit, the convict passed the condom, washed it
off and gave it to his wife to swallow. Then he swallowed more
condoms to use in future mail operations. A similar system is
used to smuggle drugs into American prisons.

Using the same method, Ginzburg and friends chronicled the
hunger strike that forced the authorities to allow the Ginzburg-
Zholkovskaya union. In 1971, the émigré-run Possev publishing
house turned those chronicles into a book called *Istoriya odnoy
golodovki, The History of One Hunger Strike.*

After being released in 1972, Ginzburg presented the authorities with a serious dilemma. He was clearly not rehabili-
tated. Also, he was well known in the West, which meant that
any action against him would threaten the "Leninist policy of
coexistence with the capitalist states," détente. Shortly after
Ginzburg's release, Arina was called in to the KGB and asked if
she would like to file for an exit visa to Israel.

"You would like to leave, wouldn't you?" she was asked.

"I would, but my husband wouldn't," she said.

In Moscow of the 1930s, Ginzburg would have simply vanished. But in Moscow of the 1970s, people didn't just disappear.
There had to be an investigation, a trial.

The KGB knew that Ginzburg was ideally positioned for
continuing his "life of crime." The agency probably knew about
the friendship between Ginzburg's wife and Solzhenitsyn's wife,
Natalya Svetlova, and about the ideologically unstable circle of
academics who lived around the Ginzburg apartment. Through
that circle, he was certain to get to Sakharov, another of the
KGB's major headaches.

Almost immediately after his release, Ginzburg started helping Solzhenitsyn give away a portion of his 1970 Nobel Prize
money to the families of political prisoners. When Solzhenitsyn
was exiled, the KGB realized that Ginzburg, working with foreign reporters, was sending Solzhenitsyn's archives to the West.

In 1974, in Zurich, Solzhenitsyn announced the formation of his Russian Social Fund to aid Soviet political prisoners. The writer called the fund's formation the return of Christian charity to Russia. He named Ginzburg the fund's administrator in the USSR. To give money to political prisoners, one had to know who those prisoners were. To do his new job properly, Ginzburg had to tap some of his camp connections.

Shortly after the fund was formed, Arina Ginzburg appealed to her co-op board to ask for a larger apartment. As the Ginzburg family grew, the old one-room place became too small. Arina, Alik, and their two toddlers slept in the one room. Their teenaged adopted son slept on a folding bed in the kitchen. Still, applying for a larger apartment was close to futile since the processing of such requests took years. Within weeks, however, the Ginzburgs were told that the residents of a two-room apartment on the seventh floor had emigrated to Israel, and the Ginzburgs were welcome to take their place.

They moved the furniture down two stories, spread out in the new apartment and threw a nice party. As the days went by, Ginzburg began to wonder why it had been so easy to get the new place. After all, other co-op residents had spent years waiting. Later, one of the co-op officials mentioned that a man who lived just above their new apartment had been jailed for economic crimes and it appeared a KGB team had moved in to replace him.

Ginzburg grew increasingly curious about what went on upstairs. His chance to find out came with a summer storm that knocked out power in the building. Ginzburg picked up a flashlight, went up the stairs and knocked on the door. The door opened.

"Has your power gone out?" asked Ginzburg, aiming his flashlight inside the apartment. He caught a glimpse of a massive tape recorder.

The door closed.

After his release from the camps, Ginzburg started to receive visits from a man who identified himself as "Vasya, a friend of Vladimir Andreyevich."

Vasya was a courier for the underground publishing house

set up by Ginzburg's camp acquaintance Shelkov, head of the Seventh-day Adventist Church, then in hiding and on the KGB's most-wanted list. Vasya was tall, husky, a bear of a man. Sometimes he was accompanied by a man who identified himself simply as Kolya. Following the unwritten law of former *zeki,* Ginzburg never asked Vasya and Kolya for their last (or real first) names.

During their walks at the Snakepit, Shelkov had offered Ginzburg few ideas about ways he could obtain religious books. Now, every ten days or so, Vasya appeared with reading materials for Ginzburg and rich honey cakes for the children. The manuscripts Vasya brought called for "nonviolent struggle for the basic rights and freedoms of each man and each citizen." Their author was Shelkov himself.

God created man in his image, but man loses his godly image the instant he acts against his conscience, Shelkov wrote in one of the works he sent Ginzburg.

Shelkov's number-one interest was the relationship between church and state. The ideal state, Shelkov wrote, is a "pure state," one that is neutral toward all religions and ideologies. Such a state builds roads, provides for education and citizen welfare. The USSR isn't a "pure state." It is based on the doctrine of atheism, which in itself is a religion, and it has aligned itself with other religions by making all churches register with the officially recognized church body, the All-Union Council of Churches.

Shelkov, an ethnic Russian, was opposed to Russian nationalism, too. "The current dominance of state atheism has created an ideological chaos and moral decay in our country," he wrote. "Therefore, we hear voices calling for the resurrection of the national conscience of the Russian people and the Russian Orthodox Church, in accordance with Russia's past. It is said that only national self-realization and the national church can save Russia. Yet, the Russian Orthodox religion, in its days of dominance and unity with the state, had stained itself with human blood by suppressing freedom of conscience and belief among nonconforming citizens. It was the Russian Inquisition that had destroyed 12 million Old Believers and hundreds of thousands of Evangelical Christians."

The titles of the manuscripts and books Ginzburg had received from the old man included *The Relationship Between Religion and the State, The Law on Cults, The Basis of Truly Free Conscience and Equal Rights, The Struggle for Free Conscience,* and *Legal Battle for Freedom of Conscience Against the Dictatorship of State Atheism.* All materials were published by the True Witness publishing house, using a nineteenth-century press, with type that scarred the paper's surface. For each of the True Witness publications, Ginzburg saw the final typed copy, the blue-ink mimeographed version, and finally, the meticulously bound final volume. Shelkov expected Ginzburg to use his connections to get the books to the West.

Ginzburg passed the books along, and though they made it into various archives, they didn't have the broad appeal necessary to be mentioned in the press.

Since every word in the Ginzburg apartment was monitored by the KGB, Ginzburg and Shelkov's courier Vasya avoided meaningful conversations.

"How are the children?" Vasya typically asked, riffling through his massive leather briefcase. It looked like the kind of leather briefcase a Gosplan bureaucrat would lug to work Monday through Friday. It was made of thick leather, with flaps on both sides. Yet it was no ordinary piece of luggage. It had a secret compartment in the middle.

"The children are fine," Ginzburg usually said. "The flu season's over."

"I brought something for them," Vasya said, producing a stack of papers or a booklet or two.

On one of his visits, in late June 1976, Vasya reached into his briefcase's secret compartment, pulled out a thick stack of paper, about one thousand sheets in all, and handed it to Ginzburg. The top sheet was inscribed: PUBLIC GROUP OF ASSISTANCE TO IMPLEMENTATION OF THE HELSINKI AGREEMENTS IN THE USSR. Ginzburg thumbed through the pages. All the sheets were the same. It was stationery.

Vasya's face broke into a smile.

On another June night, a knock on the door awoke the Ginzburgs.

"Who is it?" asked Ginzburg.

"Alik! This is Fedya!"

It was Sidenko, Ginzburg's Pentecostal friend from the

Snakepit. Sidenko had heard a foreign radio broadcast mention Ginzburg as one of the members of something called the Public Group of Assistance to Implementation of the Helsinki Agreements in the USSR. More than a decade after his attempt to get a Japanese guest at the hotel Vostok to help him emigrate, Sidenko was ready to try again.

This time, however, he wanted to try to bring out thousands of his brethren.

CHAPTER 11

KHODOKI

Vladimir Pavlov, a bus driver from the northern Caucasus, came to Moscow to find Yuri Orlov. He asked for the physicist's phone number at an address information booth.

"No such person resides in Moscow," said the clerk. Moscow address and telephone books are generally unavailable, and information booths don't give out the addresses of dissidents.

Pavlov decided to try another method. He went out to Moscow's Gorky Street and started asking the more academic-looking passersby if they could direct him to Sakharov or Orlov.

This wasn't the most promising way to locate a resident of a city of nine million, but Pavlov, then forty-seven, was a desperate man. He wanted to get out of the USSR. The odds were against him: He wasn't Jewish, he wasn't a German, he wasn't an Armenian, he had no relatives in the West, and he was certainly not internationally famous. Over the radio he heard that in Moscow a man named Yuri Orlov had set up a group to monitor Soviet compliance with the Helsinki Final Act. Pavlov decided that the group could help him.

"Could you direct me to Yuri Orlov or Andrei Sakharov?" he kept asking.

"No," said some.

"I don't know who they are," said others.

Many simply quickened their pace, saying nothing.

"Why do you need to talk to them?" someone finally asked.

Pavlov launched into an explanation: On September 3, 1971, he was sentenced to three years in the camps for slandering the Soviet state. Pavlov disagreed with the word "slander." All he had said was that the USSR is not a democracy, that the Communist party is incapable of dealing with the country's economic problems, that the 1968 Soviet invasion of Czechoslovakia was unlawful, that he wished he had been on a Soviet plane hijacked to Turkey in 1970, and that the Americans were being too humane to their Communist Angela Davis.

In August 1975, a year after his release, Pavlov read the text of the Helsinki Final Act. The document spelled out that free exchange of information was not only permissible, but was to be encouraged. Thus, Pavlov concluded, there was no longer such a thing as slander of the state. He petitioned the Soviet Union's highest court to clear his criminal record. In May 1976 the court rejected the plea, and Pavlov decided to ask Orlov to help him emigrate.

"Let's go," said the passerby and took Pavlov to a friend's apartment. The friend asked Pavlov to repeat his story. Apparently convinced that a KGB provocateur wouldn't resort to such a method of locating the founder of the Moscow Helsinki group, he gave Pavlov Orlov's address.

Pavlov was one of the *khodoki*—an especially folksy Russian word for "messenger"—who brought their complaints to Orlov's group. He was also one of the minority of such messengers whose stories group members found fit to be included in their documents. (His problems made Document 13, with his court papers included.) The Helsinki group had tapped into something characteristically Russian: the need to petition for official intervention.

For centuries peasant *khodoki* brought their troubles to

czarist officials. After the revolution, they were said to have brought their problems to the Bolsheviks, inspiring a famous Socialist Realism painting called *Lenin Chats with the* Khodoki. Now, the Helsinki group offered the ultimate in *khodok* appeal: It could amplify any complaint by getting it to the Western press, Western radio stations, heads of thirty-five governments, and a commission of the U.S. Congress.

Once, a Moscow ambulance paramedic showed up at Alexeyeva's, complaining about not being able to get an apartment. He said he had first heard about the group from another supplicant in the lobby of the Presidium of the Central Committee. Alexeyeva explained that the problem of unfair allocation of residential space isn't a component of European security and human rights as defined in the Final Act of the Conference on Security and Cooperation in Europe. However, she said, she could introduce him to Western reporters, which she did.

On another occasion, a Byelorussian peasant showed up saying he had been thrown out of the collective farm and wanted to get back in. He, too, had to be told that his problem had nothing to do with European security, but group members referred him to a Moscow attorney.

Some of the *khodoki* stories went something like: "And I says to the brigade chief, 'Why is it so? It's not right!' And he says, 'You go complain to the regional committee.' And I says, 'I will, I will.' And my brother's first wife, who isn't his wife no more, says, 'You know where that will lead you.' And I says, 'Where else it could lead me?' And it turns out she was right." Orlov, who on an average day received at least one of the *khodoki,* could listen to such narration for hours. "Yura listened as long as they talked, never interrupting," said Alexeyeva. "He has the patience of an elephant."

Khodoki even affected group members' diet. Most of these visitors were from out of town, most didn't have the money for a good meal, and few ever turned down a cup of tea and a plate of borshch. "It was best to offer them hot food that stuck to their ribs," said Alexeyeva. So every other morning, she filled a two-gallon brown enamel pot with water, threw in two pounds of beef or pork, two pounds of potatoes, a head of cabbage, five beets, five onions, five carrots, a can of tomato paste, and a bay leaf. This enormous volume of borshch, usually served with sour cream, chopped dill, and garlic, rarely lasted two days.

The first of the *khodoki,* a Ukrainian woman, came to the group with a burning problem: On October 23, 1975, three months after the Helsinki Final Act was signed, a local court ruled to take her three children away. As a Baptist, she was not bringing up the children "in the spirit of the moral code of a builder of Communism," the court held.

The mother protested, writing letters to Brezhnev, the Committee of Soviet Women, and *Soviet Woman* magazine. She gave the authorities a choice: return the children or let her and the children emigrate to Canada. She also threatened to appeal to "international organizations." Soon she received a puzzling response from a local prosecutor: "The court decision of October 23, 1975, will not be enforced. Children will remain with you." It was a bureaucratic solution: Let the court's decision stand, just don't enforce it.

So the mother turned to the closest thing Russia had to an international organization, the Moscow Helsinki group.

"The court's decision hasn't been overturned, and that means the children live under constant threat of being taken from their mother," the group's Document 5 said.

Here, Orlov and the group refrained from doing a hatchet job on the authorities. The Baptist's case was an exception, the document pointed out: "Such a practice [of taking children away from religious parents] was widespread from 1964 to 1974. But following the signing of the Final Act of the Conference on Security and Cooperation in Europe, the number of [such] rulings decreased, most likely because of international exposure of the practice and the reaction of the world community."

"When we saw improvements, we pointed them out," Orlov said.

The Moscow synagogue seemed an unlikely place for an old, bearded ethnic-Russian peasant using a stick for a cane and wearing a homemade shirt and baggy pants tucked into rubber boots.

The old man, looking as if he should be selling potatoes at a collective-farm market or starring in a Mosfilm production about peasant life under the czars, came up to a group of Jews who were milling around across the street from the synagogue. He asked if he could be directed to Vladimir Slepak.

Finding Slepak, one of the refusenik elders, the peasant introduced himself as Grigory Varnavsky. He said he was Jewish, as were the members of all the 130 families in his village of Ilynka in the woods of the Voronezh oblast, about four hundred miles south of Moscow. At least half of those families wanted to emigrate to Israel.

The villager's ethnic-Russian features didn't lend credibility to such claims. "The old man was insulted when we thought he was not Jewish," said Slepak to a reporter later. "He is illiterate but can read Hebrew prayers. He is more religious than most of the Jews of Moscow."

That day at the Moscow synagogue, eighty-one-year-old Varnavsky said the Ilynka villagers were descendants of Jews who at least a century ago went into the woods of central Russia to hide from the pogroms. After the revolution, the families united into a collective farm and called it "Yevreysky Krestyanin," "The Jewish Peasant." Ilynka's rabbi, a ritual slaughterer, and a *mohel* were killed during Stalin's purges. Yevreysky Krestyanin was absorbed by a larger cooperative called Rossiya.

But the peasants kept the faith. They gave their children Jewish first names including Samuil, Yakov, Mordekhai, Sara, and Fira, which clashed with the typically Russian last names. For years after the ritual slaughterer vanished, the Ilynka peasants ate no meat. Later, they had to compromise, eating only the meat of animals they had raised themselves. "It isn't kosher, we know, but it's the best we can do," the old man said. The tradition of circumcising the boys was alive and well in Ilynka. Week-old infants were taken on a 650-mile journey to the northern Caucasus, where the ritual was performed by Sephardic Jews living in secluded mountain villages. In the early seventies, eight Ilynka families emigrated to Israel, and sent official invitations to virtually half of the village's population.

But there was a problem. Victor D. Tarasov, chairman of the Rossiya collective farm, got hold of the invitations before they were delivered and locked them in his desk. "Don't even hope to receive these," Tarasov told the Ilynka residents. "We don't want you to go to Zionists." Would-be émigrés thought they had found a way around Tarasov by having the invitations sent to their relatives outside Ilynka. Still, Tarasov prevailed. He simply refused to give applicants papers certifying that they were collective-farm members in good standing and that they owed no money to the farm. Without such documents, the Soviet visa office refused to accept exit applications.

The Moscow Jews were skeptical about the old man's claims to being an ethnic Jew rather than a descendant of Russian peasants who for some reason converted to Judaism. Jewish emigration activist Lydia Voronina remembers one Moscow Jew engaging the old man in this discussion:

"You aren't a Jew," the Moscow Jew said.

"Of course, I am a Jew."

"You don't look like a Jew. How can you be a Jew?"

"I am a Jew, I say, a Jew."

After hearing out the old man's stories, Shcharansky went to Toth to tell the reporter about an old man who looked Russian but claimed to have come from an all-Jewish village in the heart of Mother Russia. Those people must have converted three or four hundred years ago, Shcharansky said.

He also wanted to know if Toth would be interested in joining several Moscow Jews on a trip to Ilynka. "My interest was in the sociology of such a forgotten place more than in Jews who wanted to emigrate," Toth said later.

Toth looked at his map. Voronezh, the closest town to Ilynka, wasn't closed to foreigners. Earlier that year, acting in post-Helsinki spirit, the Soviets had changed their regulations, saying in effect that reporters no longer needed to request permission to travel to "open" parts of the country. All they needed to do was "register" the trip. Toth wanted to go, thereby testing the system. He wasn't asking permission, he was telling the ministry to register the trip, implying that the new regulations allowed him to go to Ilynka and that he was following the letter of the law by informing the ministry about the trip.

"The trip is not registered," the ministry bureaucrat told him. In the past, the same official would have said, "The trip is not approved." Thanks to Helsinki, the words had changed, but their sense had not.

Toth told Shcharansky to go ahead without him. The story

would have to be written from Shcharansky's words, he said. Of course, Toth knew that not having the Ilynka dateline detracted from the story's value and would probably mean the piece would wind up buried behind travel-agency ads. Still, it was better than the consequences of defying the Foreign Ministry ruling.

A few days after the old man's appearance at the Moscow synagogue, Helsinki-group members Shcharansky and Slepak went to Ilynka. They were driven by Sanya Lipavsky, the round-faced mustachioed doctor who always made himself—and his Volga—available to drive other refuseniks anywhere.

"It's a lost place, isolated, without roads," said Shcharansky in an interview with Toth after returning to Moscow. The three men were stopped three miles short of Ilynka, held for three days, then turned back. On June 27, the story made page 12 of the *Los Angeles Times.*

"They gave us five excuses at different times," said Anatoly Shcharansky. First, they said, they were told they were murder suspects, then potential murder victims, and, at one point, told they would be interrupting the weeding of sugar beet fields by villagers.

They said they asked collective farm chief Victor D. Tarasov to suggest a better time to return.

"We will never permit you to go there," they quoted Tarasov. . . . "You know as well as we that there is a tense situation there and we will permit no one to increase the tension. . . ."

"Exactly why, we don't know," said Shcharansky, "but the atmosphere was hostile around there. People in the neighboring town spoke as if [Ilynka] had the plague. And the head of the collective, Tarasov, told us an anti-Semitic anecdote. . . .

"The police were astonished that we got so close in a car—only Jeeps and trucks get that far—and complimented Sanyo [sic] Lipavsky who did the driving."

When the old man came to Moscow asking for help, he knew nothing about Yuri Orlov or his Helsinki group. He couldn't have foretold that in a matter of weeks his story would wind up in the *Los Angeles Times;* that five months later, on October 12, the Helsinki group would use it as the basis of Document 9; that two other documents would be written in the next three years, one of them claiming that Ilynka Jews were in effect turned into serfs.

In the years that followed, the *Los Angeles Times, The New York Times, The Washington Post,* and *The Baltimore Sun* ran stories about the village.

All this attention had distracted *kolkhoz* chairman Tarasov from beet growing and other day-to-day business at the farm. He had to make repeated trips to Moscow to serve as a witness at the Orlov, Shcharansky, and Ginzburg trials. During legal proceedings, he referred to Ilynka residents as "those what-chumacallem Jews, as they call themselves."

In the fall of 1976, Toth wrote a story about a Russian family with a curious last name, Vilyams. "The Russian family Vilyams is distinguished on several counts, starting with its name, which was once Williams," the story, which made page 1 October 16 began.

> The first Vilyams was born in America and came to build bridges for the czar. His son became one of Joseph Stalin's most favored and tyrannical scientists. His great-grandson was one of Stalin's political prisoners.
>
> Family history is coming full circle in another way too. Nikolai, now 49, last of the male line of Vilyamses here, wants to emigrate to the United States.

The story proceeded to outline the Vilyams family history, from bridge-builder Robert Williams, who arrived in Russia around 1830, to his son Vasily Robertovich, who became one of Lysenko's henchmen, to Vasily's grandson, Nikolai, who spent five years in Stalin's camps.

The story liberally quoted Mrs. Vilyams, Ludmilla Alexeyeva. It didn't mention Ludmilla's membership in the Public Group of Assistance to Implementation of the Helsinki Agreements in the USSR.

That detail didn't seem important at the time, Toth said later.

CHAPTER 12

THE KING
OF TASMANIA

Sitting in Alexeyeva's kitchen, Mykola Rudenko said he realized that his plan to form a Helsinki monitoring group in the Ukraine was dangerous. As he talked, Alexeyeva mulled over the tragic irony of the situation: The round-faced man sitting before her was talking about the future, knowing that he had none.

"I said to him, 'You are a brave man,'" Alexeyeva recalled. "But I did not need to tell him what kind of risk he was taking. He knew it better than I."

Virtually all other known Ukrainian dissidents had been arrested in a crackdown that had begun in 1972, five years earlier. By some unofficial estimates, the Ukrainians accounted for 70 percent of all Soviet political prisoners. Rudenko's past status of writer laureate of the Ukraine seemed to deter the authorities from arresting him. But he had lost the job as editor of *Dnipro* magazine, his membership in the Writers Union, his high salary, his official car, his past. Rudenko, then fifty-nine, was working as a night watchman. The job gave him time to forge his verses about love, death, and the Ukraine. And since his privileges were not taken away at once, Rudenko was the only night watchman with a country house in the government compound near Kiev.

The logistical problems of starting the Ukrainian group were staggering. Since no foreign journalists are stationed in the Ukraine, to publicize its findings, the group would have to dispatch couriers to Moscow. That would expose the couriers to the risk of arrest each time the group decided to speak out. Considering the government's fear of Ukrainian dissent, arrests would be certain to follow the group's formation.

Of course, Alexeyeva said, the Moscow group would gladly pass Ukrainian documents to the West, and, of course, the Ukrainians would be welcome to address Western reporters at the Moscow-group press conferences. But before Rudenko left, Alexeyeva asked, "Whom are you going to form the group with? All your dissidents are in the camps. All that's left are women and children."

"You are right," said Rudenko. "Sometimes I feel that I am the only dissident left in the Ukraine." He said he would return with a list of Ukrainian-group members and the first documents.

It was a daring, suicidal plan, and Rudenko knew it. Around that time, he wrote a poem called "The King of Tasmania."

I am alone. The last. That makes me king.
Tasmanian sea is here, as is Tasmanian land,
And both need their king. That's what I heard from Him,
The one who gave this role to me.

All thrones rest on human bones
And I am building mine with human skulls.
It's not for honor, but in honor of my people's plight
I take their skulls from dogs.

From dogs, from trees . . . Just look at gardens
With apple trees, that are fertilized with blood.

And that's the reasons we were slain:
Sweet fruits will grow from human bodies.

The Ukraine was Tasmania, and Rudenko, "the last dissident," was the king preparing to share the martyrdom of his people.

On November 9, a hail of broken bricks shattered windows of Rudenko's house in Pushcha Voditsa, an elite country compound where high-level officials from Kiev went to hunt wild boars. When it was over, eight broken bricks lay among the shards of glass on Rudenko's floor. One brick hit Rudenko's guest, Oksana Meshko. Meshko, then seventy-one, was no ordinary old lady. She had served six years in Stalin's camps, and her son was serving a ten-year term for "anti-Soviet agitation and propaganda."

The brick-throwing hoodlums appeared on the very day Rudenko, Meshko, and several others gathered to form the Ukrainian Helsinki group. When Rudenko reported the incident, the police refused to take the complaint. A week later, still without accepting the complaint, the police confiscated the bricks "to study the fingerprints," they said.

Ignoring this less-than-subtle warning, the following day, Rudenko and Ukrainian Helsinki-group recruit Oles Berdnik, a science-fiction writer, set out for Moscow. Their plan was to recruit several more people, then announce the group's formation at a press conference.

On November 11, in Moscow, Rudenko met with Grigorenko, an ethnic Ukrainian who had spent most of his life in Russia but was rediscovering his ethnic heritage and brushing up on the Ukrainian language. (Later in life, he preferred to be called by his Ukrainian name, Petro.) The former general agreed to join the Ukrainian group, retaining his membership in the Moscow group. That day, Rudenko's traveling companion Berdnik showed up at the Moscow hospital where Ukrainian dissident Nina Strokata was being treated for a bleeding ulcer.

The authorities considered Strokata, a fifty-year-old physician and microbiologist, too dangerous to live in the Ukraine. She was married to Svyatoslav Karavansky, a dissident who had served a Stalin-era twenty-five-year term and was now serving a ten-year term. On top of that, in the late 1960s she served as a link between the Ukrainians and Moscow's human-rights movement. It was a close relationship. In the camps, Karavansky became friends with writer Yuli Daniel, and on a visit Strokata became acquainted with Larisa Bogoraz, then Daniel's wife. On the way back to the Ukraine, she stopped at Bogoraz's Moscow apartment, where she got acquainted with Alexeyeva.

In later years, Strokata supplied much of the information Alexeyeva published in *Khronika*. By 1976, Strokata had served a four-year prison term for anti-Soviet propaganda, and was living under police surveillance in the town of Tarusa near Moscow. The house she lived in was built by Bogoraz's second husband, Moscow Helsinki-group member Anatoly Marchenko. While Marchenko was in exile in Siberia, the house was shared by Strokata, *Khronika* activist Cronid Lubarsky, and Bogoraz's parents. One drawback of life in Tarusa was that Strokata could not get adequate medical care for her ulcer, which in the fall of 1976 became aggravated. Having no confidence in local physicians, Strokata's friend Alexeyeva asked Dr. Sanya Lipavsky if he would be able to arrange for Strokata's care in Moscow. Lipavsky obliged.

When writer Berdnik appeared by her bedside, Strokata was becoming more optimistic about her chances of survival. She was in Moscow, away from the dreary country hospitals and safe from incompetent doctors. She was receiving excellent care arranged by Lipavsky, who had impressed her as an upbeat man and an extremely competent doctor.

She had a new lease on life, and now Berdnik, a tall, mustachioed Ukrainian had come to suggest a new way to risk it. A few months earlier in Tarusa, she had told Ginzburg that she thought monitoring Soviet performance under the Helsinki Final Act was something worth dying for. Monitoring compliance in the Ukraine appeared even more worthwhile.

There were, however, a few problems. One, Strokata had been away from the Ukraine since 1971, and, two, the authorities would not allow her to return. (Even coming to Moscow for medical treatment required escaping from the police.) What's more, living away from the Ukraine, she would not be able to place her signature on group documents, Strokata said.

After some discussion, a solution emerged: Strokata drafted a letter in effect giving Ukrainian Helsinki-group member Meshko the legal right to affix Strokata's signature to any group document, provided that the document was not based on a "Marxist atheist world view."

On November 12, at Orlov's apartment Rudenko announced to foreign reporters that a number of Ukrainians had formed a Helsinki monitoring group. Asked to name the group members, Rudenko said the list was incomplete. Nor did he know the number. Asked if the group had any statements to make, Rudenko said it had yet to draft one.

"It was clear that he was a poet, not an organizer," said Alexeyeva. "The act of announcing the group meant more to him than the organizational details."

To compensate for Rudenko's apparent oversight, Alexeyeva drafted a Moscow-group document. "Considering the conditions in the Ukraine, the formation of the Ukrainian group of assistance is an act of great courage," the Moscow group document said. "On the day of the group's formation, an assault was organized against Mykola Rudenko's apartment, and group member Oksana Meshko was wounded with a rock. We would like to point out the danger of employment of *criminal methods* against such a group, whose work corresponds with the letter and the spirit of the Final Act. . . .

"We implore the world community to protect the Ukrainian group and, in the future, not to let it out of its field of vision."

The Ukrainian group's first document arrived three weeks later, on December 5. It was handwritten, it was in Ukrainian, and it was long. Looking at the weighty stack, Alexeyeva lingered on the edge of panic. The contact with whom she sent documents to the West was scheduled to make a pickup the following day, and it would be totally unacceptable to hand him a lengthy document handwritten in Ukrainian. It would not attract the publicity the Ukrainian group needed.

And, considering that the Ukrainian KGB was no doubt plotting a crackdown on Rudenko's group, Alexeyeva did not have the luxury of bouncing the document back to Kiev and asking for a typewritten and edited-down Russian translation. The document had to be translated in Moscow—by the following day. But how? Alexeyeva did not even own a Ukrainian-Russian dictionary.

Later that morning, Anatoly Shcharansky showed up at Alexeyeva's apartment to teach an English class. "The English language lesson is hereby canceled," Alexeyeva announced to him at the door. "Instead, we are doing the Ukrainian." Shcharansky, who grew up in Donetsk in the Ukraine and spoke Ukrainian, sat at the desk, leafing through what Rudenko's group called "Memorandum No. 1." Alexeyeva sat down at the Russian typewriter.

The document began by recapping the history of the Moscow group, gave a short biography for each of the ten Ukrainian Helsinki monitors, recapped the Ukraine's staggering losses in Stalin's collectivization, World War II, and the camps. It restated the details of the Stalin-era case of Levko Lukyanenko and Ivan Kandyba, two young lawyers who relied on the Soviet constitution and other documents to draft a brief arguing for the legality of the Ukraine's secession from the Union of Soviet Socialist Republics. They served fifteen years each and joined the Ukrainian Helsinki group.

"Prisons and punishment cells, concentration camps and psychiatric hospitals, strict KGB surveillance and near starvation—those are the rewards for faith in the sanctity of the letter and spirit of the Soviet Constitution," the document continued.

It was somber material, but fatigue makes translators irreverent, so Shcharansky and Alexeyeva started to make little remarks about dissident clichés that made their way into the memorandum. By the time the two got to the document's final stanzas, it was dark. "Civilization is a unity—that can be clearly observed from the Cosmos," Alexeyeva typed. "A ray traveling from the Sun recognizes no borders upon the Earth. Man is the creature of the Sun's radiation; he is the child of the Sun. So who has the right to limit his thoughts, which seek the Infinite?

For the sake of life on Earth, for the sake of our grandchildren and great-grandchildren, we say, 'Enough!' Together with us, this is said by the Universal Declaration of Human Rights and the Helsinki agreements, which were signed by the Soviet government."

"What would we have done if it weren't for you, Tolya?" Alexeyeva said to Shcharansky. "Thank God you are unemployed."

Less than a month later, Rudenko and group member Oleksa Tikhy were under arrest.

CHAPTER 13

THE INSPECTOR GENERAL

Early in October 1976, Ginzburg got a visit from Tomas Venclova, a Lithuanian poet he knew from the *Sintaksis* days. Venclova said he wanted to have a letter passed along to his friend Iosif Brodsky, a dissident poet who had emigrated to the United States.

"Go to Alexeyeva," said Ginzburg. "She is having a party. Alla Natanson will be there." Alla Natanson was actually Allyn Nathanson, U.S. Embassy vice-consul who had spent so much time with the dissidents that they gave her a Russian first name and replaced the *th* in her last name with the easier to pronounce *t*.

When Venclova knocked on the door, Alexeyeva was finishing fixing the salad for the dinner party.

"My name is Tomas Venclova. Alik suggested that I come to see you," the middle-aged, stocky, broad-faced Lithuanian said in perfect Russian.

"If Alik suggested it, come on in," said Alexeyeva.

"There's a little matter I wanted to discuss with you," said Venclova, motioning for a note pad. The apartment was undoubtedly bugged and he didn't want to be overheard. Venclova jotted down his question: "Will Alla *Amerikanka* be here?"

"Yes, in half an hour," wrote Alexeyeva.

Nathanson didn't show up that night, but Alexeyeva and Venclova did a lot of talking. After a few minutes, Alexeyeva noticed her guest's charming, self-effacing humor. Venclova's Russian was so artistic and so precise that, if transcribed word for word, it would have made fine prose. Yet there was a lilt in his voice, as if his Baltic jaws were so wide that he had to sing some sounds. It was a rare kind of accent. It made the Russian better.

What was not mentioned in that night's conversation was as interesting as what was. Alexeyeva didn't mention that for two years she had been involved in sending *The Chronicle of the Catholic Church in Lithuania,* the Baltic republic's equivalent of *The Chronicle of Current Events,* to the West. She found a Catholic among the U.S. Embassy staff and got him to send the Lithuaninan *Chronicle* to *Draugas,* a Lithuanian newspaper in Chicago.

Alexeyeva's embassy connection told her that he was defying embassy policies and risking his career. As for Alexeyeva, she was taking an even greater risk. Her predecessor as a courier for the Lithuanians, Sergei Kovalev, was serving a ten-year sentence.

Alexeyeva didn't think it prudent to mention such things to Venclova. What if Venclova was asked about it at a KGB interrogation? Wouldn't he be better off being able to say truthfully, "I don't know"? And what would he think of a person who mentioned casually to a new acquaintance that she was involved in what was clearly considered a crime against the state?

As for Venclova, he didn't mention that for several months he and two friends, Viktoras Petkus and Eitan Finkelstein, had been taking regular walks along the Neris River in Vilnus to discuss ways of using the framework of the Helsinki Final Act to demonstrate human-rights abuses in Lithuania.

One of the options was to form a Helsinki monitoring group in Lithuania. Another was to form a Baltic Helsinki group that would also include the Latvians and Estonians. However, at the time Venclova, Petkus, and Finkelstein agreed on one course of action: getting the Moscow group to present a document on Lithuania.

Venclova and Alexeyeva didn't talk much about politics that night.

Alexeyeva was curious about Venclova's road to dissent. It was so much like hers, yet so different. Venclova's was an artist's dissent, the passionate rebellion of a romantic. Her dissent, first and foremost, was driven by reason, her lawyerlike awareness of justice and individual rights. These differences notwithstanding, Venclova and Alexeyeva were on the same side in the same battle.

The Lithuanian's story had Zhivago-like historical sweep. He was born in 1937, three years before Lithuania was invaded by Soviet troops. His father, Antanas Venclova, also a poet, welcomed the Soviets, later becoming a Communist and Soviet-Lithuania's first minister of education. Antanas spent World War II in Moscow, worrying about his wife and son who, because of the rapid onslaught of German troops, didn't have time to evacuate. Tomas and his mother awaited the Soviet Army, their liberators.

After the Soviets returned, the younger Venclova went through the school system his father had designed. He thought of himself as an exemplary Young Pioneer, then an exemplary Young Communist. One exception to that loyalty was his interest in "unapproved" poetry. It began innocently with the sanctioned Vladimir Mayakovsky, then led to an interest in the more rambunctious early Mayakovsky, then to Mayakovsky's contemporaries, including Boris Pasternak, Osip Mandelshtam, Anna Akhmatova, Marina Tsvetayeva.

Some of these poets were banned in the USSR, and their works, for the most part, were available only in thin, yellowed thirty-year-old booklets that predated Stalin's terror. Most of these works had never been translated into Lithuanian, so young Venclova started to pen some translations. As translators go, he could have been considered lucky. He was taking brilliant verse and translating it from one poetic language, Russian, to another poetic language, Lithuanian. Yet there was something ironic about Venclova's avocation: He was introducing Lithuania to the poetic splendor of the nation that had enslaved it.

The 1956 Soviet invasion of Hungary turned Venclova into a rebel. Even the Soviet invasion of Czechoslovakia twelve years later didn't hit him as hard. "Probably because I was no longer nineteen in 1968," he said.

National shame, which has a way of striking the young, made Venclova imagine himself in Budapest, placing red carnations under the monument to Józef Bem, a Polish general who had led the Hungarians into a battle for independence a century earlier. It was by that monument that many of the disturbances occurred, leading to the 1956 Hungarian uprising.

In 1958, after Venclova's idol, Pasternak, received the Nobel Prize for Literature, Venclova attended a meeting where Lithuanian writers denounced Pasternak for having bypassed Soviet censors and publishing *Dr. Zhivago* in the West. It was a revolting sight: Lithuania's leading philistines, out of "Communist duty" were decrying one of Russia's finest writers and poets.

Venclova, then twenty, couldn't let this travesty pass. "I can't criticize Pasternak for *Dr. Zhivago,*" he said. "It has not been published in the USSR, and I am certain that none of the speakers here have read it. I don't know about others, but I can't criticize something I haven't read." That speech, in effect, ended his chances of becoming an officially recognized author. So, like Pasternak, Venclova decided to make his living translating.

Later, a Moscow friend arranged for Venclova to meet Pasternak at his dacha in the writers' colony at Peredelkino, about thirty miles from Moscow. The young man was introduced to the author as his Lithuanian translator, but Pasternak wanted to talk about neither Lithuania nor translating.

He wanted to talk about literature. Writers, Pasternak said, are divided into two groups, wordsmiths and genuine writers. One prominent wordsmith, he said, was Thomas Mann, a prolific German author who had churned out many a hefty novel. Another example, Pasternak said, was his own early poetry.

"I like your early poetry more than you do," Venclova objected.

Apparently not interested in debating the point, Pasternak said, "I want to spend what time I have left writing true literature, like Hemingway." Pasternak died six months later.

Venclova had met Akhmatova, too. Akhmatova asked Venclova to read Lithuanian translations of her poetry. Not knowing a word of Lithuanian, Akhmatova listened to the rhythm, the tones. "This sounds like I meant it to," she said of some passages. "This doesn't," she said of others.

In 1959, in Vilnius, Venclova met Aleksandr Ginzburg. Ginzburg, who was visiting a mutual friend, told Venclova he was publishing an uncensored journal called *Sintaksis,* and he wanted to publish the work of Lithuanian writers and poets. Venclova, who despite his superb Russian wrote poetry only in Lithuanian, gave Ginzburg literal translations of his verses. Ginzburg said he would have someone in Moscow turn it back into poetry.

"I am a Leninist," Ginzburg said to him then. "I wish everything were the way it was under Lenin. What I am fighting is the remnants of Stalinism."

"I am afraid I am past that," said Venclova. "I am not even a Leninist. You might say I am an anticommunist."

The evening's conversations made both Venclova and Alexeyeva feel old. The invasion of Hungary was twenty-years in the past, Ginzburg's Lithuanian *Sintaksis* never got off the ground, and Ginzburg himself had since served two jail terms and had long forgotten his "Leninist period." As for Venclova, he was at the end of his rope. In the past, he had been able to live comfortably, translating, among other things, T. S. Eliot's *The Waste Land,* Shakespeare's *The Tempest,* Alfred Jarry's *Ubu Roi.* The authorities knew about his ideological unreliability, but apparently didn't want to touch him as long as his illustrious father was alive.

After Venclova the elder died in 1971, Tomas could no longer find work. But he had an offer from the Slavic Department at the University of California at Berkeley, and he wanted to take it.

This evening of literary namedropping had a delightful finale: Venclova invited Alexeyeva and Williams to visit Lithuania. They accepted.

Two weeks later, when Alexeyeva told Orlov of her travel plans, the physicist seemed delighted. "Could you do a little investigation?" he asked.

Through the dissident network, Orlov heard that seven boys

had been expelled from the high-school graduating class in Vilnius, Lithuania's capital. Neither the boys nor their parents
seemed to be able to get straight answers about the expulsion.
However, there were some apparent reasons: The seven students regularly attended Mass and visited Viktoras Petkus, a
Catholic and a human-rights activist who had served a total of
thirteen years in jail. Petkus was a friend of Venclova's and one
of the three men who at the time were discussing starting a
Helsinki group on the Baltic. A few Moscow dissidents, including Ginzburg, had met Petkus in the camps.

Orlov continued. If the seven boys had been expelled because of their religious beliefs and their association with Petkus,
this could make a fine document for the group.

Alexeyeva agreed, transforming what was to be her long
weekend in Vilnus into what group members began to call an
"announced visit."

These "announced visits" were among Orlov's more inge-
nious creations. Each time a group member went out of town on
group business, the group issued an announcement to the Western press, or simply told reporters over their monitored telephones. If the press knew about the trip, and if the KGB knew
that the press knew, group members would be less likely to encounter "unfortunate accidents" in their travels, Orlov decided.

On Friday morning, as the train pulled into the Vilnius railroad station, Alexeyeva spotted Venclova. He was with two
other men, whom he introduced as Petkus and Antanas
Terleckas, a Lithuanian dissident and former political prisoner.

There was another escort, too. Four KGB tails, keeping
about fifteen paces behind, followed the group to the hotel.
"This one is mine," said Alexeyeva pointing at an agent who
had followed her on the train from Moscow.

"The rest are ours," said one of the Lithuanians.

Alexeyeva, Williams, and Alexeyeva's son Michael checked
into the hotel, then went over to Petkus's for lunch. That wasn't
a tea and sandwich affair. A crisp starched tablecloth was spread
over the table in Petkus's room in the Vilnius Old City. There
were starched linen napkins, an assortment of Lithuanian hors
d'oeuvres, chilled vodka, bottles of Lithuanian Cabernet.

Petkus was urbane, amazingly so for a forty-seven-year-old
man who had spent nearly a third of his life in prison. He wore a

suit, a white shirt and tie. He gave the guests a guided tour of his collection of Lithuanian poetry, saying his goal was to compile a library of official and unofficial poetry. Judging by the number of books, Alexeyeva concluded her host was close to his goal.

During lunch, Petkus subtly steered the conversation to little jokes and pleasant anecdotes. It was so civilized, so different, so Western.

"In Moscow we didn't dress up for out-of-town dissidents," Alexeyeva recalled. "We'd have them come in the kitchen and slurp borshch with us."

There was an irony in the situation. Alexeyeva had heard many an ethnic-Russian friend tell stories about being unable to get directions in the streets and being deliberately ignored by Lithuanian waiters and store clerks. In those stories the word *nationalism* was used with disdain, usually in phrases like "They are horrible nationalists," with the subtext of "How can anyone dislike us, the Great Russian People."

That dislike came easily to many Lithuanians. In 1939, without their say in the matter, Hitler and Stalin signed a pact giving their country to Russia. In 1940, Soviet troops invaded. Then came the arrests of Lithuanian intellectuals, followed by invasion by the Germans, whom many Lithuanians greeted as liberators. The Soviets returned in 1944, triggering a guerrilla war that lasted for twelve years. Lithuania's losses in that war are estimated between 50,000 and 270,000 people. On top of that, an estimated 350,000 Lithuanians were sent to Siberia.

Clearly, Alexeyeva wasn't held responsible for the deeds of her nation. Quite the opposite, she was being greeted by the honor guard of the Lithuanian national movement. Petkus's hospitality was famous even in Moscow, thanks to the party he gave for Sakharov in December 1975, when Sakharov, in Vilnius for Sergei Kovalev's trial, had been awarded the Nobel Peace Prize.

So there was, after all, a way for a Russian to win the respect of Lithuanians, Alexeyeva thought. It takes renouncing Russian imperialism and being prepared to die for your own freedom and theirs.

After lunch, Alexeyeva got to the business that had brought her to Vilnius: "Let's talk about the seven boys. I'd like to meet them."

"Of course," Petkus said. "We can have them here at six."

"We can't just talk to the children," said Alexeyeva. "Let's talk to the Ministry of Education, too."

"Fine," said one of the Lithuanians.

Later that evening, when Alexeyeva once again stopped by the Petkus apartment, the seven boys were waiting. They were a clean-cut bunch, all of them around eighteen. Alexeyeva set up two chairs by Petkus's window and sat down in one of them, leaving the other for each boy to use while recounting the events surrounding his expulsion from Vienuolis High School in Vilnius. All seven had been part of an informal club that for more than a year had gathered at Petkus's apartment. Petkus, the boys said, talked to them about Catholicism and Lithuanian history and literature.

School officials and the KGB learned about these gatherings, and for more than a year, the boys said, they were being called in for interrogations. Finally, at the start of the 1976–77 academic year, the seven were told that on June 17, 1976, the school's teachers' council had decided to expel them from the school. That meant the boys had to attend night school. To qualify for that, they had to take daytime jobs.

Alexeyeva wanted more details on the events that preceeded the boys' expulsion. "What did they ask you when they called you in?" she asked one of the boys.

"They asked whether we drink vodka and wine here," the boy said.

"Do you?"

"No, only tea."

From the corner of her eye, Alexeyeva was watching the activity at the table on the other side of the room. There was a teapot in the center of the table, and next to it a mug and a porcelain kettle with strong tea. The boys poured tea into the mug, diluted it with hot water from the teapot, then passed the mug around, each taking a sip, then filling the cup again. That had the air of a ritual, a symbol of brotherhood.

As Alexeyeva continued the interviewing, another boy said he had been held in a cell for two days, as officials threatened him with expulsion from school.

"They wanted me to say things about Viktoras Antanovich [Petkus]" one of the boys said to her.

"What kinds of things?" asked Alexeyeva.

"Terrible things," the boy said, blushing. "I don't want to repeat them."

"I have to know."

"They said that I must tell them that Viktoras Antanovich and I are homosexuals. That's a lie. We are not."

None of the seven boys ever corroborated the KGB's charge that Petkus gave them alcohol and engaged in homosexual acts with them. In subsequent months, as pressure mounted, the young men stood their ground. But the authorities weren't about to give up on the old-*zek*-buggers-youths line of investigation. Later, as Petkus stood trial, a young army recruit, never one of Petkus's students, was brought in to testify that Petkus once "attempted" to seduce him.

"I am sure he wasn't gay," Venclova, a close friend, said of Petkus later. "Of course, I didn't keep an eye on him through the keyhole, but I think I can see that in a man. You know, at the same trial he was also characterized as an alcoholic. He didn't drink. I drink, and every time I tried to offer him a drink, he refused."

"I had observed Petkus in the company of those boys for an entire evening, and I am certain about his fatherly feelings for them, and the complete absence of any other feelings on his side and theirs," Alexeyeva said later. "I am an adult and I am a mother, and I would have seen it if the boys were telling lies."

It's not good form to be late for a meeting with Lithuania's minister of education. The minister took visitors until 11:00 A.M. every Monday. Since there were no appointments, the unfortunates who didn't get in had to return the following Monday.

Venclova and Alexeyeva were late. The day before, they had driven to Lithuania's northwestern corner to see two Catholic bishops who for over a decade had been banned from conducting their religious duties. The bishops weren't charged with any crime, but were serving what amounted to a term in internal exile. The trip, which Alexeyeva's Lithuanian hosts hoped would lead to a Moscow-group document, lasted till dawn Monday.

At 10:45 A.M., sleep in their eyes, Venclova and Alexeyeva

rushed into the waiting room of Minister Rimkus, only fifteen minutes before the minister was to close his office doors to the public. Venclova jotted his and Alexeyeva's names on a piece of paper. A secretary took the paper to the minister.

"It seemed hopeless," Alexeyeva recalled. "But she came out within a minute, as did the minister, who politely invited us to his office."

Venclova apologized for his late arrival.

"The son of Antanas Venclova is a welcome guest in my ministry at any time," Rimkus said. Antanas Venclova used to occupy that very office.

Venclova the younger once again thanked the minister and said that in this case he was merely an escort to "Ludmilla Mikhailovna Alexeyeva from Moscow."

"I am a member of the Moscow Group of Assistance to Implementation of the Helsinki Agreements in the USSR," Alexeyeva completed the introduction.

"Which organization is this group attached to?" asked the minister, obviously unaware of the group.

"It's a public group," Alexeyeva said.

"And who is in charge of it?"

"Professor Yuri Fedorovich Orlov, Corresponding Member of the Armenian Academy of Sciences."

The title seemed to reassure the minister, making it easier for him to swallow the question about the expulsion of the seven boys.

"This has nothing to do with the Helsinki Agreements," he said. "They were expelled for behavior unbecoming of Soviet schoolchildren."

"What kind of behavior is that?" Alexeyeva asked.

"Boguses [one of the expelled students] was rude to the headmaster and then brought a religious picture into his classroom, and that's forbidden by the constitution. After all, the church is separated from the state in our country."

"And this was the reason for his expulsion?"

"No, it wasn't that," said the minister. "I know only the general outlines of the case and cannot tell you exactly what each one of them did, but the expulsions were perfectly legal. The school could tell you about it in greater detail."

The minister, clearly, was passing the buck. Venclova and Alexeyeva thanked him for his time and headed to the school.

"This is straight out of *The Inspector General*," Venclova said on the way. *The Inspector General,* a century-old play by Nikolai Gogol, begins with a corrupt mayor of a provincial Russian town announcing to his cronies: "I have called you together, gentlemen, to tell you a most unpleasant piece of news: *K nam yedet revizor,* an Inspector General is coming to visit us."

"An Inspector General?" exclaims one of the cronies.

"An Inspector General?" echoes another.

MAYOR: "An Inspector General, from Petersburg, incognito; and with secret orders."

"That's a pleasant surprise!" the cronies continue the reverberation.

"As though we hadn't trouble enough!"

"Good God! And with secret orders!"

At the school, the head of studies, a number of teachers, and the extracurricular-activities supervisor recalled transgressions by each of the boys, but could not explain why they had been expelled.

It turned out that Dobinas, head of studies, did not have the record of the school council meeting at which they had been expelled. As the conversation was coming to an end, the telephone rang. The call was from the minister—judging by the replies to him, he had already discovered what kind of a group Professor Orlov headed.

"Dobinas, quite literally, began to tremble with horror," Alexeyeva recalled. "I realized that the meeting, if continued, could turn unpleasant, and started to say good-bye.

"Besides, we had attained our goal. It was obvious that minutes of the meeting at which the decision to expel the students was allegedly made simply didn't exist. And that meant there had been no such meeting."

Alexeyeva concluded that the decision to expel the boys was made by the school administration on KGB orders. That was a violation of expulsion procedures.

"Walking out of the school, we were literally shaking with laughter," said Alexeyeva, recalling the joy of making Soviet bureaucrats grovel. The school's head of studies clearly had a bad day. At first he groveled before her, "the Inspector General from Moscow," then before the minister when it turned out Alexeyeva wasn't a high-placed official but a Moscow subversive.

"Tomas said that on an occasion like this it would be a sin not to have a drink," Alexeyeva recalled. "We walked into some bar, where Venclova ordered a glass of champagne and drank it in a single gulp. As for me, my head was spinning without champagne."

Three weeks later, in Moscow, Alexeyeva learned that five Lithuanians including Venclova had decided to form a Helsinki monitoring group.

The announcement of the Lithuanian group was dated November 25, 1976. The press conference was scheduled for November 27 at Orlov's apartment. As usual, several Moscow-group members got to work preparing the documents, feverishly writing, editing, typing, correcting, retyping, making sure there were enough copies for the reporters. In the finest dissident tradition all the work was left to the last minute. "That's partly because we didn't want to risk losing such materials in a KGB search, and partly thanks to our genuinely Russian carelessness," Alexeyeva said.

Petkus and Venclova came prepared. Their group documents were neatly typed, and there were enough copies to go around. Silently they observed the dissident sweatshop around them.

After a while, Venclova came up to Alexeyeva and whispered, "You know what Viktoras just said? He said, 'Observe the way they work. Observe it. Now that's the way the Lithuanian Helsinki group *shouldn't* work.'"

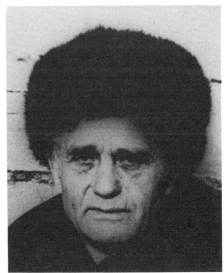

Above—NEW YEAR'S: Yuri Orlov on January 13, 1977, at the Gregorian New Year's party he hosted   LYDIA VORONINA

Right—A decade later, in internal exile in the Yakutian village of Kobiay   HELSINKI WATCH

Left—Ludmilla Alexeyeva
Right —Aleksandr Ginzburg

General Petr Grigorenko (*right*) and his wife, Zinaida, visiting Ukrainian-group founder Mykola Rudenko and his wife, Raisa, at the Rudenkos' dacha near Kiev, summer 1976

HUMAN RIGHTS DAY, 1976:
The traditional December 15
demonstration under the
Pushkin statue in Moscow
Inset—Sakharov in the crowd

GEORGE KRIMSKY

Bonner making tea at the Moscow apartment in 1979, months before Sakharov's exile to the industrial city of Gorky   HELSINKI WATCH

Below—A TOUR: Anatoly Shcharansky and *Los Angeles Times* reporter Robert Toth outside the Cathedral of New Jerusalem near the house of Shcharansky's parents
LYDIA VORONINA

Writer by calling, laborer by trade, Anatoly Marchenko digging the foundation for his house near Moscow. He never finished the house. Within months after this 1980 photo was taken, Marchenko was arrested and the house bulldozed.　HELSINKI WATCH

Lydia Voronina and exiled Jewish refusenik Boris Tsytlenok by
the Yenisey river
LYDIA VORONINA

ГРУППА СОДЕЙСТВИЯ ВЫПОЛНЕНИЮ
ХЕЛЬСИНКСКИХ СОГЛАШЕНИЙ В СССР

№ _____

„ • _____ 197 г.

ПРОЦЕСС РУДЕНКО - ТИХОГО

За попытку быть гражданином – 10 лет тюрьмы, 10 лет мучений

Олексу Тихого осудили за то, что его имя стоит под меморандумом Украинской Группы, заявляющими о намерении защищать права человека. Именно это в Стране Победившего Социализма называется антисоветской – антигосударственной деятельностью – особо опасным государственным преступлением.

Миколе Руденко, кроме его правозащитной деятельности в качестве руководителя Украинской Группы, инкриминируется также его исследование "Экономические монологи", критикующее марксистскую теорию прибавочной стоимости.

Руденко и Тихий приговорены к максимальному наказанию по статье "антисоветская агитация и пропаганда".

Руденко – 7 лет лишения свободы в ИТК (исправительно-трудовая колония – лагерь) строгого режима плюс 5 лет ссылки (в Сибирь). Годы в ИТК – это фактически смертный приговор: инвалид войны (тяжелое повреждение позвоночника) почти шестидесятилетний Руденко вряд ли вынесет те условия, на которые его обрекают.

Тихий, ранее уже отбывавший длительное заключение по аналогичному обвинению, – осужден на 10 лет лишения свободы в ИТК особого режима плюс 5 лет ссылки. Для 50-летнего человека, здоровье которого подорвано предыдущими наказаниями, этот приговор означает пожизненное заключение.

Возможности властей неограничены: могли бы обвинить и осудить и на открытом суде. Однако предпочли – особо тайный, особо закрытый процесс.

Подследственные содержались в тюрьме Донецка, вдалеке (около 1 000 км) от Киева, где жил до ареста Руденко и где совершались инкриминируемые действия.

Adventist leader Vladimir Shelkov and a Helsinki-group document on stationery produced by his clandestine publishing house, the True Witness AID TO RUSSIAN CHRISTIANS

Above—Pentecostals: Varvara and Nikolai Goretoy and Fedor Sidenko

AID TO RUSSIAN CHRISTIANS

Right— Lithuanian-group founding member Tomas Venclova, after emigrating to the United States in 1977, reads his poetry to a Lithuanian audience in America.

JONAS KUPRYS

EXPELLED: AP reporter George Krimsky, his wife, Paula, and daughter, Alissa, at Moscow's Sheremetyevo Airport. In the background, the KGB agents are ducking the camera: One is leaning over his walkie-talkie, another pulls a scarf over his face.

Below—Krimsky's photos of one of his KGB tails

GEORGE KRIMSKY

THE ORLOV TRIAL: KGB photographing spectators outside
the barricades surrounding
the courthouse   HELSINKI WATCH

CHAPTER 14

FISHERS AND HUNTERS

You could say Lydia Voronina was a dissident's dissident. She was born Russian, but neither her genes, nor her grandmother's lullabies, nor reading Tolstoy and Pushkin made her feel Russian. Not ethnically; not culturally. Voronina was involved in the human-rights movement, but never actually considered herself a "democrat." She was involved in the Jewish emigration movement, but didn't embrace either Judaism or Zionism. She helped many a group, signed many a document, but never joined any group formally. If she was to be reduced to a category, it would be philosopher by education and inclination. Voronina questioned everything.

Wandering was in her blood. Her grandfather switched his loyalties from the Socialist Revolutionaries to the Bolsheviks to the Mensheviks. Her father, a military attorney during World War II, left the family and dropped out of society, becoming a stoker in the Soviet merchant marine and, later, a gold prospector. Her mother believed there were limits to wandering. She rose steadily in the Ministry of Jurisprudence, becoming one of its key legal theoreticians. In her off-duty hours, Voronina's mother drank heavily.

Once Lydia informed her mother that her phone had been disconnected. "You have a right to appeal," the mother said. This wasn't sneering. She wrote the law that authorized the interruption of telephone service to dissidents, and now she was informing her daughter of her rights.

Given such a background, Voronina advanced a philosophical concept of her country's history. "Progress of Regression," she called it. "Progress" because political changes, after all, do occur; "regression" because with every change Russia slides deeper into barbarity. Deeper, because of such technological advances as barbed wire and automatic weapons. Thus, Peter the Great, the reformer, killed more people than his predecessors. Lenin, the revolutionary, killed more people than the czars. Stalin killed more people than Lenin. Khrushchev allowed an intellectual "thaw," then froze it. Brezhnev the freeze. All new beginnings are doomed; only the backlash prevails.

Voronina believed that democracy was preferable to the alternatives, but didn't expect democratic political institutions to arise on Russian soil. Democracy isn't among the cravings of the Russian soul, she said. In 1976, people like her were getting away with a lot, but things were destined to get worse because, according to Voronina's theory, for Russia, regression means progress.

Voronina wasn't universally accepted by Jewish activists.

In 1975, Voronina, then twenty-eight, angered her fellow refuseniks when, at a seminar on Jewish culture, she presented a paper analyzing the national identity of Soviet Jews. True, she said, Soviet Jews are currently in a state they refer to as religious uplift. But for most of them this uplift is nothing other than a defensive reaction to dehumanizing conditions of life in the USSR, Voronina said. Would this identity survive once Soviet Jews found themselves in a free society, perhaps a society with a synagogue on every street corner? Would they keep going to those synagogues?

Soviet Jews have been brought up not knowing Hebrew or Yiddish, not knowing Jewish history. What's worse, most have no feel for Judaism as a way of life. And since Judaism *is* first and foremost a way of life, no book knowledge, no beginners' classes in Hebrew can be expected to make Soviet Jews genuinely Jewish, she said.

Compare a Moscow Jew to an Israeli-born sabra, even a secular one, or a Brooklyn Hasid. The two, though different from each other, grow up feeling Jewish, thinking like Jews, emulating their Jewish parents. What's more, these people aren't trying to *become* Jewish. They *are* Jewish. Unlike Soviet Jews who cannot see beyond their zeal, genuine Jews are able to practice reflection, and they are capable of self-criticism, she said.

Soviet Jews, by contrast, use their Judaism as an instrument for protesting the Soviet philosophy, the Soviet way of life. Some have traded their Communist views for Judaism and Zionism. Therefore, Jewish awareness among Soviet Jews is psychological rather than cultural. It is a method of protest and a means of defense.

As a result, Voronina continued, such Jewish self-awareness has to be short-lived. When Soviet Jews are allowed to leave, they will no longer need to rely on their contrived Jewishness. They will then discard it.

Voronina's presentation caused an uproar, with the prominent figures of the Soviet Jewish movement countering with more traditional—and less discomforting—arguments, invoking the "Chosen People," "the Jewish Spirit," and the millennia both had survived.

"Who brought her here?" Voronina heard a distinctive whisper.

"Did we kill your Christ, too?" mocked a fellow refusenik.

When Orlov formed the Helsinki group, Voronina wasn't prominent enough to be invited to join. But as Shcharansky's roommate and Alexeyeva's maid (the job was designed to protect her from prosecution under "parasitism" laws) she was never far from the group. Frequently she volunteered to help with errands and typing. It was informal help, the only kind that could be expected from Voronina.

In late November 1976, Shcharansky asked Voronina if she would mind interviewing some Pentecostal *khodoki* to see how their complaints could be boiled down to a Helsinki-group document. "They are funny people. They talk about God and want to emigrate," he said.

"Well, if it's God, it's my department," Voronina said.

*   *   *

On December 2, 1976, four men walked into Alexeyeva's apartment and proceeded to take off their shoes.

"You don't need to do that," Alexeyeva said.

"No, we can't wear dirty shoes in the house of a respected person," said one of the four men.

They were Pentecostals who had come to Moscow to meet Western reporters. Among them was Ginzburg's Snakepit friend Fyodor Sidenko, who by then had moved from Nakhodka to the village of Starotitarovskaya, a small town in the northern Caucasus mountains. The others were Vasily Patrushev and Boris Perchatkin. The men brought a thick file that contained handwritten autobiographies of 520 Pentecostals who sought emigration.

Unshod, their pant legs tucked into thick socks, the men walked into the main room of Alexeyeva's apartment. Reporters were already waiting, Moscow mud oozing off their heavy Sierra boots.

"We want to leave the USSR for any noncommunist country," one of the Pentecostals said. "This government has a goal: to eliminate religion and God and to create heaven on Earth. We believe in God, and our goal is to get to the real heaven. This country does not need us. Our grandparents perished in Stalin's camps, our children go to jail rather than serve in the Soviet Army, none of us get more than high-school education because our faith makes us 'ideologically suspect' and therefore ineligible for education. So we want to leave, as a community and on religious grounds."

At the end of the press conference, Orlov announced that Lydia Voronina, at the request of the group, would travel to the Pentecostal communities in the Far East and the Caucasus. For Orlov, this was to be a straightforward fact-finding mission, not too different from the one Alexeyeva had completed during her trip to Lithuania. For Voronina the trip meant much more.

The Pentecostals intrigued her. Like her, they were Gentiles. Like her, they saw no future for themselves in the Soviet state. Like her, they wanted to emigrate. But her dissent was intellectual. It came from that volatile combination of knowledge, experience, and introspection. Their dissent came through faith. Their children were born into it, becoming fourth-generation dissidents. Unlike Voronina, they didn't have to break away from a hard-drinking Communist legal theoretician mother.

"I would have jumped on that chance to go even if there had been no Helsinki Final Act," Voronina said later. "I would have done it if there had been no Orlov; I would have done it if there had been no Shcharansky. I would have done it even if there had been no Public Group of Assistance to Implementation of Helsinki Agreements in the USSR."

What Voronina had in mind was a philosopher's journey to explore the Pentecostal structure of consciousness. Her goals went beyond fact-finding and journalism.

Voronina's traveling companion was Vasily Patrushev, a member of the Caucasus Pentecostal community. He was a little man, wearing thick glasses and a big overcoat, toting a schoolboy's vinyl briefcase.

"He is precisely what you call a 'humble man,'" Voronina recalled. But when she got Patrushev talking, Voronina began to fathom the tremendous pressures this seemingly humble little man endured with natural ease.

"When this compact man opened his mouth, I understood there was something extraordinary about him," Voronina recalled. "He, as other Pentecostals, lived in a different system. They saw God as their roommate. This is not a metaphor. God to them was more real than the building superintendent and a whole lot more real than some regional Communist party boss or some General Secretary."

Talking to Patrushev, Voronina began to gather some details about the object of her inquiry:

Pentecostals were teetotalers. They had a strong work ethic. They didn't practice birth control. Statements such as "The Lord told me . . ." or "God said . . ." quite clearly didn't raise eyebrows in their circles. Consequently, they were hated for being different.

The Lord didn't retire after the Creation or after the martyrdom of his son. He was around and about, and not above speaking to folks. The Lord appeared insulted by Bolshevism, its godlessness and ruthless persecution of the faithful. He also said the Bolsheviks would be punished and that the righteous wouldn't share the fate of the evil ones.

They would be delivered, for, as the Lord's avenging angel told Abraham by the walls of Sodom, not one righteous person would perish within the sinful city.

Another key revelation was Jeremiah's: "Therefore, behold, the days are coming, says the Lord, when it shall no longer be said, 'As the Lord lives who brought up the people of Israel out of the land of Egypt,' but 'As the Lord lives who brought up the people of Israel out of the north country and out of the countries where he had driven them.' For I will bring them back to their own land which I gave to their fathers.

"Behold, I am sending for many fishers, says the Lord, and they shall catch them; and afterwards I will send for many hunters, and they shall hunt them from every mountain and every hill, and out of the clefts of the rocks. For my eyes are upon all their ways; they are not hid from me, nor is their iniquity concealed from my eyes. And I will doubly recompense their iniquity and their sin, because they have polluted my land with the carcasses of their detestable idols and have filled my inheritance with their abominations."

The "north country" had to be Russia. The "detestable idols" that pollute it were the statues of Marx, Engels, and Lenin—and most certainly Lenin's publicly displayed corpse.

But what about the "fishers" and "hunters"? That was a reference to the Exodus that was to take place. A "fisher" casts for a specific fish; he won't use the same hook for a shark as he would for trout. So when the "fishers," in this case the West, decided to secure freedom for Solzhenitsyn, they cast for him and him alone; Fedya Sidenko could not have been pulled out with the same hook. Hunters are different. When they move through the forest, all the animals run, the bird, the wolf, the deer. They are indiscriminate, so when the Lord's hunters arrive, Exodus will no longer be limited to the Solzhenitsyns of this world. It will also include the Sidenkos.

"Orlov, Shcharansky, and members of that congressional commission would never have guessed that these people considered them part of God's plan for the redemption of humanity," Voronina said later.

Every day, Pentecostal religious leaders sat by shortwave radios, listening to the Voice of America and correlating world events with the Bible and their personal revelations.

The time for the Jewish and Pentecostal Exodus had come, Pentecostals told Voronina. Pentecostals, the Righteous, would follow the Chosen People.

The Pentecostals seemed to be spread out throughout the Soviet Union, but their greatest concentration was in the seaport of Nakhodka in the extreme southeast, about six thousand miles from Moscow and three hundred miles directly across the sea from Japan. It was from Nakhodka, some believed, that the Lord would deliver the faithful. Some believed it would be accomplished by another Noah's ark.

Voronina also gathered that Nakhodka was unlike any city she had seen. The town was long and narrow, built around a horseshoe-shaped bay. *Sopki,* the rounded wooded mountains of the Far East, formed the city's western border. At its widest, the city cut half a mile into the *sopki.* During the day, the mountains looked as if they came off a Chinese watercolor, except for the many hills disfigured with dynamite to make room for the city.

The city was built by prisoners shortly after World War II. Most of them weren't prisoners of war but Soviet citizens turned into slaves during Stalin's purges. In the early fifties, the city was closed to virtually everyone except the people building it. Not least among them were the inmates of thirteen labor camps that were located inside the city. The new city was to serve as a base for the Soviet fishing fleet.

After the prisoners built the seaport and the town, labor camps were moved outside the city limits, and the abandoned barracks filled up with settlers. The authorities didn't mind seeing the Pentecostals move in. Most of them were good workers who, unlike many Russians, took pride in their work and could be counted on. Over the years, some Pentecostal settlers dismantled the shabby structures and used them as lumber, but the majority simply moved into the barracks, leaving them essentially as they were. The barracks remained intact until 1974, when the authorities cleared these remnants of Stalinism, anticipating the visit of President Ford. Ford came to Vladivostok, about 120 miles to the north, but never made it to Nakhodka.

Voronina also got a taste of Pentecostal folklore, which

mostly consisted of poignant anecdotes of God's acts in history. In the 1930s, He was said to have commanded thousands of Pentecostals to head for the China border. They did, and quite a few made it across.

There was also a story of God's messages to Yefrosinya Kulabakhova, a barely literate woman laborer. As she tells it, in 1948, she heard the Lord say: "First you will pass through imprisonment, then you will pass through Vienna and Rome and go to a faraway land, America."

A few months later, as Yefrosinya began frying potatoes for a late dinner, the Lord said to her, "They are coming for you." By the time the potatoes were cooked, the police were in her house. She was sentenced to ten years in Stalin's concentration camps, but was released six years later and soon moved to Nakhodka.

In 1975, Yefrosinya was allowed to leave and, after passing through Vienna and Rome, settled in the Los Angeles area. Hers was one of the fewer than half a dozen families allowed to emigrate, Voronina was told.

Voronina and Patrushev's plane landed at the Krasnodar airport around midnight. Since the next bus to Starotitarovskaya wasn't due until morning, the two had to camp out at the "bus station," a tiny building with an outhouse behind it. A couple of drunks were stretched out on the benches.

It would have been a typical Russian scene if not for the static of hand-held radios that could distinctly be heard from treetops and from behind the nearby shrubs.

"The subject is moving toward the outhouse. Over," Voronina heard from behind the shrubs on her way to the outhouse.

"Continue the surveillance. Over."

A dozen young operatives brought in by the local KGB were botching their first surveillance exercise.

When she got back, Voronina found Patrushev curled up on the bench, the little schoolboy's backpack under his head, the large coat over him. He was asleep.

Starotitarovskaya, once a settlement of Cossacks, was crisscrossed by unpaved roads. Since winters in the northern Caucasus are mild, the roads were barely passable, giving the entire village the sweet smell of freshly disturbed mud.

Patrushev took Voronina to the house of Nikolai Goretoy, former schoolteacher and war veteran who was once the leader of the Far Eastern Pentecostals. A decade earlier, after a rift within the sect, Goretoy packed up his bags and moved to the Caucasus. In Goretoy's house, a couple of dozen people were waiting for their turn to tell Voronina about their troubles.

The complaints were similar:

The older Pentecostals told about serving long terms in Stalin's camps or hiding in the wilderness to avoid persecution. The middle-aged told of growing up without knowing their parents and grandparents. The young talked about being unable to get admitted to universities, and about their fear of being drafted.

There was yet another complaint: On the day of Voronina's arrival, the collective-farm chairman, the head of the militia, and the regional KGB "operative for the matters of religion," started to call in the Pentecostals for informal chats. "You are religious people. You should be concerned about spiritual matters, so what are you doing talking to a Moscow girl who got herself entangled in politics?"

Still, the Pentecostals kept coming to Voronina. One young man grumbled about his parents not allowing him to go to dances. "I understand it's evil, but it's hard to deal with temptation to go," he said.

When she asked Goretoy's wife why her third-grader son's arm was in a cast, she was told, "Other boys broke it in a fight." A couple of weeks earlier the boy saw village kids tie a Young Pioneer red tie around a dog's neck. He tried to stop them, saying that they were desecrating their Communist symbol and mocking a dog. So the boys broke his arm.

The boy's mother, too, had a story to tell. Several years earlier, while her husband was in prison, she had to find a job to support herself and four children. She settled for the job nobody else wanted, a custodian at a children's hospital. She worked well. The floors were clean. She didn't miss work, and never fought with management. After a while, the hospital administrator summoned her to his office. "You are a good, honest worker," he said. "It would have been nice if I could promote you to replace one of those thieves in the kitchen. But I can't do it. Everyone knows you are a religious fanatic and, frankly, I am afraid you will poison the milk."

There was also the story of a girl who refused to write a school essay called "Take a Lesson from a Communist."

"The Communists killed my grandfather," she explained to the school principal.

"But the party has corrected its mistakes and there are good Communists now," said the principal. "Take me, for example."

"You are not a good Communist," the girl said. "Everybody knows you steal bricks from the school."

She was brought up to be honest.

To find out about the deeds of the Lord, the Pentecostals turned on their shortwave radios.

They monitored the conditions in South Africa, Northern Ireland, the Middle East. They could rattle off the names of the last three chancellors of Austria, describe the participants in Italy's latest coalition government, and cite pacts Voronina had never heard of.

But most of all the Pentecostals were up on information about Jimmy Carter, a Southern Baptist who had just been elected president of the United States. Baptists, they pointed out, are close to Pentecostals. In conversations, the Staro-titarovskaya Pentecostals referred to President-elect Carter simply as *nash,* "one of us." "*Nash* has come to power. He'll help us," they said.

"They knew everything about him," Voronina recalled. "They knew about Rosalynn, about Miss Lillian. They knew their children by name, they knew everyone's age. They knew about Plains, Georgia, they knew the name of the Washington church the Carters had chosen, and they knew the street it was on.

"We, the so-called educated people, are conditioned for concepts, so we don't take things literally and therefore miss a lot in the world," said Voronina later. "But they were childlike. Their world was an integrated entity, a single living system, and they were a component of that system. They weren't outsiders to it.

"There they were, living in this remote village, up to their knees in mud, but the world wasn't as removed from them as it was from me, a Muscovite.

"These people were unspoiled. With their stories, they were affecting my level of consciousness, changing forever the way I see the world. What do you think happens when a child tells you he's had his arm broken for trying to protect Communist symbols from being desecrated? It changes you."

The day Voronina arrived in Nakhodka, her hosts slaughtered a calf.

The children were cutting the meat into slices, then feeding them into a grinder. Another group of children was preparing pastalike dough for *pelmeni,* a Siberian dish similar to the Italian *tortellini.*

Voronina tried to chat with the children, to bring them out, to find out what it meant to be a fourth-generation dissident, what it meant to be hated by others, what it meant to live a double life from the start.

The children were small. Some looked three years younger than their age. They were polite, but not verbal. They always answered, but their answers were short, usually "yes" or "no." They never looked Voronina in the eye, as if trying to hide something about themselves from her. They didn't look like young heroes. If anything, their eyes showed the scars of being persecuted at school and growing up in a strict home. Their eyes showed emotional overload.

Voronina wanted to study those children, so she took out her camera and started to click away.

A lot happened that week. She trekked through the snow to a clandestine prayer meeting. She resisted many an overture to join the Pentecostal "brothers and sisters" in their eternal bliss, and she heard many a saga of Pentecostal families and their suffering for the faith. On the last day, one of the leaders, thanking Voronina for her help, asked if there was anything they could do for her. "Yes," she said. "Let's get some candy and have a party for the children."

The following day, the children gathered in one of the Nakhodka houses. They sucked on hard candy, talked in hushed tones, and were polite and restrained with Voronina. Voronina got out her camera, looked at one of the children through the viewfinder, zoomed in, and suddenly, she, too, felt awkward, like a grande dame throwing a party at an orphanage.

The old Zaporozhets huffed along the coastal highway north, to Vladivostok.

The people next to Voronina were continuing with stories about the Lord, about their conversations with Him, about the abundance of guidance He offered the righteous as they struggled with the forces of evil. Even after three weeks, the attribution "the Lord said" hadn't lost its shock value to Voronina.

The ocean to her right was the color of steel. The *sopki* to her left were dark brown. The squat shrubs on them were oaks, a creeping version of the grand trees of Europe. Their leaves were anchored in so strongly, they didn't shed in the fall. That's how they froze: dark, glistening, and dead. The sun was setting over the *sopki,* giving a purple tinge to a full quarter of the sky.

Between the road and the *sopki,* cutting into the rock, were labor camps and cemeteries. Voronina saw the *zeki* behind barbed wire, the guard towers, soldiers with machine guns. Where the camps ended the cemeteries began. These were ordinary Soviet tributes to their dead: marble obelisks with bronze stars, iron wreaths, and Socialist Realism statues that probably rolled off some assembly line of emblems. These were the fallen heroes of the Soviet fleet.

Dirty snow was packed on the road, and under a bright far-eastern sky, the road meandered between the *sopki* and the sea. Voronina saw an orange dot on the horizon. The dot split into two. The objects were still too far to see, but they were getting closer. After a few minutes, Voronina made out the shapes of two trucks. As the trucks approached, she began to make out the shape of the load: They were hauling cages. As the trucks whizzed by, she looked at the cabs. They were foreign, probably West German. The drivers wore military uniforms, two soldiers to a cab. Inside open cages were people . . . prisoners.

"This is *syur,*" Voronina muttered, *syur* being a Russian slang abbreviation of "surrealism." She looked around again, taking note of the dark gray waters of the Pacific, the squatting frozen oaks, the purple sky, the obelisks and guard towers, the meandering white road, the orange trucks hauling people in cages. Life was imitating Salvador Dali. "I've gone nuts," Voronina concluded.

On January 1, 1977, this story, written by Toth, appeared on page 1 the *Los Angeles Times*:

Persecuted Minority of 400,000
PENTECOSTALS SEEK TO LEAVE RUSSIA

The Pentecostal religion is unique here. It alone arrived after the Communist Revolution and took root despite communism's militant atheism.

Russian-born Ivan Voronayev, converted in the United States, returned to Odessa in 1918 to preach the faith.

Now Pentecostals claim to number up to 400,000 in the Soviet Union . . . About 200,000 Soviet Pentecostals have made an uneasy compromise with the authorities by registering with the government as members of a "religious society," according to Vasily Patrushev, 46, of the Pacific port of Nakhodka. He gave that estimate to a representative of a Moscow dissident group last month.

But an equal number, he said, has refused to register. While registration would allow them to worship openly, it also requires obedience to all Soviet laws, some of which—like service in the army—violate the Pentecostal faith. . . . Not to register means risking penalties from a $133 fine for holding a service to five years in jail for organizing one.

Many of the Pentecostals, including Patrushev, have served terms for their faith, according to Lydia Voronina, who visited their communities in Nakhodka and Krasnodar near the Black Sea on behalf of a private group here dedicated to publicly seeking fulfillment of the humanitarian aspects of the Helsinki accords.

Believers today suffer fewer arrests and fines than a decade ago, Miss Voronina said last week in an interview. But the pressure from authorities continues. Sometimes it is sudden police searches. . . . Sometimes it is attempts to incite the people against the Pentecostals.

Miss Voronina cited a lecture in Nakhodka in which the speaker charged that the Pentecostals live better than their Russian neighbors not because they are thrifty, hard working and non drinking, but, the lecturer said, "because American helicopters come over at night and drop money into the backyards of these servants of US imperialists."

Many of the unregistered Pentecostals—90% of the Nakhodka community of between 3,000 and 5,000 . . . as well as some of the registered believers, want to leave the Soviet Union for any place they can freely practice their religion, Miss Voronina said.

The Pentecostals want to emigrate "not only because of their awful conditions at work and for their children at school," she said, but because ". . . they think emigration is supported by words in the Bible which say that one day God will take from this land all of his people."

"The emigration movement of Soviet Jews to Israel was a very important religious sign for them, since they believe Jews are one of God's people, and confirmed their decision to try to leave," she said.

The Pentecostals also view dissident physicists Andrei D. Sakharov and Yuri Orlov as instruments of God, Miss Voronina added, and also see the election of Jimmy Carter—since he is a Baptist, a faith similar to Pentecostalism here—as yet another favorable sign that they soon will be delivered from the Soviet Union. . . .

Nikolai Goretoy, about 50, a major spiritual leader of the unregistered Pentecostals who lives in Staro-Kitorovka [sic] in Krasnodar, said he was invited by the KGB secret police to apply for an Israeli visa. . . . According to Miss Voronina, he refused, because, he said, "I am closer to my community here than I am to any relative abroad."

"They want to emigrate as a community now, if possible, to America or Canada or Australia where there are large Pentecostal communities already," she said. . . .

"They are given the worst jobs wherever they are," Miss Voronina said. "Even though they are the hardest workers and don't steal and don't drink. You cannot appreciate how unusual that is among Soviet workers. . . .

". . . They want education for their children, who usually are very bright. But the kids are not allowed into higher education institutes because they refuse to join Communist youth groups like Pioneers and Komsomol. Their 'character references' are not good enough," she said.

Patrushev told her the story of a girl who was directed to write an essay titled: "Take a lesson from a Communist." She refused, and the principal demanded to know why.

"Communists killed my grandfather and imprisoned my father," she said.

"But there are different Communists now," he said. "Like me."

Voronina was more than a source for this story. She was more even than an expert—she was a surrogate reporter, and neither Toth nor his editors in Los Angeles saw this as an impediment. The affiliation with the Moscow Helsinki group was now an advantage.

"I didn't think the Orlov group had much going for it until that moment, until they began to do broad surveys," Toth recalled.

CHAPTER 15

I HAD EXPECTED
THEM SO LONG . . .

A t 7:30 A.M., January 4, 1977, a long ring of the doorbell awoke Yuri and Irina Orlov. "Only provincials and police use a long ring," the professor said to foreign reporters later that week. The Orlovs, who wanted to see neither visitors from the provinces nor militia, remained in bed. The ringing continued, then came the shouts.

"*Otkroyte!* Open up!" It was indeed the militia.

Orlov had a lot to do before he could open the door. He and Irina ran frantically around the apartment picking out papers and documents that could incriminate them and others. The sound of the flushing toilet mixed in with shouted threats to break down the door. About twenty minutes later, when the door was broken, the men were greeted by the scent of burning paper.

At about the same time, other search teams entered Alexeyeva's and Ginzburg's apartments.

Ginzburg wasn't home. He was putting together a bed and a

bookshelf at the apartment of writer Lev Kopelev. The head of the seven-man team, identifying himself as Investigator Borovik, asked Arina Zholkovskaya to hand him all materials "containing deliberately false information slandering the Soviet government and social order."

Zholkovskaya declined, and the search began. "During the first ten minutes, Investigator Borovik proceeded to search the bathroom, demanding that Zholkovskaya stand by his side," the Helsinki group reported in a document later. "Then, turning with his back to Zholkovskaya, he opened the door of a bathroom closet, poked around there (one couldn't see what precisely he was doing), and produced an envelope with money. He looked in the vicinity of the bathtub, then, with an envelope in his hands, returned to the large room, where the other searchers waited." The envelope, the authorities later claimed, contained $130 and 1,400 deutsche marks.

Subsequently, the search inventory said that foreign currency was kept in a secret compartment, next to an envelope from America signed by V. Turkina. Veronika Turkina, Solzhenitsyn's distant relative, had emigrated to New York two years earlier and was running an office that supplied books to anyone willing to take them to the USSR. A large empty envelope from Turkina was indeed kept in the bathroom closet, the Ginzburgs said after the search.

On the surface, it was a plausible scenario: During a search of the apartment of the administrator of Solzhenitsyn's charitable fund, an envelope bearing no signs of having gone through the mail and inscribed with the return address of Solzhenitsyn's relative living in New York is found to contain foreign currency. The implications of Borovik's alleged find could have been grave for Ginzburg. Foreign currency operations are a capital crime in the USSR.

A decade later, Ginzburg said some of the money he received indeed circumvented Soviet currency laws, but, he said, he never accepted foreign currency. Sometimes, Ginzburg said, activists abroad bought Soviet rubles in the West, then had them smuggled into the USSR. This bypassed the official exchange rates and the steep tax on fund transfers from abroad. Once, students from Scandinavia showed up at Ginzburg's offering him foreign currency. "I told them to take their money to the Beryozka store, buy some hard salami and come back with it," Ginzburg recalled. "That was the only kind of hard currency we could accept."

At 9:15 A.M., half an hour after the search began, Ginzburg walked into the apartment. Seven men were rifling through his belongings. *"Nu vse. Pizdets,"* Ginzburg said to himself. "That's it. The fucking end."

An old *zek,* Ginzburg didn't underestimate the authorities. Surely, with all the listening equipment in the apartment upstairs and with the help of informers, the KGB must have been able to trace his every step. He always knew that the search was coming, and that the arrest would be next.

He watched as the searchers sifted through piles of evidence he and they knew would be found incriminating in Soviet court. The searchers' gray linen bags were bulging with books, manuscripts, letters, money. Ginzburg had 4,000 rubles in Solzhenitsyn-fund cash. Every now and then over the previous couple of years he had thought of getting his books and papers out of the apartment, but there was so much. And it kept growing. Every day, messengers brought more documents, manuscripts, appeals. Foreigners brought books, letters, still more books. Gradually, Ginzburg grew accustomed to keeping the stuff at home. Even without it, the KGB had enough evidence against him, he thought.

"It couldn't have ended any other way," he thought as the searchers were rummaging through his apartment. Cold air from the open windows mixed with the acrid smoke of their cigarettes and his. Ginzburg felt no fear, no anger. He didn't even feel the cold.

By noon, AP reporter George Krimsky was tipped off about the ongoing searches. When he got off the elevator at Ginzburg's floor, he found Andrei Sakharov sitting on the stairs.

"There's a search on," said Sakharov, who had just made an unsuccessful attempt to get inside. Krimsky walked up to the door and listened. It seemed there were at least half a dozen voices.

He knocked on the door. There was silence, then, as if prodded, Ginzburg asked, "Who is this?"

"Alik, eto George!" Krimsky knew Ginzburg would appreci-

ate hearing his voice. An appearance of an AP reporter would tell the KGB inside that the story of the search would hit the wires and be broadcast by the Voice of America long before they finished sifting through Ginzburg's belongings.

"I am busy. Can you come back later?" said Ginzburg. There was a lackluster tone to his voice.

"How are you? What's going on in there?"

"*Ukhodite, eto ne vashe delo.* Go away, it's none of your business," answered a man's voice from behind the door. It wasn't Ginzburg.

Krimsky glanced at Sakharov. The physicist sat on the stairs, watching Krimsky's attempt to get in. Yet he wasn't entirely there. He had that vacant look of a theoretician who had taken a quick glance at the real world, then escaped back into theory. If the KGB was on his mind, he was pondering it; he was pondering his oppressors much as he pondered the hydrogen atom.

Over the years, Krimsky saw Sakharov in a way few others had seen him: a saintly man conspicuously lacking in political savvy, a man who seemed to become slightly disoriented whenever he got out of the stratosphere of theory. Krimsky had seen Sakharov with crumbs and food stains all over his shirt, eating what seemed to be one of the staples of his diet, cottage cheese with sour cream and sugar; he had seen Sakharov's vacant gaze; he had heard him stop at midsentence, looking like a child lost in a department store.

The sight of Sakharov made Krimsky recall stories about Albert Einstein forgetting his own address on the way home in Princeton. Yet, Dr. Einstein didn't become Germany's or America's leading dissident. Would Dr. Einstein have slapped a militia man at the Dzhemiliev trial in Omsk, as Dr. Sakharov had nine months earlier? Something pure and theoretical must have been at stake that day in Omsk.

Krimsky sat down next to Sakharov.

The searchers took Alexeyeva by surprise. She and her husband, Nikolai Williams, were expecting a friend. The friend, who wasn't a dissident, wanted to borrow a book, and, perhaps, stay for a cup of tea.

At 7:30 A.M., the friend rang the doorbell. The instant his

index finger touched the bell button, seven men jumped out of the nook by the garbage chute. When Alexeyeva opened the door, Williams's friend stood before her, mouth ajar. He was flanked by two men; five more were behind him.

"*Obysk.* A search," one of the men announced to Alexeyeva. The men in plain clothes walked in; Williams's friend stayed behind.

"Forgive us, but it seems it would be better if you came later," Alexeyeva said to him.

"Yes, yes, I will. Of course."

She closed the door.

The searchers were in the bigger of the two rooms in the apartment. It served as the living room, Alexeyeva and Williams's bedroom, and a study.

"Present your documents, please," said Alexeyeva.

"You can trust us that we are here on official business," said the same man who had announced the search.

"How do I know that you are on official business? It's not written on you. Documents, please."

The man, obviously head of the search team, produced a Moscow city prosecutor's office ID.

"Now everybody else," said Alexeyeva.

"I think my documents will suffice. They are with me."

"I demand to see their documents."

"Ludmilla Mikhailovna, I am afraid your demands cannot be satisfied." They were polite.

Meanwhile, the searchers moved to the two cabinets in the room. Her family members referred to one as the *samizdat* cabinet, because that's where she kept her voluminous collection of unofficial literature. The other was the Helsinki-group cabinet.

It seemed the searchers had a sense of smell for subversive literature. But it was more likely that they had made "unofficial" visits to the apartment, Alexeyeva thought.

The *samizdat* cabinet was yielding its treasures. There were Solzhenitsyn, Sakharov, Pasternak, Zinoviev, Marchenko, more Solzhenitsyn. The Helsinki-group cabinet was being emptied out, too. Just a day earlier, Alexeyeva had prepared some information to be sent to the West. It was in a thick envelope stuffed with other, smaller, envelopes. The thickest of those smaller envelopes was addressed to Khronika Press in New York; others were to go to the Voice of America and Radio Liberty.

The materials were to be sent out the previous night, but Alexeyeva's courier, a U.S. Embassy functionary, showed up to say that Ambassador Malcolm Toon had renewed his crackdown on embassy-staff contacts with the "natives" and specifically prohibited running dissident documents through State Department mail. The embassy official apologized profusely. In the past, the smuggling of documents was prohibited, too, but officials frequently looked the other way. Now, after the latest directive, the official said, he could no longer run documents.

Now the documents were in the hands of the KGB. The envelope addressed to Radio Liberty was the most incriminating of the bunch. The Munich-based radio station is financed by the U.S. government. It was started during the Cold War with what Americans were told were "private contributions." Subsequently, it was revealed that most of the radio station's startup costs had been picked up by the CIA. Later, the United States abandoned the private-contributions myth, openly financing the station through congressional appropriations. Even during détente, when the Soviets stopped jamming the Voice of America, Radio Liberty was being jammed.

At 8:00 A.M., Valentina Yefimenko, Alexeyeva's mother, got up to cook breakfast. She and Alexeyeva's younger son, Michael, were sharing another, smaller, room. That room seemed to be of no interest to the searchers.

"Mother, don't be afraid; there is a search on," said Alexeyeva, as Yefimenko heated oil in the skillet.

"Oh, a search." Yefimenko took a handful of boiled cabbage, flattened it into a cutlet, and dropped it in the oil.

Alexeyeva returned to the big room. The pile on the table had grown. The searchers were beginning to put some of the papers into gray linen sacks.

"There must be books in mother's room, too," Alexeyeva thought. "They have to read something before they go to sleep, and it sure isn't *Pravda*."

There were at least two *samizdat* books in the small room, and that meant Alexeyeva's mother, too, could become a target of interrogations.

"Mother," Alexeyeva said, returning to the kitchen. "I am sure you have some books in your room."

"Yes."

"Mother, there should be nothing in your room."

At about 9:30 A.M. the doorbell rang. Alexeyeva and one of the searchers lunged at the door. The searcher got there first and put his index finger to his mouth.

"I can't open the door. They won't let me. There is a search on. Who is this?" hollered Alexeyeva.

"This is Valya Turchin. There is a search at Orlov's and at Ginzburg's."

Out of the corner of her eye, Alexeyeva saw Yefimenko return to her room. Then she saw her come out. "Good work," she thought.

At 10:00 A.M., Shcharansky and Voronina came up to Alexeyeva's apartment building. They were struck by the unusual number of cars parked by the entrance. There was a black Volga across the street. There was also a dark gray van, its windows draped. A man Shcharansky saw by the van looked like one of his old tails.

"I think something's going on," said Shcharansky. "If we go in, we could be stuck all day. Shall we go in or not?"

"Let's go."

This time, the KGB didn't keep Alexeyeva from opening the door. They must have wanted Shcharansky and Voronina to come in.

Alexeyeva, Williams, Shcharansky, and Voronina retreated to the kitchen. There, on top of the refrigerator, Alexeyeva saw three books her mother had brought out of her room. They were Anatoly Marchenko's *My Testimony,* Alexander Zinoviev's *The Yawning Heights,* and the most recent issue of *Kontinent,* a magazine published by Russian émigrés in Paris.

The books were out of her mother's room, but leaving them out in plain view somehow seemed too much of a giveaway. Alexeyeva stuffed the *Kontinent* and *My Testimony* under the kitchen table, so the searchers would at least have to bend down to see them. *The Yawning Heights* seemed to be appropriate reading for the situation, so she kept it on the table.

The Yawning Heights, a weighty parody on Soviet history and culture, is set in an imaginary place called Ibansk (the name is derived from the obscene word for sexual intercourse). Ibanskians "are a whole head taller than everybody else, with the exception of those who are following their example." They "do not live but carry out epoch-making experiments," one of which is the pursuit of "Soc-ism," "an imaginary social order which would come into being if individuals were to behave completely in accordance with social laws. It can, in fact, never be attained because of falsity of the premises on which it is based."

Alexeyeva's guests and Williams started turning to their favorite passages, drinking in the irony of the situation. After some artistic reading, Alexeyeva walked out into the main room to see what was going on.

The searchers were looking through the desk where she and Williams kept private correspondence and Williams's mathematics papers. The gray linen sacks were filling up. String around the openings of the couple of sacks had been drawn, tied, and sealed with the prosecutor's office seals.

"This is a violation of the rules!" Alexeyeva screamed, though she wasn't quite sure which rules were being violated. "You could have put anything in those sacks! I demand that the sacks be unsealed and their contents checked against the inventory."

The head of the search team declined to unseal the sacks.

"Then I ask everyone to leave the room in protest." By 2:00 P.M. the guests were hungry. Alexeyeva warmed up some borshch, then fried some perch and potatoes. As KGB officers were leafing through onionskin papers, the scent of fried fish wafted through the apartment. Five people sat around a kitchen table; there were no documents to write, no appointments to keep. It felt like a normal gathering, except the laughter, Alexeyeva noticed, was unusually loud. It seemed to release more emotions than any laughter she had heard before.

Six hours later, the search leader walked into the kitchen.

"Ludmilla Mikhailovna, we are done. The inventory is on the table."

"Good-bye."

"*Vsevo horoshevo.* All the best."

Then, coming up to Voronina, he pulled out a warrant for the search of her apartment. They were to proceed there immediately, he said. When Shcharansky demanded to come along, he was told he would not be admitted.

Alexeyeva walked into the big room. It seemed the searchers had made an effort to put everything back in place. The furniture was just where it had been in the morning. The pictures were slightly off, but in the same places. There was no time to waste. Reporters had to be informed.

Telephoning foreign reporters from the house was out of the question; the authorities would simply turn off her phone. She ran out to the nearby phone booth. At the *New York Times* bureau, Christopher Wren told her that even before the searches were finished, Tass had moved a story saying that evidence had been uncovered connecting Orlov, Ginzburg, and Alexeyeva with the Frankfurt-based right-wing Popular Labor Alliance, abbreviated in Russian as NTS. NTS, a Russian émigré organization, had sided with the Nazis during World War II.

Alexeyeva called Krimsky at AP, then made a couple of calls to other news agencies, hoping someone there spoke enough Russian to take her story. Nobody did.

Alexeyeva returned to the apartment. The phone rang.

"I heard you had a search." It was a friend.

"Yes."

"Did they take a lot of *samizdat*?"

"No. They were fuckups. They missed a pile of books under my kitchen table."

The phone was bugged, so why not give those guys some problems at the office, she thought. Let them be called in and be chastised for not having found all the books. That could lead to bad evaluations, perhaps even demotions.

Alexeyeva came up to a window. She pressed her forehead to cold glass. Since it was hardly a secret that she was involved in *samizdat,* Alexeyeva had had five searches in nine years. The first one was rough; she felt violated. Strangers had invaded her apartment, leafed through her private papers, putting their fingerprints on everything from her family albums to her volumes of Mandelshtam to her sons' underwear drawers. The place wasn't a wreck. In fact, one couldn't really see that it had been combed through. Yet the apartment wasn't the same, it was no longer *hers.* If she could, she would have moved, burning the old place behind her. Her second search was no easier. Neither was the third, nor fourth. Now, the fifth had left her as violated as the first. Alexeyeva's thoughts turned to a poem her friend Viktor Nekipelov had written a few years earlier about a search of his own.

I had expected them so long,
That when they finally came
I felt so numbed by their sight
Inert, and beached, and lame.

I cast a glance at them
Down low, they were a ghost pack:
With goat legs, the skins of rats
And little snouts, pig-like.

Like bees on honey they had
swarmed
On diaries of mine.
And their droppings have remained
On jackets of my books.

An album then attracted them.
They whipped it out and oinked.
I pressed my face against the glass
Against its soothing cold.

I looked away into the woods,
At my beloved three pines.
I saw that all but them's for naught,
Nightmares of our time.

Out there, to spite my foul guests,
From freedom's ocean waves,
The sun was climbing up the sky—
The dawn was deep, rich, red.

And in the clouds' foam,
Unshackled and unchained
Immortal poetry floated on
Unstrained, untouched, unstained.

Without fear; without grief
The sun was coming up . . .
I knew it was the order that
Nobody could foul up.

And looking round at my beasts
And all that they had wrought,
To them, through slumber, I had
said,
"It's mine. I'll sign the protocol."

Alexeyeva came up to the table where the search team had left the inventory. The searchers got the complete archive of Helsinki-group documents, a new typewriter, a stack of blank stationery, back issues of *Khronika,* an issue of *Kontinent,* a 1972 issue of *Possev* magazine, published in Frankfurt by NTS.

She leafed through the inventory, then put it down. Next to it on the table lay an envelope. It was hers. "Radio Liberty" read the inscription.

The envelope was the most damaging piece of evidence in the house. The KGB couldn't have overlooked it. It appeared they didn't want it, and that meant the agency had decided to throw her out of the country instead of arresting her.

The drive from Alexeyeva's apartment to Voronina's usually took ten minutes. This time it took over an hour. Not that Voronina's place was hard to find. She lived near Vokzalnaya Ploshchad, Railroad Station Square, next to three railroad stations. Circling Moscow had to have been part of some mysterious KGB directive, perhaps a way to demoralize the subject.

The drive was uncomfortable. The two KGB agents in the backseat with Voronina were wearing heavy winter coats, their walkie-talkies stuffed in the pockets. There was no elbow room. There was the smell of gasoline and the scents of five people, most of them smoking, in a stuffy heated car. Old odors were coming out of the upholstery, new odors were being born.

Voronina's apartment was only slightly more spacious than the car. In the room were four bookcases, a couch, a desk, and a chest of drawers.

The search leader asked Voronina to surrender "all documents of deliberately false and slanderous content."

"Precisely what sort of materials do you mean?" asked Voronina, mostly to be difficult. "I don't understand this 'deliberately false and slanderous. . . .' "

"The works of Solzhenitsyn, Sakharov, documents of the Helsinki group."

"Is that all?"

"Yes."

"I am not of the opinion that the works of Sakharov and Solzhenitsyn and Helsinki-group documents are materials of the character that has been described in the search warrant. Furthermore, I state that I am not in possession of any slanderous materials, and that like any Soviet, or for that matter, non-Soviet citizen, I have a right to read and write any materials I see fit. Therefore I consider any search aimed at confiscation of books, newspapers, letters, etcetera, illegal and in contradiction to pledges the USSR made by signing the Helsinki accord."

The search leader browsed through Voronina's bookcase, which took up the entire wall. On the shelves were volumes of Plato, Aristotle, Hegel, Marx, Engels, Lenin. The operatives picked up each book, shook it, then put it aside. Sometimes snapshots of people who had dropped out of Voronina's life fell to the floor.

"Oh, good, I've been looking for it," Voronina said each time. "Thank you."

The KGB checked the kitchen, too. An operative opened the refrigerator door. Inside were four pounds of oranges. They were beautiful big oranges, a rare find in the winter. Shcharansky had used his connections to buy them, intending to give them to his parents and nephew at a family gathering the next day. The searcher took out an orange, bounced it up like a tennis ball, caught it, took a knife, and stuck it in the fruit.

"Why ruin the oranges?" asked Voronina. "What are we going to hide in them? Bullets?"

The KGB operative picked up another orange. He had the look of a man who loved his job.

There was a knock on the door. Voronina lunged toward it, as did one of the searchers.

"Lida, this is Volodya Slepak. They said on the Voice of America there is a search on."

It was just as likely that Slepak had heard the news from Shcharansky, Voronina thought. Shcharansky had probably asked him to stop by and keep Voronina company.

The operatives refused to open up; Slepak refused to leave. The standoff continued until the operatives realized that the refusenik was carrying a large suitcase. Slepak with a suitcase was too good an opportunity to pass up.

The instant Slepak walked in, an agent ripped the suitcase out of his hands. Inside they found a copy of *Das Kapital.*

At Voronina's, the search yielded 438 letters from Israel, nearly all of them written to Shcharansky by his wife, Avital, a copy of a Russian-language Israeli newspaper, several letters addressed to the Moscow Helsinki group, and volumes of Bulgakov, Tsvetayeva, and Korzhavin. Also confiscated were Voronina's English notebooks.

At Orlov's apartment the searchers took 141 items including the issues of *Time* for May 5, 1975, January 16, 1976, and October 18, 1976; *Newsweek* issues of January 4, 1974, February 25, 1974, and September 8, 1976; the June 21, 1975, issue of *The Economist;* a twelve-year-old issue of *L'Express;* a copy of Woodward and Bernstein's *All the President's Men;* Andrei Amalrik's *Involuntary Journey to Siberia;* Gyuzel Amalrik's *Childhood Memories;* E. H. Carr's *The Bolshevik Revolution 1917–1923;* Isak Dinesen's *Russia, China and the West 1953–1966;* a book called *Livre Blanc sur Internement Psychiatrique;* a two-page typed letter that began with "To all scientists of the world," and ended with "Andrei Sakharov and a list of other names"; documents typed on Group of Assistance to Implementation of the Helsinki Agreements in the USSR stationery. There were also issues of *Khronika,* published in Russian in New York, a letter from Dante Fascell, head of the newly formed congressional Commission on Security and Cooperation in Europe, and a petition in which eleven hundred Meskhetians living in Azerbaijan demanded to be returned to Georgia.

George Krimsky was pounding away on his typewriter. The sun was coming up. In Moscow it was past 6:00 A.M., Wednesday,

January 5. In New York, eight hours behind, it was just past 10:00 P.M. In Connecticut, his father was about to turn on the evening news.

At 10:41 P.M. Eastern Standard Time, AP's New York headquarters moved Krimsky's story about the searches.

MOSCOW—Police searched the homes of three leading dissidents Tuesday and the official Tass news agency said evidence was found linking them to an anti-Soviet organization.

Tass reported material was found in the homes of Yuri Orlov, Alexander Ginzburg and Ludmilla Alexeyeva which came from the Paris-based Popular Labor Alliance, NTS.

The dispatch said the NTS is supported by "intelligence agencies of certain Western countries" and "acts of anti-Sovieteers were paid for by foreign currency."

None of the dissidents was arrested.

"I have never had any NTS connection or met any of their people," Miss Alexeyeva told reporters. "Of course there was NTS material in my apartment." She also added that Ginzburg and Orlov also were not connected with the NTS.

Orlov called the Tass claims "absolutely absurd." Ginzburg could not be reached for comment.

Tass published the accusations hours before the day-long searches had ended, and dissidents said this was proof that authorities were fabricating evidence against them.

Orlov's apartment was searched for 12 hours, Ginzburg's for more than 15 hours, and Miss Alexeyeva's for 10 hours.

Orlov heads an unofficial group established last year to monitor Soviet compliance with human rights provisions of the Helsinki pact signed in August 1975 by 35 countries, including Russia and America.

Ginzburg and Miss Alexeyeva are also active members of the monitoring group that has been tagged illegal by Soviet authorities.

Orlov and Miss Alexeyeva said police confiscated materials relating to alleged human rights violations here, Western periodicals and typewriters.

Andrei Sakharov, the Soviet physicist and human rights

activist who won the Nobel Peace Prize in 1975, waited outside Ginzburg's apartment while the search was under way.

He told newsmen the police action was a test of the administration of President-elect Jimmy Carter, who will take
office January 20.

"I think a main reason for this at this time is to test the
new American president to see how far he will go on the
human rights question in this country," he said.

Orlov said four plainclothes officials—two from the
KGB secret police and two from the prosecutor's office—
remained at his apartment throughout the search. He
charged there was no way Tass could publish a report on
confiscated evidence nearly five hours before the search
ended. . . .

Voronina wasn't prominent enough a dissident to be included in Krimsky's story. At 11:21 P.M., AP editors in New
York made this addition to the search story:

The wife of exiled Soviet author Alexander Solzhenitsyn
telephoned the Associated Press in New York and said the
search in Ginzburg's apartment was an effort to bar money
her husband sends to families of Russian political prisoners.

In her statement, Natalya Solzhenitsyn said, "The purported link with NTS denounced by Tass is a shameless lie
which the Soviet government needs in order to persecute
Ginzburg and to deprive of assistance the families of prisoners and victims of political persecution in the USSR.

Mrs. Solzhenitsyn declined to say where she was calling
from.

That night, wire editors at *The Washington Post* and the *Los
Angeles Times* didn't pick up the story. The next day, new developments made the search story obsolete.

CHAPTER 16

GOOD REASONS
TO HURRY

The door at Orlov's didn't look broken, but it budged slowly, with a squeak, dragging on the floor. It was back on its hinges, but out of balance. The morning after the search, when a group of dissidents gathered at his apartment, Orlov and his wife had the look of people who had spent the night talking—they were alert, pale, and exuding nervous energy.

Orlov said that before the search team left, he was handed a summons to appear at the city prosecutor's office the next morning. He refused to go. From now on, Orlov said, he would try not to go outside unless absolutely necessary.

However, he added, it was absolutely necessary to go to Ginzburg's later that day. Since the authorities had planted foreign currency at Ginzburg's, his would be the logical place for a Helsinki-group press conference. That would give the Ginzburgs a chance to tell the world just how the KGB placed the money in the bathroom closet. Who knows, maybe the presentation of this information to the court of public opinion would force the Soviets to drop their foreign-currency-operations accusations, Orlov said.

As for his own search, Orlov was particularly upset about the loss of the petition from the Meskhetians. There would be no way to collect the eleven hundred signatures again, especially if the authorities sustained the crackdown. "When will we learn not to keep these things at home?" he said to Alexeyeva.

Orlov handed her a letter he and Grigorenko had written about the searches.

The letter said the searches were evidence of Soviet stifling of internal criticism in preparation for war. "I had heard that there was an intensive installation of rockets," Orlov recalled. "Grigorenko and I thought there was some military action in the works." The letter didn't say whether the USSR would fight its war in Poland, the Sinai, Namibia, or Afghanistan. Nor did it say when the war would begin.

The letter, which Orlov wanted to pass along to the press later that day, was handwritten. His typewriter had been taken by the KGB, most likely to ascertain whether it had been used in "production" of anti-Soviet documents.

To decrease the risk of his arrest on the way to the press conference, Orlov asked group members to meet at his apartment, then walk him the six hundred feet to Ginzburg's.

Meanwhile, Orlov said, he had some urgent personal business to take care of. He wanted to install two locks on his entrance door, and a lock on each of the doors inside the apartment. "When they come, I will retreat one room at a time," he said calmly. Orlov was preparing his last stand.

Symbolism, after all, was important.

A lot of work had to be done quickly. Documents to be presented that day included the brief announcement of the formation of a Helsinki-group offshoot, the Working Committee to Investigate the Use of Psychiatry for Political Purposes. There was also an appendix with brief case histories of several psychiatric-institution inmates, and there was Orlov's letter about the searches.

"Thank God we aren't sending this to thirty-five heads of

state," Alexeyeva said on the way to Turchin's where the typing had to be done. The documents were typed only once—with an original and nine onionskin copies. It was a bit past 9:00 A.M. The press conference was scheduled for noon. About ten people gathered at the Turchin apartment. Voronina and Alexeyeva sat down at the typewriters, while Grigorenko and Shcharansky prepared the paper for typing, stacking carbon paper on top of onionskin.

Just before noon, Alexeyeva took the prepared and collated copies, rolled them up in a tube, and put them in her purse. Now the task ahead was getting Orlov to the press conference.

As usual, about a dozen KGB men were stationed in front of Orlov's apartment building. It was unpleasant work, and on especially cold days the *toptuny*, the stompers, as they are called in Russia's law-enforcement-oriented slang, stomped their feet, clapped their hands, slapped themselves to get the blood pumping a little faster. Their assignment was to watch the apartment-building doorway, and every window of Orlov's apartment.

Orlov was ready for the short walk to Ginzburg's. Outside his apartment door, the dozen or so dissidents fell into a paramilitary formation. One group walked in front of Orlov, another behind him. The physicist was flanked by Voronina and Alexeyeva, who held on to his arms above and below the elbow.

This procession had marched about 150 feet from the apartment door when a man in plain clothes broke through its ranks and put his hand on Orlov's shoulder. "Are you Yuri Orlov?" he asked, and without waiting for the answer, ordered, *"Proydemte,"* Soviet equivalent of "I'm afraid we'll have to take you downtown, sir."

Orlov stopped. Alexeyeva and Voronina grabbed his arms and broke into a loud high-pitched scream. KGB operatives were running toward the group, tackling their way in, tearing Orlov out of Alexeyeva and Voronina's grip, pushing him into a car and speeding off. Other cars ripped out of their spaces, following in a convoy.

Confusion reigned at Ginzburg's. About fifteen reporters and ten dissidents arrived at the press conference, three times the crowd that had gathered there the day before.

Now, with Orlov gone, group members had to decide how to conduct the press conference. Should the description of the searches precede the announcement of the formation of the working committee on psychiatry? And what about the news of Orlov's arrest? Should that be addressed first?

Before taking over, Alexeyeva decided to get Sakharov and Bonner to sign the letter in which Orlov argued that the searches signified such total disregard for the Helsinki Final Act that it was likely that the USSR was preparing for war.

"War?" asked Bonner, reading the onionskin page.

"That's what he wrote," said Alexeyeva who had also signed the letter.

"He must have meant *cold* war."

"No, he wrote *war.*"

"But that's insane. We can't sign that."

To ward off a debate, Alexeyeva took out the ten copies of the letter, penned in *kholodnaya,* "cold," on one of the copies and handed it to Bonner. She signed it. Sakharov signed after her. They repeated the process nine more times.

The press conference was ready to begin.

First Alexeyeva told reporters that Yuri Orlov had been apprehended on the way to the Ginzburgs' apartment. She described the circumstances of the arrest, answered a few questions, then yielded the floor to General Grigorenko, the Helsinki-group member and former psychiatric-hospital inmate who planned to join the spinoff group on abuses of psychiatry. Grigorenko, in turn, introduced Vyacheslav Bakhmin, a member of the new group.

As Bakhmin launched into an outline of the group's goals, he was interrupted. "No, let's not do this. Let's talk about the search first." The speaker attempted to continue, but the questions about the search persisted.

"Here we go again. They can't stop asking about those stupid searches," Alexeyeva heard psychiatric-group member Irina Kaplun mutter in Russian under her breath. "Oh, Lord, people are being drugged in *psikhushki* and all they want to know about is searches." Kaplun's husband, Vladimir Borisov, a dissident, had been arrested and placed in a psychiatric institution eleven days earlier.

The press wanted more details. How long did the searches last? What about the foreign currency? Was it Ginzburg's or was it a KGB setup?

Ginzburg's wife, Arina, took the reporters to the bathroom, opened the closet door, and demonstrated how the search leader, turning his back to her, had produced an envelope with foreign currency. No, the Ginzburgs said, the currency wasn't theirs. Keeping it would have been a blatant—indeed, a suicidal—violation of Soviet laws. It would have been no better than keeping guns.

What about the NTS connection?

"I had an old copy of *Possev*," admitted Alexeyeva. "But I also had a lot of old and new copies of *Pravda*. Why didn't they claim I had ties with the CPSU Central Committee?"

Nearly an hour later, psychiatric-abuse study group's Bakhmin got to present his report, case histories and all.

Three hours after he was apprehended, Orlov returned. He had been informed that a criminal case had been started against him and was ordered to return the next day. For his part, Orlov informed the investigator that he regarded the previous day's searches and his apprehension as illegal. He also said he would answer no questions and would go to no interrogations.

The next day, UPI reported that "five Soviet plainclothes police shoved dissident physicist Yuri Orlov into an official black car and arrested him Wednesday as he walked down a street to address a news conference on government harassment, witnesses said." The story continued:

Orlov, currently the Soviet Union's most outspoken campaigner for human rights, was released after being questioned for five hours about copies of *Time* and *Newsweek* magazines police found in his apartment during a raid.

The Moscow prosecutor's office told him to return today, but the physicist said he would defy the order.

Orlov, who heads a dissident group set up to monitor Kremlin's compliance with the human rights decisions of the European security conference, told the prosecutor he was entitled by the Helsinki accord to buy and receive foreign news publications. . . .

The following day, the story of Orlov's apprehension made page 6 of the *Los Angeles Times*. *The Washington Post* put the story into an "Around the World" news roundup on page 9 of its B section. *The New York Times* ran a short Reuters story on page 3. "Pyotr Grigorenko, a retired army officer, said the group has set up a committee to investigate alleged abuses in mental hospitals, particularly the detention of Vladimir Borisov, a 33-year-old electrician who was put in a Leningrad institution on Dec. 25," the story read. It was the only story to mention the psychiatric committee.

After the press conference, Voronina returned to her apartment. The place needed to be cleaned, purged of the memory of yesterday's search. As she was mopping, she had two visitors, who, without introducing themselves, told her that she was no longer wanted in the USSR.

"Who are you?"

"Don't play games with us. You know who we are."

"Isn't that decision in the hands of the visa office?"

"They have been informed."

Voronina had been waiting for that moment for over two years. This was a country she found ill-fitting, a country she didn't want any part of. It wasn't good, and it wasn't bad, it just wasn't hers; even that country's internal enemies weren't like her. Most of them were "fighters," which meant their purpose was singular, they were reduced to being no more than the inverse of Bolsheviks, the opposite of her mother, yet in many ways very much like her mother. Now she was being allowed to put that land behind her. It was the moment of liberation, a moment she had envisioned many a time. Yet she didn't feel liberated, she didn't feel free, she didn't feel overjoyed. She felt numb.

Around 8:30 P.M., as soon as Alexeyeva got home, she was told that OVIR, the visa office, had been trying to reach her all day. The day before, after two years of talking about it, Alexeyeva had got around to applying for an exit visa. It was a half-hearted effort. Alexeyeva said she and Williams would not submit the required permissions from their parents, saying that she didn't want to "traumatize" her mother and Williams's.

"If you don't submit them, you won't leave," the official told her.

"Okay, we won't leave," said Alexeyeva.

Now, a day later, the OVIR official sounded eager to talk. The last call had come around 8:00 P.M., and the official left a home number asking that Alexeyeva call as soon as she could. Alexeyeva dialed the number. The official, a woman, told her that OVIR was prepared to consider her visa application. Alexeyeva was being offered a chance to bail out.

"I am sorry, but the circumstances have changed, and we'd like to delay our departure."

"For how long?"

"Till the circumstances change again."

She hung up.

Orlov repaired the broken door, installed two locks on it, then one inside each room. He spent much of his time at his desk, sometimes glancing at the KGB Volgas and the jumping, clapping, stomping, and smoking *toptuny*. It was cold outside.

The *toptuny* could be seen from every window of his first-floor apartment. Mostly, they wandered on the walkway about thirty feet from the windows, but every now and then, following an odd directive, or perhaps moved by curiosity, one or two climbed on top of a snowdrift and looked directly inside the apartment.

On January 6, Orlov sat down to write a letter: "Dear Mr. Fascell," the letter began.

Thank you for your letter. Unfortunately, it was confiscated during the search January 4, 1977.

The searches of the members of the group have done great damage to our work. We are trying to do anything we can to keep on with the job, but it is becoming harder with every hour of every day.

Aleksandr Ginzburg should be under treatment in a hospital now; he has an aggravated stomach ulcer. He did not go in for questioning and has found temporary refuge with the Sakharovs. But the KGB can seize him whenever he leaves their home or later, right out of the hospital. Ludmilla Alexeyeva has been summoned to an interrogation tomorrow, January 7, 1977.

I did not go in for my turn with the investigators January 6, 1977, and am blocked in my apartment which is surrounded by cars full of KGB agents.

Nonetheless, I hope to hold a press conference January 14 at which our group (or the part of it which is not under arrest at that point) will transmit its next set of documents which we are trying to put back together from memory.

Within the group we have just created a working commission to investigate the uses of psychiatric repression for political purposes. The Christian Committee for Defense of the Believers is working closely with us, and I am sending you their documents with the request that, if it is no trouble, you send copies to the address they indicate.

Considering our situation, I strongly appeal to you, Mr. Fascell, to take the most urgent steps possible to defend our activity, activity conducted within the framework of the Final Act and those international covenants on human rights which are already in force in the USSR.

Respectfully,
Yu. Orlov

But the unofficial mail moved slowly, and Fascell didn't receive the letter until May 3. It was accompanied by this note from the commission's deputy staff director, Alfred Friendly, Jr., formerly *Newsweek*'s Moscow bureau chief:

TO: DBF
FROM: Alfred Friendly, Jr.
     LETTER TO YOU FROM YURI ORLOV
For your information, I attach a translation of a letter Yuri Orlov wrote you on January 6. It was among a large batch of documents from the Orlov Group I picked up in

New York last weekend, including letters to me and Rep. Fenwick very similar in tone and content to the one addressed to you.

No particular action is required by the letter. Since Orlov is in prison, there is no way of sending him a personal reply. On the occasion of the next Commission session dealing with the Orlov Group, however, you should make another public statement supporting it and Orlov personally. . . .

If you like, I can arrange to circulate this letter to all Commission members. It's a gesture, but probably not a very important one.

After the searches, Orlov began to try to persuade Alexeyeva to leave the country. "Lyuda, you were planning to leave for America; what about the application? How is it?"

Alexeyeva was adamant. Her departure this soon after the search and the Tass story accusing her of having ties with the NTS would look like an escape, and that would damage her good name and the group's, she said. Besides, if the KGB has resolved to let her out, as it appears to have done, there would be no harm in making them wait. That argument didn't seem to satisfy Orlov. "How's your application? Have you filed it yet?" he asked Alexeyeva at every opportunity.

Like Orlov, Ginzburg was being summoned to interrogations, and he, too, refused to go. He had developed pneumonia, which made it impossible to travel to Tarusa every seventy-two hours to comply with his residency requirements. Besides, the prospect of going to a hospital didn't appeal to him. The Sakharovs suggested a way out: Ginzburg could stay at their place. Bonner, a doctor, would take care of him, and the Sakharov apartment would provide a sanctuary. After all, the KGB wouldn't dare arrest him at the apartment of a Nobel laureate.

As he was being driven to the Sakharovs, Ginzburg thought his *zek* thoughts. The authorities weren't ready to make an arrest, they weren't interested in dragging a sick man out of bed— that's too powerful an image. But they were certain to make an arrest the day he got back on his feet. No, Ginzburg decided, he wouldn't evade them. He would go by the old *zek* adage: "The sooner they get you, the sooner they let you out."

Alexeyeva decided she couldn't ignore her summons. If she did, she reasoned, the authorities would take her to interrogations by force, just as they had done with Orlov. The prospect of getting arrested before her elderly mother's eyes didn't appeal to her.

The summons didn't come from the KGB. It was from the Moscow prosecutor's office. The address was Novokuznetskaya 27.

The investigator was courteous. "It seems you have a lot of work, trying to document Helsinki agreement violations in the *entire* USSR."

"It's not easy," said Alexeyeva. (Later that day, after she described the interrogation to Orlov, the physicist suggested, "If he says this again, invite him to join.")

She filled out a form. It was an ordinary form asking her name, her internal passport number, nationality, and membership in organizations. "Member of the Group of Assistance to Implementation of the Helsinki Agreements in the USSR," Alexeyeva wrote. Then she said she would sign nothing and answer no questions in protest of the "illegal search" of her apartment.

"Are you afraid something was stolen."

"No, I am afraid something was planted."

"But the sacks were sealed."

"That's right. You can seal them, unseal them, plant whatever you want, then seal them again."

For the rest of the day, the interrogator sat at his desk, reading back issues of *Khronika* that had been confiscated from Alexeyeva. "*Ochen interesno.* Very interesting," he muttered every now and then. At the end of the day, he issued another summons.

The following day, Alexeyeva brought a book to the interrogation. She also stopped by a grocery store, picked up a ham and cheese sandwich and a pastry. She was about fifteen minutes late, but the interrogator didn't seem to mind.

Information gathering wasn't the point of that exercise. The point was to force Alexeyeva to leave the country.

*   *   *

On January 8, a bomb exploded in the Moscow metro, killing five.

Three days later, Victor Louis, a Soviet reporter frequently used by the authorities to unofficially float official views, wrote that the explosion was so uncharacteristic for the Soviet Union that it appeared to reflect the negative effect of "uncontrolled flow of information from the West." Some—most notably Sakharov—thought Louis was implying that the explosion had been set by dissidents. The KGB continued its investigation of the blast. Dissidents, including a friend of Sakharov's son-in-law, were searched and questioned.

A lot of accusations had been hurled at dissidents in just two weeks. The KGB had attempted to frame Ginzburg by stuffing foreign currency into his bathroom closet. A Tass story had asserted that dissidents were connected with the right-wing NTS, which "serves as a front for Western intelligence agencies." Now, it seemed, the KGB was about to portray dissidents not only as currency operators, right-wing fanatics and spies, but terrorists as well.

Yet, the metro explosion was real, and five people were indeed dead. Who had set it? Who was responsible? Who stood to benefit from this act of terror?

If Victor Louis's charges were to be made more specific and if the Western press were to give some credence to them, the Soviet dissidents' reputation in the West would be marred. (It would have taken a lot of evidence to overcome the natural skepticism about any statement of Victor Louis, but evidence could have been manufactured.) That view, first expounded by Sakharov, had in a matter of days become accepted even by dissidents who could agree on little else.

Sakharov also expressed this hypothesis in a phone call to Krimsky.

"What?" said Krimsky. "What kind of evidence do you have?"

"What kind of evidence could I possibly have in this system?" Krimsky recalled Sakharov's reply. "It is only logical that they would do this to discredit us."

Krimsky put a story on the wire.

Now Sakharov planned a massive counterattack, a press conference with dissidents of every type denying any involvement in the blast and deploring terrorism. Only that, Sakharov figured, could convince the press of their innocence. There, Sakharov planned to repeat his charges.

CHAPTER 17

AND BEFORE I'D BE A SLAVE, I'D BE BURIED IN MY GRAVE, AND GO HOME TO MY LORD AND BE FREE

While Orlov was hiding behind three locks in his Belyaevo-Bogorodskoye apartment, wondering whether his group members would be charged with terrorism, foreign-currency speculation or espionage, the best minds in Washington were pondering the future U.S. foreign policy.

At every opportunity during the campaign, the soft-spoken candidate Jimmy Carter lambasted what he called the moral bankruptcy of the Kissinger détente. It was an effective strategy; Ford had stopped using the word. Now the world waited to find out what precisely Carter meant by his promises to bring American values and the American quest for decency into the shaping of foreign policy.

On January 11, nine days before the inaugural, Representative Dante Fascell dropped a note to Secretary of State–designate Cyrus Vance.

"I think it is extremely important to let the Soviets know that we are serious about the implementation of the Helsinki accords, especially those provisions dealing with basic human rights," Fascell wrote. "I have, therefore, taken the liberty of drafting some language which I hope you will ask the President-elect to consider in his inaugural address. The language is attached and is self-explanatory. I think that this is the time and the manner in which we should signal our intentions to the Soviets on this important matter. I will appreciate your consideration of this language and hope that you will pass it or something similar on to the President-elect."

The "language" was indeed attached, typed up in caps and ready to be scotch-taped into the rest of the president's inaugural address:

THERE CAN NO HIGHER PRIORITY THAN A RENEWED EFFORT TO END THE MADNESS OF THE ARMS RACE. THE NEGOTIATIONS ON SALT II AND MBFR WILL HAVE THE URGENT ATTENTION OF THIS ADMINISTRATION. THE SUCCESS OF THESE ENDEAVORS WILL REQUIRE PATIENCE—SKILL—CAUTION—DETERMINATION—AND FAITH. IN THAT REGARD—ALL SIDES *MUST* TRY TO ACT IN WAYS WHICH WILL INCREASE TRUST AND FAITH IN ONE ANOTHER'S WORDS AND COMMITMENTS.

THE PROMISES MADE IN HELSINKI *MUST* BE KEPT—ESPECIALLY THOSE THAT PROMISE TO RECOGNIZE BASIC HUMAN RIGHTS AND TO PROVIDE FOR GREATER MOVEMENT OF PEOPLE, INFORMATION AND IDEAS AMONG NATIONS. OUR NATION, OUR PEOPLE, AND THIS ADMINISTRATION ARE—AS AMERICANS ALWAYS HAVE BEEN—IRREVOCABLY COMMITTED TO BASIC HUMAN RIGHTS, INDIVIDUAL FREEDOM, AND GUARANTEED JUSTICE—NOT ONLY FOR OURSELVES—BUT FOR ALL PEOPLE EVERYWHERE. WE SHALL THEREFORE PLACE GREAT IMPORTANCE TO THE HELSINKI FOLLOW-UP CONFERENCE IN BELGRADE LATER THIS YEAR.

PROGRESS IN THE AREA OF INTERNATIONAL HU-
MAN RIGHTS IS NO LESS IMPORTANT TO WORLD SE-
CURITY THAN PROGRESS IN SALT II OR MBFR. GOOD
FAITH EFFORTS TOWARD EACH OF THESE GOALS
ARE ABSOLUTELY AND INEXTRICABLY LINKED TO
EACH OTHER IN THE QUEST FOR PEACE.

The president's speech nine days later was done in a different meter, but most of Fascell's points got tucked in among
its ruffles. One thing Carter did not mention was the Helsinki
Final Act, which, after all, was widely viewed as the product of
Republican folly.

On January 13, the Union of Councils for Soviet Jews held an
unofficial briefing at the Rayburn House Office Building on
Capitol Hill. Appearing at the briefing were Harvard law professor Alan Dershowitz, one of America's best-known trial lawyers, and Andrew Young, a former House member who had just
been appointed by President-elect Carter to represent the
United States at the United Nations.

The third attraction was a telephone call from Moscow refuseniks. Eight time zones away, the refuseniks' master fixer,
Dr. Sanya Lipavsky, was doing the work he did so well, looking
for a phone that hadn't been disconnected.

This was being done for a dozen congressmen who made
brief appearances, and for about eighty congressional staffers,
with positions ranging from intern to legislative assistant.

Bombarding his audience with the short, emphatic phrases of
courtroom orators and stand up comedians, the shaggy-haired
Dershowitz hammered down the point: The Soviets must be
pressured, and pressured hard.

"We don't know what the key is. We know one thing,
though. The Soviet system is a rational system. It is not simply a
hodgepodge. Things do operate in response to pressures. We
don't know precisely the pressure points. We don't know where
to apply the pressures. The important point is to keep the pressure on."

The pressure points of the Soviet system are political, Dershowitz said. It is a political decision that targets a dissident or a
dissident group for persecution. After the political choice is

made, the legal system is summoned to come up with a legal reason, a legal coating of the Soviet Union's superb criminal code. But what if that political force, the starting point of arrests, is influenced the other way? What if external influence, such as pressure from the United States, causes the Soviets not to make a political decision to prosecute? Wouldn't that reverse the current?

For several years, Dershowitz had been engaged in what he called "guerrilla lawyerfare" with the Soviets. In his autobiography, *The Best Defense,* Dershowitz wrote that in 1972, while defending Jewish Defense League members on charges of murdering a woman in the bombing of the offices of a New York impresario, Dershowitz frequently lunched with Meir Kahane. JDL founder Kahane, perhaps the only fire-and-brimstone clergyman in Judaism, predicted another Holocaust and called on Jews to prevent it through violence against anti-Semites, including the Soviets. A large dose of rhetoric from Kahane and other JDL leaders affected Dershowitz:

"Some of my own family—like many American Jewish families—had emigrated from what is currently the Soviet Union," he wrote in his self-aggrandizing memoir. "I wondered what I would now be doing if they had not had the foresight to leave. Would I be a dissident follower of Andrei Sakharov? Would I be a 'refusenik' Jew, seeking to emigrate to Israel or the United States? Or would I be one of the silent millions? As I thought of these alternatives, I began to feel a bond with Soviet dissidents. There but for the grace of God, and the foresight of my great-grandparents, go I."

Dershowitz's guerrilla raids on the Soviets were lawyerlike. He submitted a brief in defense of Soviet Jews convicted for the 1970 attempt to commandeer a passenger plane to escape from the USSR. The Soviets had convicted the group of air piracy; Dershowitz's brief called their action joyriding, since the Jews had no intention of harming the crew or damaging the plane.

Dershowitz enlisted the help of his former professor, Telford Taylor of Columbia University Law School, who had been a U.S. prosecutor at the Nuremberg trials. In Nuremberg, Taylor had become acquainted with Roman Rudenko, the man who became the procurator general, the Soviet Union's chief law-enforcement officer. Taylor paved the way for submitting the airplane-case brief to Rudenko's office. Rudenko didn't respond.

Now Dershowitz was suggesting a new form of pressure: a coordinated two-front assault that would be carried out by lawyers and legislators. At future dissident trials, American attorneys, taking the Soviets up on their assurances that their system operates in accordance with the letter of the law, would file briefs on behalf of dissidents. Soviet judicial canons do not explicitly bar foreign attorneys from defending Soviet clients. Dershowitz even found a loophole in Soviet law: Attorneys hired by relatives of a defendant can present the equivalent of *amicus*— friend of the court—briefs.

Thus a Soviet defendant's aunt living in the West can hire Dershowitz or any other attorney to file briefs in any Soviet court. This loophole, which would have allowed an injection of American legal expertise into Soviet courtrooms, has been traditionally ignored by the Soviets. But what if the United States pressures the Soviets on a political level to open their courtrooms to foreign lawyers? What if U.S. legislators step in, asking that briefs filed by American lawyers be considered by Soviet courts?

"It seems to me when those requests come from congressmen; when those requests come from senators; when those requests come from people in the U.S. government, it seems to me it will be difficult for those requests to be turned down," said Dershowitz.

An hour into the Union of Councils briefing, the phone rang, lawmakers and their aides got a chance to help. The first in line was Representative Bill Brodhead, a Michigan Democrat serving his second term.

"Hello." It was Vladimir Slepak, the Jewish refusenik and Helsinki-group member who a few days earlier had brought *Das Kapital* to the search at Voronina's.

"This is Congressman Bill Brodhead."

"I am very glad to know you."

"It's very good to hear your voice. We have been meeting here for about two hours, a group of congressmen and senators to see how we can be of assistance to you and others in similar

situation. We've learned a lot of things, shared a lot of ideas and
. . . there seems to be a lot of enthusiasm here to help you. I
just wanted you to know that."

"Thank you very much. Now we need your support very
much."

"Well, we are glad to do so and I hope you keep in touch
with us and encourage others to do so because we need to know
as much as we can know about your situation so we can help you
in every way. Will you do that?"

"Yea . . ."

"I want you to talk to Congressman Andrew Young who is
going to be our ambassador to the United Nations, who has just
been appointed by our new president and will be taking office in
a couple of weeks or so. I'll put Mr. Young on the phone."

"Hello."

"Hello, Mr. Young, I am very glad to hear your voice."

"Thank you very much. It's very good to talk with you."

"I am very glad to speak with representative of United States
in United Nations."

"Well, very good. I have never visited the Soviet Union, but
I look forward to doing so soon . . . and . . . I hope we could
meet then."

"I hope so. Thank you."

"Very good."

"And . . ."

"This is quite a delegation here. I got in late. And I think the
concern that they share is one that I've shared for many, many
years. In fact, in 1957, I was part of a religious community to
look into the problem of religious freedom in the Soviet Union,
as a part of a group of Christian young people that were concerned about freedom of religion throughout the world. One of
the things that we became acutely aware of was the plight of
Jews in the Soviet Union. I also worked with Martin Luther
King, and some of his concerns about human rights in this country are also naturally extended to the question of human rights
in the Soviet Union. That's the question that we are trying des-
perately to deal with in the United Nations and I am looking
forward to getting to know you in that context, perhaps."

"Yes, and I think you know about a group here which also

has representatives also from Christians, from Jews for helping with fulfillment of Helsinki agreement."

"Uh-huh."

"And now this group is under very big attack from the Soviet authorities."

"Well, very good, and it's amazing that we can talk and hear each other so clearly."

"Yea."

"Over such long distance . . . Maybe our countries will be able to hear each other better, too, because of our friendship."

"I hope so, but I am not sure that it will be easy to do." There was sarcasm in Slepak's voice.

"No, and it was not easy for us here. I guess some of the people in this room have been jailed in this country in pursuit of human rights. And we found a good measure of success here through persevering. Well, I hate to compare the situations, but I can compare the hopes and aspirations of people. People everywhere want to be free and are determined to be free. We used to sing a song that said, 'And before I'd be a slave I'd be buried in my grave and go home to my Lord and be free.' And I think that's the song that people are singing all over the world and I am sure that it will come to be. That all of us will be free."

"I am sure that all of us will be free, but it takes time and hard work," said Slepak, notes of sarcasm still lurking in his voice. It had to be contained, because, uninformed as he sounded, Andrew Young was a high-placed U.S. official.

"It sure is," said Young. "Okay, very good talking to you."

CHAPTER 18

THE PROPHECY OF
NIKOLAI WILLIAMS

Every January 13, Nikolai Williams borrowed his mother's
deck of cards, a family heirloom brought to Russia by his
aunt at the turn of the century.

Each card had a little inscription, made in accordance with
the English method of fortune-telling. A nine of hearts stood for
good luck, a queen of clubs meant an encounter with a man-
chasing woman, and an ace of spades meant death. There was
also an instruction sheet. Williams used the deck to tell fortunes
at "old" Gregorian calendar New Year's parties, held two weeks
after the official New Year. The Gregorian Russians abandoned
the calendar shortly after the 1917 Revolution.

On Old New Years' 1977, Williams and Alexeyeva were invited to the Turchins', but their hosts decided to change their
plans. The Turchins' friend Orlov was hiding behind locked
doors, not leaving his apartment except for press conferences.
With Orlov unwilling to risk walking down the block, the
Turchins decided to move their party to the Orlovs'.

The change of venue didn't go smoothly. Two U.S. Embassy employees who showed up at the Turchins' said they couldn't go to Orlovs'. Shortly after the searches, Ambassador Toon had prohibited the staff from having contacts with the dissidents whose apartments had been searched. The Americans apologized profusely, but said they couldn't defy the instruction. They remained at the Turchins', as did Tatiana, their hostess.

It was a fine party. Cold cuts and heavy salads were placed on top of the grand piano that Amalrik had "willed" to Orlov after his departure. There was beer and vodka. Irina Orlova, presumably after having some of both, did a little Russian jig, complete with the raising of her skirt and the waving of her scarf.

"I don't want to leave," Voronina said to Irina and Alexeyeva. "I've been trying to get out for years. Now I can leave, but I don't want to. For the first time, I can say I am living a full life. We are doing good work, helping people—and our conscience is clear. What else does one need?"

"*Sdelal delo—gulyay smelo!*" said Irina, a Russian proverb that translates loosely as "You've done your work, now have a ball."

Voronina still wonders why she brought her camera to that party. Generally, she didn't like interfering with the normal course of events or calling attention to herself, and what can be more conspicuous than a camera in a room full of people? It wasn't the poignancy of the situation that made her bring her Russian Zenit along, she insisted in an interview later. It wasn't that she was getting sentimental about seeing her friends for what might have been the last time. She didn't want mementos or souvenirs. She just brought her camera, and that's all there was to it. Then she took some pictures.

Williams pulled out his cards. "Whom shall we do?"

"Brezhnev," someone suggested.

"Brezhnev?"

"Yes, Brezhnev. Do Brezhnev!"

"Brezhnev? Who is Brezhnev? I don't know any Brezhnev. . . ."

"Brezhnev!" Williams had no choice.

He shuffled the deck, then, religiously following instructions, cut the cards with his left hand. A nine of hearts, the wish card, was just near the top. The General Secretary's wish would come true, Williams announced, stirring moderate jubilation.

"Who's next?"

"Alik! Let's do Alik!" Ginzburg, who was sick, had come to the party anyway.

"No, no. Let's not." Ginzburg cringed.

Nobody wanted to argue with a *zek* saying "No, no. Let's not."

"Why not do me?" suggested Orlov.

He'd had a couple of drinks; no more than a couple. There was a smile on his face; not a broad grin, but a half smile. He lit up a pipe, took a puff, and through the viewer of her Zenit, Voronina saw more than just Yuri-Orlov-the-man. She saw his soul; she saw him as art; the shutter clicked.

At least in that company, Orlov's fortune warranted a more detailed treatment than Brezhnev's. First, Williams had to assign a card to represent Orlov. He picked the king of hearts, a card that, the instructions told him, represented an enthusiastic but indiscreet man of fair coloring. He put the king face-up on the table, asked Orlov to shuffle, then laid the cards out in six stacks, with three cards in each stack.

Fortune, it appeared, smiled at the redheaded physicist. He was to be lucky in love, famous, and successful in business.

"The group! Helsinki group!" someone suggested as an interpretation of "business."

Shcharansky was next, and good things, including a long journey, were coming his way, Williams predicted.

"Next year in Jerusalem" was the shouted interpretation. "Next year in Jerusalem!" hollered virtually everyone at the predominantly Gentile party.

After midnight, Shcharansky left the party to join Slepak, Lipavsky, and others in their telephone conference with the United States. By the time he came in, Vladimir Slepak and Andrew Young had finished their frank and useful discussion. Shcharansky took the phone.

"Hello, Anatoly!" It was Irene Manekofsky, head of the Union of Councils for Soviet Jews, who had met Shcharansky on her 1974 trip to Moscow.

"Oh! Hello, Irene."

"How are you, my dear . . . Listen, I heard you on the radio the other day!"

"Really?"

"Yes! They had a broadcast of the press conference that Sakharov had. And you were the translator, right?"

"No, it was a press conference of Helsinki group. That's why I was there, but it was also at Sakharov's home."

"Yes, but I heard the English translator and it was you. It was very nice to have you in my living room."

"Irene, I was just now at a meeting of Helsinki group, and the situation is very serious. Yuri Orlov is under home arrest, and every day there are new interrogations. . . . It's bad."

"Yes, Anatoly, the Helsinki Commission is starting to become active in their case."

"Yes, it is very important."

"They are starting to do something in that case. They are working very hard and we are trying to get them to be active in their case and all of their papers are going to be published."

"Oh, Irene, listen, tomorrow there will be our current press conference, a usual press conference of our group where new documents will be represented and I'll try to send you all the documents of this group. I hope that you will make as much publicity as is possible."

"Yes. I don't have all of them but the Helsinki Commission got them. They have up until [document] number fourteen, yes? Is that correct?"

"Number fourteen? Yes, it is."

"Okay, we love you all. Hugs and kisses to everybody. Enid wants to say a couple of words to you."

Enid Wurtman, another Jewish activist, picked up the phone. Wurtman, too, had met Shcharansky, and had even taken pictures of him to be passed along to Avital in Israel.

"Anatoly!"

"Hello, Enid."

"How are you?"

"Stuart will see Avital next week, and he'll bring pictures of you we took. And Saturday night our synagogue will be honoring Stuart and myself and you and Yuli Kocharovsky [another refusenik]."

"Ah-h."

"And also on your birthday there will be another ad in *The Washington Post.* About you. You understand?"

"I see. Yeah, I understand."

"That is the day of the inauguration. And it will go to many congressmen and many dignitaries, from all over the world. They are publishing thirty thousand extra copies of the newspaper on that day. So many people will read about you."

"I hope that one day it will help."

"We think it will."

"Well, I hope that soon I will be able to see you in Israel."

"I hope so, very soon. Is there anything that you want Stuart to tell Avital?"

"Well, I want you to know that during the searches they confiscated all Avital's letters to me."

"There was excellent support expressed today from senators and congressmen from all over the United States including the state of Hawaii. They expressed their active support by being here today and they will very actively work for you on a constant basis."

"Okay, thank you very much for your support."

"Our love to you and to all our dear friends."

"Okay, best regards to all our friends from those who are present here: Dina Beilina, Professor Lerner, Ida Nudel, and Sanya Lipavsky. From all of them our regards to all those who support us in America."

There was a certain warmth—and an equal share of awkwardness in such conversations. There was so little a desperate Russian Jew could say to a secure and moneyed American except, perhaps, "Thank you," or, more emphatically, "Thank you very much."

The better-informed Jewish activists in the USSR knew about deep splits in the movement for their emigration. They knew that the Israelis were concerned about an increasing proportion of Soviet Jews who opted to settle in the United States. They knew that the Soviet Jews who came to Israel soon became known as "the Jewish goyim" because many of them lacked knowledge of Judaism and Jewish culture. They knew that Israelis joked about their Soviet brethren leaving the USSR in pursuit of villas and Volvos.

More important, it was no secret that the Israelis were suspicious of the highly visible campaign for Soviet Jewry waged by American and Western European Jews. What seemed to worry the Israelis was their lack of control over those campaigns. In the United States the Israelis operated through the National Conference for Soviet Jewry, an umbrella group that includes B'nai B'rith and the American Jewish Committee. The Israelis avoided the group of activists called the Union of Councils for Soviet Jews. In the lingo of the Jewish movement, the National Conference was referred to as "establishment" and the Union of Councils as "grass roots."

The Israeli ideal was a Soviet Jewry campaign where officials in the Soviet Jewry Office in Jerusalem would keep the lists of refuseniks and, in a coordinated manner, pass down a few names to the countries "assigned" to write to Soviet authorities and those refuseniks. So, if a given refusenik is "assigned" to France, the British would not have a right to campaign for him. Unfortunately for the Israelis, the political reality was different. Israel's "list," which was believed to have been updated when the refuseniks arrived in the transit camp in Vienna, had become a big issue to the "grass-roots" groups in the West.

The "grass roots" demanded the list in the name of "cooperation" in getting their brethren out of a hostile land. The Israelis said no. The names would be available only on a need-to-know basis, and only to establishment groups, they insisted. This turf battle took on global proportions. On at least three occasions, emissaries were sent to warn Moscow Jews about dealing with the grass-roots activists in the West. Specifically, they were told not to telephone Michael Sherbourne, a London schoolmaster who spent nights taking calls from Moscow refuseniks, including Shcharansky, translated the information into English, and passed it along to grass-roots activists around the globe. "He doesn't pass on the information," the Moscow refuseniks were told.

Yet, this strife aside, there was something captivating about the world American Jews lived in, a world where newspapers printed whatever they wanted and accepted ads for what wasn't compelling enough to print for free. It was a world where the government could be "lobbied," and where synagogues weren't just places where old men met to chant, but institutions pursuing political agendas, educating the young, feuding with each other, even "honoring" Jews living half a world away. At the end of these telephone encounters, the Americans got into their late-model Buicks to return to suburban security; the Russians remained as vulnerable as ever, but feeling a little better because some American synagogue was honoring them, lobbying for them, and placing newspaper ads on their behalf.

A strange thing happened on January 14, the day after Orlov's Old New Year's bash. Alexeyeva looked out of the window and didn't see the lights of the mysterious van and the black Volga that had become fixtures around her apartment building after the January 4 search.

Every morning, the two vehicles had parked outside her house, their motors rumbling.

At Orlov's she didn't see the usual detachment of *toptuny*.

"Lyuda, have you refiled your exit application yet?" said Orlov in what had become his standard opening.

"Not yet, Yura."

"By the way, did you notice? There's no one out there. No one by the windows."

"Same at my place. My car and my van have been moved."

That could have meant one of two things. One: The case was closed and now it was just a matter of making the arrests. Two: The authorities had decided to let up.

The second version appeared more plausible to Orlov. The time didn't seem right for the crackdown. In less than a week a new man was about to assume the U.S. presidency; there was no telling how he would react to dissidents being hauled off to jails—especially highly visible dissidents like Ginzburg and Orlov. The Soviets wouldn't want to take a chance, especially after the international outcry that followed the January 4 searches and the Moscow metro explosion—the Soviets were still sensitive to international outrage.

Besides, the authorities thought in terms of Great Dates, dates like party congresses, revolutionary holidays, summits, jubilees. Would they dare destroy Soviet dissent's most visible group before the Belgrade conference in June, when the thirty-five signatories were scheduled to review their compliance with the Final Act? Would they want to listen to indignant speeches from the United States and other Western delegations? Surely they would want to put on a good show, come home, and then have their crackdown.

"Now they won't touch us at least until after the Belgrade conference," Orlov said to Alexeyeva.

That day the Moscow Helsinki group held its best-attended press conference ever. A West German television crew set up a camera and lights at Orlov's. Cushions were put on the floor to make extra seating for reporters and Soviet dissidents representing, among others, the Moscow, Georgian, and Ukrainian Helsinki groups, Russian nationalists, and Jewish refuseniks.

Sakharov got up to speak. "I cannot dismiss the feeling the blast is the latest and most dangerous provocation by the [KGB]," he said.

Sakharov had no facts, and two days later, officials warned him that he was out on a limb and open to prosecution for a slanderous remark.

"We are losing our patience with you," a KGB official told him.

After returning from the KGB interrogation, Sakharov called another press conference to clarify his original statement: "I made no direct accusations against the KGB but expressed certain fears and feelings, and my hope that [the blast] was not sanctioned from above. I understand the sharp character of my statement, but I am not sorry for this because in sharp situations one needs sharp means."

It was an odd clarification. Sakharov wasn't taking back his words. Instead, he seemed to be saying that his original statement wasn't an accusation but a carefully crafted innuendo—and that he stood by the innuendo.

On January 20, Martin Garbus, an American civil-rights lawyer, stepped off the plane at Moscow's Sheremetyevo airport. He was in Moscow to offer assistance in the defense of Amner Zavurov, a refusenik in trouble with the law.

Soon after his arrival, Garbus telephoned Toth and asked if he could be introduced to Andrei Sakharov. Toth put Garbus in touch with Shcharansky.

Garbus was no Soviet scholar. In his 1987 book, *Traitors and Heroes,* he claimed to have met twelve members of the Helsinki Watch group (an impossible feat); identified Yelena G. Bonner as Yelena B. Bonner; said Bonner's mother was once "sentenced to eleven harrowing years" in the nonexistent city of Karagard (most likely a reference to the city of Karaganda); cited a mysterious journal called *Chronicle of Human Events;* quoted Article 70 of the Soviet Criminal Code, calling it "Section 70-190"; referred to the "famous 1966 trial and conviction of Abram Tertz and Yuli Daniel," thus putting Daniel, a real person, on trial alongside a pseudonym. (Tertz was actually Andrei Sinyavsky.)

At first, Sakharov was reluctant to grant Garbus an audience. "But when I told him I thought he should personally write to President Carter and that I would deliver the letter for him, he asked us to come over as soon as we could," Garbus wrote in his book. "Carter was coming in, and given who he was, I figured he would be interested in that kind of an issue," Garbus said in an interview.

Garbus said the idea of getting Sakharov to write a letter to Carter came to him in Moscow. "It was certainly not a long-seated plan," he said. Years later, in an interview, Shcharansky said it was he who gave Garbus that idea. On the evening of January 21, Sakharov sat down to write the letter to the president. It was Sakharov's third message to Carter. On November 3, 1976, he had sent a telegram congratulating Carter on his election, and on January 3, he had asked the president-elect to defend an artist sentenced to eight years in the camps and five in internal exile for carving a wooden replica of the Statue of Liberty and presenting it as a "gift to the American people." The telegrams got no response.

In his handwritten and hastily translated note to the president of the United States, Sakharov warned about "the provocation in the Moscow subway which should be resisted energetically."

If anything, the physicist had grown more certain that the explosion was a provocation. "We compare it with the Reichstag fire in 1933 and the murder of Kirov in 1934," he wrote. The Reichstag fire is believed to have been set by the Nazis to be blamed on the Communists; the Kirov murder is believed to have been ordered by Stalin to get rid of a powerful political figure and as an excuse to kill a variety of "enemies of the people" who were accused of the murder.

"It's very important to defend those who suffer because of their nonviolent struggle for *glasnost,* for justice, for the destroyed rights of other people," Sakharov wrote. "Our and your duty is to fight for them. I think that a great deal depends on this struggle—trust between the people, trust in high promises and the final result—international security. Now, before the Belgrade meeting . . . the authorities do not wish to make any concessions to the most vital human rights. . . . They are incapable of engaging in an honest competition of ideas. . . . They persecute the members of the Group for Assistance to Fulfillment of the Helsinki Agreement, in Moscow and in the Ukraine.

"It's very important that the U.S. President should continue efforts for the release of those people who are already known to the American public and that these efforts not be in vain. It is very important to continue the fight for the very sick and for the women—political prisoners. The detailed information about them is in Khronika Press. . . ."

When Garbus returned to the United States, he realized that he had had no idea whether Sakharov wanted the letter to be forwarded to the president confidentially or given to the press as well. "I think that we had a very large agenda, and I was there [at Sakharov's] for a short time, and there were a lot of issues to be decided," Garbus said later. "Perhaps we could have discussed it."

CHAPTER 19

THE NEW GAME

On January 14, the day Sakharov first said the KGB had a lot to gain from the blast in the metro, Helsinki Commission members were sniping at Donald Kendall, chairman of PepsiCo and a vocal critic of special-interest groups that, he argued, were derailing U.S.-Soviet détente and thus hurting the causes of emigration from the USSR and of human rights in the USSR.

Kendall chaired the U.S.-USSR Trade Council, a chamber of commerce–like group funded equally by the Soviet government and U.S. businesses. His firm had earlier built Pepsi-Cola plants in the USSR and became the distributor of Soviet vodka in the United States. Protesting this deal, a number of Jewish groups in the United States had initiated a boycott of both Pepsi and Stolichnaya.

"The Helsinki agreement . . . says you don't interfere with internal affairs of another country," said Kendall. "Let me give you an example. . . . What would you think if the Soviet Union said to us during the crisis we had in Boston, on the busing issue, that they were not going to trade with us . . . until we solved our busing issue in Boston? Now, you know we would have told them to go to hell."

Once again, Kendall found himself on hostile ground. This time he was in for a lashing by one of the sharpest tongues on Capitol Hill, Millicent Fenwick.

"I see that [argument] in the Communist press," said Fenwick. "I have read that many times. I am very familiar with that. *Pravda* as well as Tass, and *Rude Pravo* have used that argument."

KENDALL: "I used that statement a long time ago."

FENWICK: "They copied you then. They found it useful. Busing is not a matter of international accord and these things are. That is the difference."

KENDALL: "But that is your opinion and not theirs. . . ."

FENWICK: "But that human beings have a right for visas for unification of families, a right to information, to travel for professional and personal reasons, to religious freedom. These things are written down, Mr. Kendall."

KENDALL: "I don't think there is any difference. For example, you smoke a pipe and I smoke cigars—we are both after the same thing, it is enjoyment from that tobacco. And I think we are both after the same thing in the humanitarian side, only I think my way will accomplish it, and I think the way you are suggesting will not accomplish it because there is no way you are going to tell the leadership of the Soviet Union how many people they are going to have to give visas to. It is not going to happen."

Kendall and his allies lost their battle the day Henry Kissinger, the proponent of the discreet manner of dealing with the Soviets, left the State Department.

By the time Carter took office, the Soviets had gone on the offensive against the Helsinki monitoring group in their country. Was it fitting for the president to try to intercede on behalf of the group, risking an escalation of tensions in U.S.-Soviet relations? Or would it be better to let the crackdown continue, making no statements, letting special interest groups and editorial writers nationwide accuse him of reneging on the central promise of his campaign?

The Soviets had some choices to make as well. If the KGB

were to continue its crackdown on dissent, it ran the risk of triggering Carter's wrath, and, perhaps, the slowing of trade with the United States.

Yet, if the crackdown continued despite the new U.S. president's outrage and despite the demonstrations in front of Soviet embassies in Washington, Paris, Rome, and London, the Soviets would be able to put an end to the perception that they were extremely sensitive to international pressure, the perception that they could be manipulated.

Whatever choices were to be made, in late January 1977, Orlov and his group wound up at the crossroads of superpower relations. Orlov's social experiment had catapulted a group of private citizens into the arena of superpower politics. Any decisions made in the Kremlin and in the White House were to have immediate repercussions on the Moscow Helsinki-group members.

Orlov et al. weren't the players in this gripping international drama—they were the stakes.

At 7:00 P.M., January 22, the Soviet Union's Program 1 television channel aired a documentary called *Traders of Souls.* The film showed Vienna slums, home of former Soviet Jews trying to return to the USSR. It showed an open-air market in Rome where Jews were selling Russian wooden spoons, Palekh lacquer boxes and *matreshki,* trading their dignity for meager earnings from the sale of wooden trinkets. There was a brief interview with a young Jewish couple about to board a plane at Moscow's Sheremetyevo Airport.

"Is all your family leaving?"

"Yes."

"Are you leaving any relatives in the USSR?"

"Yes, our parents."

The announcer turns to another couple. "Whom are you leaving in the USSR?"

"Our parents."

"What kind of reunification of families is this, comrades?" says the announcer. "The parents remain here while the children are going to Israel. This is separation of families rather than reunification of families."

A photograph of the bearded Vladimir Slepak hugging an Israeli athlete in Moscow for the 1975 University games flashed on the screen. Shcharansky's name—and his address—were mentioned in the film. "How was it possible that Zionist cells were created in the Soviet Union?" the announcer asked the typically Eastern Bloc rhetorical question. Those cells, the film alleged, are in direct contact with worldwide forces of Zionism, and receive instructions from the likes of Senator Henry Jackson and Representative Sidney Yates.

There had been media attacks on refuseniks before, but none hit this hard. The photos of Soviet citizens hugging athletes of a foreign power as if they were the hometown team were bound to incite hatred. Flashing pictures of members of a "Zionist cell with connections in the United States and Israel" was damaging because, unlike most Soviet attacks on Zionism, this claim was factually correct.

One day in early January, as Soviet and foreign reporters shoulder to shoulder were filing out of a press conference, a short man in a baggy gray suit nudged AP's George Krimsky and said: "*Nu chto, paren', yeshche para dney.* What's the matter, guy, just a couple more days."

The man looked like a character out of a Gogol play or a Chekhov short story, a sneering little bureaucrat. Krimsky concluded that something was in the works, but what?

Soon thereafter, Krimsky's drinking friend, Valery, a Soviet artist, asked if he could take back a Salvador Dali–inspired portrait of Krimsky he had given the reporter for his thirty-fifth birthday eight months earlier.

It wasn't an ordinary portrait; in fact, there wasn't a human in the picture, just lush rolling hills—Valery was especially adept with bright shades of green—and a blowfish with a human face flying through the air. "That's you," Valery told Krimsky. The portrait hung in the Krimskys' living room.

Valery, a bear of a man with a bushy mustache who reminded Krimsky of Porthos, one of Alexander Dumas's three musketeers, was anything but a starving artist. He lived in a four-room apartment, drank Stolichnaya vodka, could get tomatoes and cucumbers in the winter and caviar year-round.

He hung out with the Soviet Union's most beautiful people: the movie crowd, sons and daughters of the party elite, even Armand Hammer, the Russian-born nephew of the American business tycoon.

"Look, Valery, I know you are at least a fucking colonel in the KGB, but I love you like a brother," Krimsky once said after downing several glasses at the super-expensive Slavyansky Bazar restaurant in Moscow.

"Don't say that."

"Why not?"

"Because you couldn't possibly love someone who is a KGB colonel."

"Why couldn't I? I know you are a KGB colonel, I know you are assigned to me, I know you are assigned to pick my brain. I know you are assigned to show me the good times in the Soviet Union so I avoid the other side of life. And I know you got that beautiful apartment not because you are a great artist but because you are working for someone on the side. But I can still love you."

It was the kind of love reserved exclusively for drinking friends, and it made KGB ties irrelevant. That day in mid-January was the last time Krimsky saw Valery—and the painting.

On the evening of January 24, Krimsky received a call from his bureau chief, David Mason.

"We have to talk. Immediately," Mason said. He sounded worried.

Krimsky drove to the bureau.

Earlier that day, Mason said, he had been called in by V. N. Sofinsky, press chief at the Ministry of Foreign Affairs. Sofinsky said the ministry was concerned about what he called Krimsky's intelligence-gathering activities, foreign-currency-law violations, and other activities incompatible with the status of a foreign reporter in the USSR. It seemed the Foreign Ministry official's tone suggested that the authorities were anxious for a backroom compromise.

"Oh, Mr. Mason, we know all about Mr. Krimsky," the official said, pointing at a thick file. Asked what was in the file, Sofinsky reiterated the accusations made in *Literaturnaya gazeta* earlier, plus some heretofore unheard evidence. Krimsky violated established procedures by hiring a Soviet citizen maid without completing all the required paperwork; then he paid her in foreign-currency certificates.

"Is that all you've got?" Mason said he asked Sofinsky. The absence of an official contract wasn't a major crime. And there wouldn't be many Westerners left in the USSR if authorities started expelling all reporters and diplomats who supplemented the salaries of Soviet maids, translators, and drivers with foreign-currency coupons. Sofinsky pointed out that the ministry didn't have any problems with the AP—just Krimsky—and that if he were transferred, the wire service would be given a clean slate.

"What if we refuse to transfer him?" Mason asked Sofinsky.

"Then we might just throw him out," the official reportedly said. "We have ways of dealing with criminals and spies in this country."

"We'll give you an answer as soon as we can," Mason said.

The problem went beyond replacing one reporter in one bureau. If Krimsky were to be quietly removed in the middle of his three-year tour, the AP would be giving in to the KGB. Also, the AP's long-standing business relationship with the Soviets would be at risk. The American wire service is under contract to carry Tass dispatches to subscribers in the West. In addition, Krimsky would become the first American journalist to be expelled from the USSR since the beginning of détente. It would be a big story, making a reporter a newsmaker, a situation no reputable news organization wants. It was the sort of dilemma chess players call "a fork," a choice of two evils.

"Do you want AP to pull you out, no shame involved?" Mason asked Krimsky.

Being withdrawn from a bureau definitely involved shame, Krimsky thought. It was the ultimate expression of lack of confidence and an implied admission of guilt, perhaps the end of a career. If he were to leave Russia quietly, he would forever have to explain that he was not a spy.

"No, Dave, I don't want AP to pull me out."

"You realize what they are implying when they accuse you of all this?" Mason said. "There could be criminal punishment. You could conceivably go on trial." That was an extreme possibility. Expulsion seemed more likely. The two agreed to keep the matter quiet. No reporters were to be told of the impending situation until the Soviets made their move.

The next day, Mason called the Foreign Ministry to inform press-relations chief Sofinsky that AP management in New York had decided not to pull out Krimsky. He got as far as the secretary. Sofinsky was ill, she said, and took a message. Mason made another call in a few days, getting the same answer. It seemed the ministry was interested in letting the Krimsky affair linger.

As the days dragged, Krimsky proceeded with his daily routine, trying to concentrate on official news and dissident gatherings while his career hung in the balance. Confidentially, he told Ginzburg about his problems. "I hope I get expelled, because if AP calls me off, I am finished."

With the KGB closing in, Helsinki monitors thought the new U.S. president was the key to assuring their survival. If he remained firm, Orlov and his group members might avoid imprisonment. If he wavered, the crackdown would continue. To them, the news broadcast over the foreign radio stations made the difference between imprisonment and exile.

The radio stations brought some good news on January 27. A State Department spokesman warned the Soviets against any attempts to "intimidate" or silence Sakharov. The statement's wording was strong enough to please the dissidents. Its timing was even better.

But there was a problem, one that baffled Washington watchers far more experienced than Yuri Orlov: The statement apparently didn't go through proper channels and was released without being approved by Secretary of State Cyrus Vance. Vance claimed he first heard about it when Soviet Ambassador Anatoly Dobrynin called to protest the State Department's "meddling in the Soviet Union's internal affairs." In the days that followed, the U.S. press—and with it the Voice of America—began to chart the story of the State Department pronouncement on Sakharov.

The statement, State Department officials said later, was authorized by Assistant Secretary of State John A. Armitage without being cleared by either Vance or Carter. Both readily admitted they didn't authorize the statement, but to stress their resolve to pursue human rights Carter and Vance issued clarifications:

"We do not intend to be strident or polemical, but . . . we will from time to time comment when we see a threat to human rights, when we believe it constructive to do so," said Vance. President Carter said the State Department statement, though it was unauthorized, reflected his views.

As officials in Washington were inserting caveats and clarifications, Moscow dissidents, unfamiliar with the mechanics of Washington bureaucratic rivalries, were struggling with a gnawing question: If everyone was in agreement with the State Department statement, why did Vance and Carter say it was unauthorized? Could that be a sign of wavering?

Alexeyeva found herself fighting off fears that the Carter administration had gone back on its promises; and she was not alone. She and others were in no position to appreciate that the Carter policy was not following a meticulously drafted plan, and that mistakes such as "unauthorized statements" are known to occur in the chaotic process of U.S. policymaking. No profound messages were being sent to dissidents or Soviet officials. It was a simple Washington screwup.

CHAPTER 20

LIARS AND PHARISEES

n the afternoon of February 2, a friend stopped by the Ginzburg apartment. He was carrying a copy of *Literaturnaya gazeta.*

"Have you read it? It's about you."

Ginzburg opened the paper.

The headline, LIARS AND PHARISEES, caught his eye. So did the by-line—Aleksandr Petrov-Agatov.

Petrov-Agatov was Ginzburg's *zek* acquaintance, a former Vladimir prison cellmate. He had done time for forgery, then more time under Article 70. After his release, he asked Ginzburg for money from the Solzhenitsyn fund.

The article identified Petrov-Agatov as a former member of the USSR Writers Union, a claim Ginzburg had heard his former cellmate make in the Vladimir prison. He said he joined the union when he was living on the Chuckotskiy peninsula, in the extreme northeast of the USSR, a place hardly known for its literary tradition.

Ginzburg and Petrov-Agatov had been on the outs for a few

months. The Chukcha writer wanted more money than the fund was prepared to give him.

"I can no longer remain silent about my own delusions and those of my former comrades," Petrov-Agatov wrote.

> These people are called either a "human rights group" or the "group for implementation of the Helsinki accords" or even "Helsinki monitors." These are very effective names and the reaction they receive from Western news agencies and various radio "voices" is extremely warm. Statements by these "dissidents" are quoted together with those of West European and American statesmen. Their moral image is praised in every way: they are supposedly "fighting fearlessly" for human rights, they "never compromise with their consciences," and they are depicted as models of uprightness and purity.

For a long time, Petrov-Agatov was one of the many old *zeki* who seemed to deify Ginzburg. After prison he stopped by Ginzburg's house in Tarusa and handed him two thick homebound volumes of his own poetry. A gushing note on the title page of one of the volumes thanked Ginzburg for being himself. The other volume wasn't inscribed. Petrov-Agatov wanted Ginzburg to pass it along to the West. The poetry was bad, typical camp lyricism reducing God and Country to drivel, but Ginzburg sent the volume to the West. He was surprised to hear that some of the stuff got published in the émigré press. As for the other volume of Petrov-Agatov's work, it was in Ginzburg's possession until the search January 4.

> I probably have more grounds for being considered a dissident than other dissidents. Two years have not yet elapsed since I finally regained freedom, after having done time "from bell to bell." I was sentenced for anti-Soviet agitation and illegally sending anti-Soviet works abroad. I recently wrote a story, called "Meetings in Prison." It, as well as a number of poems and sketches, imbued not so much with the spirit of Christianity (I am a believer while the majority of "dissidents" are atheists) as with spleen, have been published abroad. In many places, including Israel where my

poetry about Jews (I am a Russian) appeared, these imma-
ture, vicious works of mine were translated and reissued repeatedly.

The reference to religion was amusing. Rejected by the fund,
Petrov-Agatov became a Pentecostal and moved in with a
preacher's family. That arrangement turned sour. Petrov-
Agatov started an affair with the preacher's wife. The preacher
was thrown out of the house.

I saw that Ginzburg's subservience to the West springs from
his greed for money—yes, money and only money which he
receives from the West. I learned from conversations with
Ginzburg that without hesitation he could become a zealous
monarchist and anti-liberal if such a position would satisfy
his mercantile needs.
     After I was freed, I, naturally, visited those whom I
knew closely in prison. Aleksandr Ginzburg gave me 200
rubles from the "public fund" and hinted straightforwardly
that money is not given for nothing and that I should do
some work for it. He gave me an initial assignment: to write
about the condition of prisoners. I wrote what I knew, but
eventually my eyes began to open and I saw how facts are
"cooked up" for export by Ginzburg and Co.

That was a predictable scenario: a *zek* saying that Ginzburg
was buying information with foreign money. There was a grain
of truth in it. The money, indeed, largely came from abroad;
Ginzburg was indeed giving it out, and he was asking for information about the camps. All along, Ginzburg envisioned the authorities parading one *zek* witness after another, all of them
being asked: "Did Ginzburg give you money?" followed by
"Did he ask you to describe the conditions in the camps?" That
could have been presented in court as purchase of information.
All Ginzburg could do in his defense was point out that fund
beneficiaries received the same allotment whether they provided
information or not.
     That wasn't an airtight argument, but Ginzburg never had
much choice. The purpose of the foundation was to give out

money, and to distribute it intelligently, he had to have current information.

Somehow I heard a report of the Reuters agency: "Aleksandr Ginzburg, member of the Helsinki monitoring group, told Western correspondents that a policeman in civilian clothes threw 1,000 deutsche marks, about $100, into his toilet." Nonsense. Aleksandr Ilych [Ginzburg] was simply denying illegal currency dealings. If I had been that correspondent, I would have supplemented this reportage by saying: "How bad the Moscow militia is—managing to have found only $100!" After all, Ginzburg operated with far bigger sums. . . .

That was obvious. The KGB wanted to retain the option of pressing the currency-manipulation charge, and needed a "witness" to corroborate it. Interestingly enough, Petrov-Agatov stopped short of claiming that he had seen—or even heard of—an illegal currency transaction involving Ginzburg.

I was closely acquainted with other "dissidents," especially with Orlov. Yuri Orlov, who aims to be the leader of dissidents, has more than once spoken about his displeasure over the fact that the West talks mainly about Sakharov "while Ginzburg and I do all the work."

"I wouldn't have Sakharov in leadership anymore." He was also indignant with Sakharov's wife, Yelena Bonner, who, in his words, "has earned herself fame and received material advantages." The implication—and for me it is an extremely disagreeable implication—of these declarations is that both "fame" and the "material advantages" should by right belong to Orlov and Ginzburg. As for Orlov's views, in essense they do not differ at all from Ginzburg's "opinions."

Yes, the moral qualities of the "dissidents" are by no means what they assert and what Western propaganda publishes.

Very briefly about the character of Aleksandr Ilich Ginzburg, whom the West refers to as a "writer." (Agence France Press recently called him a poet though he has never written a verse in his whole life.) So this "writer" is not picky concerning his contacts with women.

Incidentally, this is like Yuri Orlov who is married for the third time and has abandoned his children, leaving them without support. Ginzburg's drunken orgies are well known, and one of them ended with him, to use the language of a police statement, falling out of an open window and breaking an arm. This kind of life-style demands more than a little money. I have already said where it comes from.

Petrov-Agatov seemed to be an extraordinarily well-informed former *zek*. He had "somehow" heard about a Reuters story, and he had read enough Agence France Press dispatches to find a faux pas in one. His confession also seemed to draw on remarkably detailed biographical information.

The information about Ginzburg's drunken orgies, which Petrov-Agatov described in "police report language," probably came from actual police reports. In 1958, Ginzburg got very drunk and fell out of a fourth-story window, breaking an arm. And Petrov-Agatov was right: There was a woman in the room. (After the fall, in the hospital, through the haze, Ginzburg saw his mother's face. "He who is meant to hang will not drown," she said.)

Ginzburg didn't feel betrayed. If anything, the story gave him a glimpse of the tactics the KGB planned to employ. The KGB wanted to conduct the crackdown openly and in public, but while dissidents used foreign radio stations to communicate with their countrymen, the authorities were going to use their own press. The government planned to take the lead on the Soviet dissident story away from foreign radio stations.

Dissidents would be accused through the Soviet version of investigative journalism, in which the investigations are conducted by the "competent organs" and propagandized in the press. Soon after accusations appeared, the dissidents would be arrested. That way, presumably, a Soviet citizen listening to the Voice of America reports of arrests would know why the arrests took place.

"Pizdets," Ginzburg said to himself. "The fucking end." Since his January 4 search, the word had become the lowest

common denominator, the basic undercurrent, of everything he thought and said.

A separate story in the same issue of *Literaturnaya gazeta* accused Krimsky of espionage and currency violations.

The story ran with a photo of the note Krimsky had written "John," the would-be source on his Soviet GI story. "Call me every Monday—232-7015 office, 281-1533 home," the note said.

"We'll arrange the time. One day early. One hour later. If we agree Wednesday at 4 p.m., it means Thursday at 3 p.m."

"DO YOU RECOGNIZE YOUR HANDWRITING, MR. KRIMSKY?" the cutline read.

The reporter's phone began to ring.

.

Two women, looking bereaved, greeted reporters at a press conference at the Ginzburg apartment. Ludmilla Ilynichna Ginzburg, Aleksandr's mother, had seen her son go to jail twice; Arina, his wife, had seen it once.

Ginzburg seemed calm. In his mind, he was setting the slow, measured pace he would have to sustain for days, months, years. It was as if he had gone into meditation, floating out of his own body, outside his two-room Belyaevo-Bogorodskoye apartment, away from his wife, his mother, his two sons, an adopted son, friends, reporters. He knew this was going to be the hardest and longest of his stints in the camps. There was no anger in his voice, no fear, no feeling at all, as if someone else were about to face the twelve-year term, as if someone else would get out at age fifty-three—if at all.

That morning through unofficial channels Ginzburg heard that warrants for his and Orlov's arrests had been issued by the KGB.

The information came through a KGB captain, a man named Viktor Orekhov. Earlier that year, Orekhov had befriended a dissident, Mark Morozov. It was an odd, suspicious friendship that made everyone wonder what made the captain tick. Was he acting under orders to penetrate the dissident circles, exchanging some KGB inside information for dissident inside information? Moreover, why would he pick Morozov, a man who was very much on the periphery of dissent, mostly because he couldn't keep his mouth shut? In one conversation with Morozov, the KGB captain confessed that he had great respect for Orlov, "first, because he is a scientist, second, because he is a Russian."

Captain Orekhov's motivation was a frequent topic of discussion, with some dissidents believing in his sincerity and others doubting it. Alexeyeva, for instance, banned Morozov from her house, while Turchin treated Morozov's tips with great interest. Two months earlier, in late December, Morozov showed up at Slepak's to tell him that Orekhov had warned him about the search warrant for Slepak's apartment. Slepak told Morozov to leave and never to return, but the next day the KGB, indeed, showed up with a search warrant.

Now, on the morning of the *Literaturnaya gazeta* story, Orekhov's information about the warrant for Ginzburg's and Orlov's arrests seemed entirely believable.

Ginzburg got up and faced the press and friends. He picked up a copy of *Literaturnaya gazeta*. "Now I will tell you how the fund really worked," he said. For the next twenty minutes, Ginzburg outlined the workings of the Russian Social Fund. It was established by Aleksandr Solzhenitsyn. It was chartered in Switzerland and was chaired by Solzhenitsyn's wife, Natalya.

Since its founding two and a half years earlier, the fund had spent 270,000 rubles, 70,000 of which had been raised inside the USSR and the rest transferred from the West. In 1974, the year the fund was formed, it helped 120 prisoners and their families. In 1975 it helped 720 prisoners and families, and in 1976 it helped 630. The fund disbursed Soviet currency only.

This was the first time any financial information about the fund had been disclosed, and Ginzburg was making his report to prevent another *Literaturnaya gazeta* exposé.

Ginzburg's 270,000 ruble figure was an accountant's nightmare. It reflected money spent on food, clothing, and medication, but didn't specify whether the food and the medication were bought in the USSR or in the West. If the medication was bought in the West, how did Ginzburg convert the purchasing price into rubles? Was he using the official exchange rate or the market rate? And what about food and clothing purchased with Soviet hard-currency coupons? How were they converted into rubles? Ginzburg, understandably, did not address those questions.

Ginzburg said he distributed the rubles to his helpers. He mentioned no names. Some of the money was kept in Ginzburg's account. He held up the passbooks. As the fund's administrator, Ginzburg said, he drew no salary since the payment of salaries is inconsistent with the traditions of Russian charitable foundations. The Ginzburgs lived on Arina's salary, payments for his odd jobs, and the 70 rubles a month he earned as Sakharov's secretary. From now on, Ginzburg said, his wife, Arina, along with Malva Landa and another dissident, Tatiana Khodorovich, would act as administrators of the fund.

There was another matter Ginzburg wanted to get off his chest: The same issue of *Literaturnaya gazeta* had attacked AP reporter George Krimsky. The story represented blackmail by the KGB, Ginzburg said. "If the Associated Press gives in to this blackmail and transfers Krimsky, its reporters will no longer be welcome at our news conferences." Ginzburg, the most likely next victim of the crackdown, was trying to pressure the AP much as he had tried to pressure the Soviets.

Throughout the press conference Alexeyeva marveled at Ginzburg's calmness. "It was as if he was reacting not to his own arrest, but to someone else's, as if he had turned some psychological lever, as if he was already there, in the camps," she recalled.

Christopher Wren of *The New York Times* stayed at Ginzburg's apartment after the press conference. The following day his story said that when the fund was founded, the money from the West was sent through legal transfers, but the authorities blocked further payments. Now, Ginzburg told Wren, he received money—all of it in rubles—through Russian intermediaries who said the money was Solzhenitsyn's but did not explain how it arrived.

This remark, made in an interview with Wren, constituted nothing less than Ginzburg's admission that he was an accessory to currency manipulations carried out by the Solzhenitsyn fund. The remark was tucked in at the end of Wren's story, which ran on page 2 of the *Times* on February 3.

Currency operations of this sort would not be illegal in the West, but could constitute a capital crime under Soviet law.

Nonetheless, for decades Soviet citizens have been bringing out suitcases full of rubles to the West. The rubles are sold to banks, which resell them at market rates, typically to people traveling to the USSR. Some of the most prestigious banks in the West trade in rubles.

In 1977 a dollar bought about 75 kopeks at the official exchange rate. Money transfers were then taxed at a 65 percent rate. So, a dollar transferred legally bought 26 kopeks. At the same time, in the West, a ruble could be bought for 20 to 25 cents.

Years later, after his release from prison, Ginzburg said that fund officials purchased Soviet currency in the West, then smuggled it into the USSR. He has repeated that story in his lecture tours. The Russian Social Fund, chartered in Switzerland, does not release its financial statements, but a source familiar with the fund confirmed Ginzburg's account of the fund's operations.

If Ginzburg's story is correct, everyone from the fund administrator down to released *zeki* and their families were made vulnerable to prosecution on currency charges. This was unknown to most of the fund's activists in the USSR.

"If I knew it was the case, I would have stayed away from it," said one former fund activist. "It's one thing to go to jail for helping prisoners. It's something else to go to jail as an accessory to a currency crime."

By February 2, 1977, the Solzhenitsyn fund's ruble-smuggling was very much on the surface. The KGB could read Ginzburg's broad hints about it in *The New York Times*. However, it seems the KGB found the matter too sensitive to discuss in the press or bring out at a trial. An admission that large sums were leaving the country and getting smuggled back would have exposed an international black market the Soviets weren't ready to acknowledge.

Besides, Ginzburg was open to prosecution as a repeat offender under Article 70. That was enough to put him away for a long time.

That day, through Mark Morozov and Turchin, Orlov got Captain Orekhov's warning about his impending arrest. Later that night, when the *toptuny* under his apartment window took a supper break, Orlov turned out the lights and climbed out onto the snowbank. Later, the police showed up at his door. "He isn't here," said Irina.

Ginzburg spent the following day, February 3, at home, waiting for the KGB. In the evening, he went out to make a phone call and didn't return. "I slept through my first week in prison, sometimes waking up for lunch and dinner," he recalled later. "I dreamt of myself as the most free man of all, as free a man as I was only once in this life—during the year of 1976."

At a Helsinki-group press conference February 4, after the news of Ginzburg's arrest was announced, Irina Orlova approached the nearest American reporter. "You betrayed us!" she said to him.

Packed into that "You betrayed us!" was Irina's feeling of doom and her fear; perhaps there was also something her friends referred to as the immaturity of a pampered wife. But that wasn't all. The U.S. State Department–White House snafu seemed far more significant across the Atlantic. It wasn't just the case of a bureaucrat speaking out of turn and the U.S. president gratuitously clarifying that the statement didn't come from him, though he agreed with it. In the Moscow dissident circles, this incident of Washington bumbling was seen as hesitation by the American president to make human rights the centerpiece of his policy. With "You betrayed us!" Irina was saying that the U.S. president's hesitation had sent a message to the KGB that the United States wouldn't stand up for the dissidents. That implied message, she seemed to believe, led the KGB to issue warrants for Ginzburg's and her husband's arrests. Rightly or not, at that moment, Irina must have felt stranded.

Also on February 4, Foreign Ministry officials informed the Associated Press that the presence of George Krimsky was no longer desired in the USSR. He was being expelled.

"We ought to keep a log of our calls," suggested Paula Krimsky, who was fielding most of the phone calls generated by the *Literaturnaya gazeta* article.

"Great idea. It would make a great memento," George

agreed. Altogether, the Krimskys logged about eighty calls. Two thirds of them were supportive:

"Is your husband really a spy?" callers usually asked.

"Of course not," Paula answered.

"I didn't think so. Please don't think so badly of us."

Some messages were even more supportive: "I am calling from a pay phone and I just wanted to say that we don't believe what we read in our newspapers. . . ." Click.

There were half a dozen negative calls, including what amounted to the reading of a prepared statement: "Imperialists come to our country, a peace-loving nation, to undermine and subvert our social values . . ."

Paula interrupted.

The caller hesitated, then started from the top: "Imperialists come to our country, a peace-loving nation, to undermine and subvert our social values . . ."

The rest of the calls had to be classified as "other."

"I read in the newspapers that your husband has been expelled."

"Yes."

"Are you going back to America?"

"We don't know yet, but we think we are."

"Would you mind taking a tape my group and I did back to Ray Conniff?"

Krimsky's expulsion inspired a member of the psychiatry monitoring group to scribble a little poem:

> Hello, George
> You are a fine pal
> You're what your people call "okay"
> You've seen a lot of our troubles
> May God now grant you better days.

Another note, typed on onionskin paper, with smudges over periods and holes for *o*'s, commended Krimsky for his "meaningful dispatches on the human-rights movement in the USSR." Those stories "have become part of international *glasnost*," the letter said. It was signed by Orlov, Turchin, Landa, Zholkovskaya, Alexeyeva, Williams, and Father Gleb Yakunin, a Russian Orthodox priest who had just started the Christian

Committee for the Defense of the Rights of Believers, another Helsinki-group spinoff.

U.S. Ambassador Malcolm Toon called, too, with the news of the Carter administration's plan to retaliate by expelling a Soviet reporter from Washington. Toon said the administration would target a Soviet reporter who wasn't a spy. On February 6, the State Department ordered Tass reporter Vladimir I. Alexeyev to leave the United States.

Toon's promise notwithstanding, Alexeyev was anything but an ordinary reporter. He had been suspected of spying at least since election night, 1976, when he attempted to recruit Ronald L. Humphrey, a U.S. Information Agency employee. Humphrey reported the incident to his superiors and was asked to report on further contacts with the Russian, which he did. (In 1978 Humphrey was convicted on an apparently unrelated charge of stealing classified cables and passing them on to the North Vietnamese.)

On February 10, her last day in Moscow, fourteen-month-old Alissa Krimsky walked for the first time. She got to walk partway to the AP's ancient Chaika, a massive old clunker of a car that looked like a 1950s Chrysler.

Driven by the bureau's chauffeur, an old rummy named Tolya, the Chaika chugged along to the Sheremetyevo airport, staying just below the speed limit. Krimsky was to leave "clean as a hound's tooth," his bureau chief Mason directed. No farewells with dissidents, no Soviet currency, not even a copper kopek, no unofficial art, no speeding on the way to the airport. Mason sat in the front with red-nosed Tolya, making sure the departure proceeded smoothly.

The Sheremetyevo airport foyer was lined with men in heavy overcoats, their faces covered with scarves; the KGB *toptuny,* like AP's Mason, were making sure nothing went wrong. They were the last *toptuny* the Krimskys would ever see. Friends, mostly foreigners, were there, too, lurking between scarved men, saying good-bye. Alissa wobbled through the crowd, her mother holding her hand and saying to anyone and everyone, "Look, she is walking."

The procession had passed through the turnstile, when Krimsky heard, *"Podozhdite! Podozhdite!* Wait! Wait!" Sakharov and Bonner were elbowing their way through the crowd. Over the turnstile, Sakharov planted a wet kiss on Krimsky's face, followed by something like "We are grateful to you."

It was precisely the kind of scene Mason was trying to avoid, and it was getting worse. "This is from us," Sakharov said, handing the reporter an English copy of *My Country and the World,* Sakharov's compendium of essays. Krimsky turned to Mason. He was white, absorbing the scene: Sakharov openly handing Krimsky his tract over the Sheremetyevo airport turnstile. If the KGB escort had had cameras, this would have made a fine picture for next week's *Literaturnaya gazeta.*

"Andrei Dmitrievich, I cannot accept this," said Krimsky. "Please give this to one of my friends and they will get it to me."

The answer seemed to stun Sakharov. His jaw dropped; he looked crestfallen. Krimsky had known Sakharov long enough to see what he was thinking: Why wouldn't he take a gift? Why wouldn't a free man commit his final act of defiance of the Soviet oppressors?

Standing at the turnstile, Krimsky couldn't explain that now his oppressor wasn't the Soviet state, that he had other obligations: to himself, to his family, to his career. When he had passed through that turnstile, he had become an American once again.

An hour later, an attractive Pan Am stewardess brought the Krimskys glasses of Stolichnaya on the rocks.

George took a small sip. The vodka went down smoothly. He took a deep breath. There wasn't a trace of the odor of sweet perfumy disinfectant and thick Russian tobacco.

"*Slava bogu,*" said George. "Thank God."

"*Slava bogu,*" said Paula.

CHAPTER 21

"I AM NOT HIDING"

Around 3:00 P.M. February 9, a short man wearing a shabby jacket, a pair of Russian village felt boots, glasses, and a fur cap with earflaps down walked past the KGB men stationed by Alexeyeva's apartment building. He looked like one of the many supplicants from the provinces who had passed through Alexeyeva's apartment since May. He walked in, got in the elevator, pushed the sixteenth-floor button.

He rang the bell. Alexeyeva's mother opened the door, the man took off his hat, a shock of red hair sprang out. He put a finger to his lips. It was Orlov. He walked in and took off his coat. Yefimenko, Alexeyeva's mother, picked up a Magic Pad and, with a pen, wrote, "Would you like some tea?" The ink curdled into droplets on the gray plastic. "No, thank you. Where is Lyuda?" Orlov wrote back.

"I don't know," wrote Yefimenko. She kept using a pen.

"Could you call Tolya Shcharansky, please," Orlov wrote.

Yefimenko dialed the apartment where Shcharansky was staying. "Lyuda asked you to come here," she said.

In a few minutes, Shcharansky was at the door.

"Find Lyuda and reporters," Orlov wrote.

Shcharansky went to Turchin's, then the two headed for Grigorenko's where Alexeyeva was helping type an appeal to the authorities for conditional release of Aleksandr Ginzburg because of his poor health. Soviet law allows for conditional release of criminals into their "working collectives." The letter said that in view of Ginzburg's poor health, he should be released into the "collective" of his friends, Grigorenko among them. The letter did not promise to "reeducate" Ginzburg.

Around 3:00 P.M., Turchin stormed into Grigorenko's apartment. He picked up a board and wrote, "*Begi skoreye domoy. U tebya Orlov.* Run home fast. Orlov's there." Without explanation—after all, Orlov wanted to see her, not the entire group—Alexeyeva excused herself.

At the apartment, using the note pad, Orlov explained his reappearance. He knew the situation was desperate. Over the radio, he had heard Ginzburg had been arrested.

He had found a hideout, sharing an apartment with a friend's elderly mother outside Moscow. But at a time like this, he felt the leader of the Moscow Helsinki group shouldn't act like a fugitive from justice. "Americans wouldn't understand why I am hiding," Orlov wrote. He planned to reappear just for a short time, make a statement to the press, then put on his disguise, and go back into hiding.

To the best of his knowledge, Orlov wrote, he hadn't been followed to Alexeyeva's apartment. Besides, her *toptuny* were attuned to following her. They wouldn't pay much attention to a man wearing thick glasses, with a scarf hiding his face and a hat hiding his hair. But, just in case, Orlov wrote, he would try to walk out with the reporters. The KGB would hesitate to arrest him before their eyes.

"Will you write or speak at the press conference?" Alexeyeva wrote on the pad.

"Speak," Orlov wrote. "The leader of the Helsinki group should not act like a fugitive in front of reporters."

At 6:00 P.M., Shcharansky and Turchin returned. With them were Toth of the *Los Angeles Times* and Mason, AP bureau chief. As soon as they walked in, the reporters were asked not to refer to Orlov by name.

Orlov tried to make the press conference as normal as possible. To do so, he presented a document calling on all Helsinki Final Act signatories to declassify information in a number of areas now labeled secret. That, the physicist argued, would facilitate the exchange of information and help bring about trust between nations. The appeal stayed within what was becoming the Helsinki-group tradition: presentation of documents to reporters who were interested only in quotes from people reacting to the crackdown. It was a short document, after which Orlov moved on to his own problems.

Meanwhile, Alexeyeva's mother was talking to a friend over the phone. As soon as Orlov began to talk, the phone clicked, disconnecting the call. She tried to redial, but couldn't get the tone. The KGB staffer monitoring the apartment through listening devices recognized Orlov's voice and the phone was disconnected.

"Are you in hiding?" one of the reporters asked.

"No, I just don't live at home."

"Why not?"

"I simply don't want to surrender to them. I am not guilty of any crime, as the others are not."

No, Orlov said, his arrest was by no means imminent. Not after the international uproar that followed Ginzburg's arrest. The Soviets would hesitate to face the wrath of the West all over again by arresting him. However, Orlov continued, if he were arrested, he would probably be tried for slander against the state under Article 190-1 of the RSFSR Criminal Code. At the most, he would be facing three years in labor camps.

Orlov said he was afraid the authorities would prosecute Ginzburg on fabricated charges of currency manipulation and under Article 70, slander aimed at the foundations of the state. That article carries the punishment of up to seven years' imprisonment followed by up to five years in internal exile. Ginzburg, he said, was more vulnerable to harsh punishment because of his work with the Solzhenitsyn fund.

The press conference lasted about twenty minutes. As reporters began to leave, Orlov decided not to risk walking out with them. Instead, Shcharansky went to check if there was any surveillance.

A man and a woman were kissing in the apartment-building

entryway. Many Moscow couples kiss in apartment-building entryways, but typically, they are young people with no place else to go. This couple was different. They were both middle-aged and wore imported suede coats. Shcharansky walked around them. The man and the woman kept kissing.

"I know this guy," Shcharansky said to reporters. "He has tailed me a few times before."

The kissing continued.

The reporters left and Shcharansky returned to Alexeyeva's apartment to map out another escape route for Orlov. The building had three stairways, each with a door to the attic. If those doors were unlocked, Orlov would be able to go up to the attic, walk to the door of the other entryway, catch the elevator, and walk out at the other end of the building.

Shcharansky put on his coat and hat and lowered the ear-muffs. He walked up to the seventeenth floor, pulled on the attic door. The door opened. The door on the other side of the building was unlocked, too. The escape appeared possible. Shcharansky took the elevator down, then walked out into the street. As soon as he did, he was stunned by the glare of flashlights. The KGB operatives, expecting Orlov, not Shcharansky, allowed him to leave.

The open attic doorways were a trap, Shcharansky said after returning to Alexeyeva's. The KGB wanted to catch Orlov escaping through the roof like a common criminal. It would make good copy for *Literaturnaya gazeta.*

At 7:00 P.M., Shcharansky left. An hour later, Alexeyeva, Williams, and son Michael had to go to a farewell party in their honor. On February 1, the visa office had told her that her exit-visa request was approved, though she had never completed it.

The party was a social obligation that Alexeyeva couldn't ignore. Orlov stayed in her apartment, with the lights out. When Alexeyeva returned, she and Orlov went to the kitchen, where, with lights still out, they proceeded to plot the group's future. It was an odd strategy session, held by a man who was about to be arrested and a woman whose plane for the West was to leave twelve days later.

"Who will lead the group?" Orlov wrote. His bravado was dissipating. With the KGB couple kissing downstairs and goons in every doorway, the secret police were making it clear they weren't going to let Orlov slip by.

"You will," Alexeyeva wrote.

She paused, waiting for Orlov to ask for the note pad. He didn't. "Leadership in the group will emerge by itself," she continued.

She paused again. Orlov wanted her to continue to develop her thought. Not asking for the slate was the silent form of "What do you think?"—his favorite expression.

"Why put responsibility on others?" Heading the Moscow Helsinki group was a certain way to get on the KGB's most-likely-to-get-arrested list.

Orlov wrote nothing, letting the subject drop.

Then, in a whisper, he turned to the next subject—his fear for his wife. "She is so helpless," he whispered. "She has never dealt with money. She doesn't understand what's cheap, what's expensive. . . ."

He paused, perhaps waiting for Alexeyeva to say something wise, offer some insight. In her mind, Alexeyeva searched for that insight, that comforting thought, but found none. She conjured Irina's image—her wide, surprised eyes, her youthful figure. She was almost thirty but looked fourteen and sometimes acted eighteen. Irina was all emotion; what Orlov thought, she felt. Now the sheltered Irina would get a chance to grow up—and it would be painful, Alexeyeva thought.

"Where will she find a job?" Orlov continued. "Who wants a French art historian? And being Orlov's wife . . ."

At 5:00 A.M., Orlov went to bed. Alexeyeva heard him tossing and turning, each turn echoed by the squeaking of the cot. Sigh . . . toss . . . squeak; sigh . . . toss . . . squeak . . . sigh. The symphony of doom.

At 6:00 A.M., Alexeyeva woke up her son Michael. "Misha, would you get dressed and walk around the building," she said. "See if they are still there." He threw on some clothes, and, still groggy, opened the door. There were men on the staircase. He closed the door.

In the morning, Orlov seemed cheerful.

"Oh, good, there's something for me to do," he said looking out at the snowbank on the balcony. "I'll clear it."

At 11:00 A.M., there was a knock on the door. It was about time for Turchin, Shcharansky, and Irina to show up.

"Who is it?"

"*Prokuratura.* The prosecutor's office."

"Shall I open or let them break in?" Alexeyeva asked Orlov.

"No, open it."

She opened the door. Eight men, one of them in plain clothes and the rest wearing crisp new militia uniforms walked in. The militia uniforms were a nice touch, she thought. Of course, these men were from the KGB, not the prosecutor's office, which doesn't deal with crimes against the state. But for some reason, the KGB crackdown plan called for a little costume party. The uniforms looked as if they came straight off the shelf, creases and all.

"Is this a search?" Alexeyeva asked.

"No. We have evidence that you are being visited by your like-thinkers."

"Of course, I am not visited by *your* like-thinkers."

The man in plain clothes opened the hallway closet.

"I will not allow you to look at anything in the apartment in the absence of a search warrant."

"Well, why are you keeping us in the hallway? Why not invite us inside the apartment?" said one of the uniformed militia men. Alexeyeva recognized him from the January 4 search.

"Come in," she said, opening the door into the small room.

But the man in plain clothes had already opened the door to the other room where Orlov was sitting on the couch.

"Here's the man we want," said the man in plain clothes. "Present your documents, please."

Orlov showed the man his passport.

"Get dressed, please."

Orlov put on his coat and walked out into the hallway. Now he was surrounded by the men in police uniforms.

The eight goons led the diminutive physicist to a car. From above, Alexeyeva watched the van leave.

The next day, this story made page 1 of the *Los Angeles Times:*

MOSCOW—Soviet police Thursday arrested Yuri Orlov, chairman of a dissident group that has tried to investigate and publicize Soviet noncompliance with human rights provisions of the Helsinki accords. . . .

Western diplomats said the Soviet crackdown seems almost calculated to affront the US Congress and the Carter Administration which has spoken out for civil rights in the Soviet Union.

Orlov was arrested in his apartment after almost a week of hiding. He told foreign correspondents here Wednesday night that he felt safer after the U.S. State Department had voiced its "concern" over the arrest of Alexander Ginzburg, 40, a week earlier.

But neither the State Department's expressed concern nor President Carter's promise to speak out against Soviet human rights violations appears to have made an impact on the Kremlin.

Similar stories made page 1 of *The Washington Post* and *The New York Times*. *The Christian Science Monitor* referred to the U.S.-Soviet tensions caused by the arrest of "red-bearded Dr. Orlov." In his search for color, David K. Willis, the *Monitor*'s man in Moscow, apparently confused clean-shaven Orlov with red-bearded Bernshtam. When the Helsinki-group story hit page 1, reporters like Willis had to catch up with the story they had ignored or played down since the group's founding nine months earlier.

Days after Jimmy Carter's inauguration, attorney Martin Garbus informed the State Department that he had in his possession a letter from Nobel laureate Andrei Sakharov and that he wanted to present it to the president personally, in a public ceremony. In the event the administration refused to accept the letter, the press would be informed, Garbus told State Department officials.

It was an ultimatum. What's more, the very existence of the Sakharov letter to Carter challenged the new president to deliver on the promises he had made during his campaign and in the inaugural address January 20.

"The passion for freedom is on the rise," Carter had said at the inaugural. "Tapping this new spirit, there can be no nobler nor more ambitious task for America to undertake on this day of a new beginning than to help shape a just and peaceful world that is truly humane."

Sakharov could not have imagined that the letter he had scribbled in a rushed evening with Garbus would launch Carter's quest to transform mankind.

But first the administration had to decide what to do with the Sakharov letter. "At first [Under Secretary of State] Philip C. Habib . . . did not want the letter publicly delivered," Garbus wrote in *Traitors and Heroes*. The prospect of the president of the United States openly accepting a letter from a private citizen in the USSR was a diplomat's nightmare, especially considering that the memory of Henry Kissinger and his preference for handling the matter of human rights quietly was still fresh at State.

"We negotiated over three days on the phone," Garbus wrote. "I then met Habib and three of his associates. Habib continued to want the private delivery of the letter to him. . . . I told Habib that if he did not take the issue public, I would hold a press conference and state that the administration refused to publicly accept the letter that Sakharov wished me to personally deliver to the president."

That was an interesting point since at the time Garbus had no recollection of Sakharov's mentioning whether the letter was to be kept confidential or made public. Garbus consulted several people who knew Sakharov, all of whom told him that Sakharov does not work behind the scenes, Garbus recalled. Anything Sakharov writes is meant to be public.

"Ultimately, we compromised," Garbus wrote. "Habib refused to allow Carter to accept the letter publicly from me, but it became front page news when the letter was delivered by me to Habib, who accepted it on the president's behalf."

The text of the letter appeared in *The New York Times* on January 29, just eight days after it was written. "Mr. Garbus, who made the letter available to *The New York Times,* said he was representing Dr. Sakharov in discussions with the United States Government," the paper reported in a front-page story.

Under the circumstances there was nothing the administration could do to avoid dealing with the Sakharov letter: Refusing to accept the letter or not answering it was certain to bring back memories of Gerald Ford taking Kissinger's advice and refusing to meet with Aleksandr Solzhenitsyn for fear of unnecessarily infuriating the Soviets.

"We all felt that the President had to reply," Carter's national security advisor Zbigniew Brzezinski wrote in his memoir. "The prestige of the author was such that failing to do so would invite adverse comparisons with the widely criticized refusal by President Ford to meet with Solzhenitsyn. Had the Nobel Peace Prize winner been a resident of Chile, the liberal press would have been outraged by Carter's failure to respond. Moreover, American-Soviet relations had not been hurt by Brezhnev's direct contacts with Gus Hall and other pro-Soviet American activists, nor did we take public exception to Soviet proclamations that the world was destined to experience a global revolution. We had every right to insist that human rights was the wave of the future, not to speak of the fact that it would have been cowardly to ignore Sakharov's letter."

The president's reply was written by Brzezinski and Secretary of State Cyrus Vance. "Vance and I drafted a carefully worded reply to Sakharov couched in language that made it clear that the President's concern was global in character and not focused specifically on the Soviet Union," Brzezinski explained in his book.

On February 17, Sakharov was invited to the U.S. embassy and handed a letter. The words THE WHITE HOUSE were on the top of the stationery. The signature on the bottom read, "Jimmy Carter."

"I received your letter of January 21, and I want to express my appreciation to you for bringing your thoughts to my personal attention," said the letter dated February 5. After many years of trying to get the Kremlin into a "dialogue with society," Sakharov was now in a dialogue with the White House.

"Human rights are a central concern of my administration," the U.S. president wrote to Russia's premier dissident.

> In my inaugural address I stated: "Because we are free, we can never be indifferent to the fate of freedom elsewhere." You may rest assured that the American people and our government will continue our firm commitment to promote respect for human rights not only in our country but also abroad.

> We shall use our good offices to seek the release of prisoners of conscience, and we will continue our efforts to shape a world responsive to human aspirations in which nations of differing cultures and histories can live side by side in peace and justice.
>
> I am always glad to hear from you, and I wish you well.

Without leaving the embassy, Sakharov sat down and composed a response:

> I have numerously written and said that the defense of basic human rights does not constitute interference into internal affairs of other countries, but, instead, is one of the central aspects of international relations, which is inseparable from the basic problems of peace and progress. Today, having received your letter, the extraordinary nature of which I clearly understand, I can only repeat this.

Moving on to the specifics, he informed the president about the wave of arrests of the Helsinki monitors. "Heads of all states that have signed the Helsinki Final Act must all take actions to assure that all members of the Helsinki group are freed so the group could continue its important work," Sakharov wrote.

The president of the United States, by affirming sympathy to Sakharov, was openly pressuring the Soviets. Meanwhile, the KGB was dealing with an entirely different set of problems: Prisoners had to be interrogated; foreign reporters had to be put in their place; and final touches had to be put on yet another crackdown extravaganza, the Case of Anatoly Shcharansky.

Despite symbolic gestures from Washington, the crackdown continued.

More than a decade later, Garbus had a hard time passing judgment on his role in bringing about a superpower confrontation. "I really don't have a viewpoint on it," he said in an interview. "Sometimes I feel one way, and sometimes I feel another."

The story of the Sakharov letter has a curious postscript. During her 1986 visit to the United States, Bonner told Alfred Friendly that she and Sakharov were surprised to hear that the letter had been made public.

Apparently it was a confidential memo after all.

*   *   *

It took more than a crackdown to get the Western press to start writing about Orlov's group. It also took the president's interest in the subject and with it the likelihood of an East-West confrontation over human rights. The stories started out as a trickle after the January 4 searches. By February, the trickle turned into a gush.

Newsweek first took notice of the Helsinki group on January 24, when it reported the searches that had taken place more than two weeks earlier. The story, which combined the Czech crackdown on Charter 77, a dissident group, and the Soviet crackdown on Orlov's group, ran with a mug shot of Czech writer Pavel Kohout and a photo of ten smiling people sitting at a holiday table. Andrei Amalrik's bespectacled square face stared at *Newsweek* readers from the group shot, which was taken by Krimsky at Amalrik's birthday party nine months earlier. Behind him, sitting on the couch at the table, were Valentin Turchin, Arina Zholkovskaya, Yuri Orlov, and Gyuzel Amalrik. Paula Krimsky, bushy-haired Aleksandr Ginzburg, and Tatiana Turchin were sitting on the far end of the table, with George Krimsky half kneeling over Paula and Ginzburg. It was Orlov's pert young wife, Irina, who made the shot perfect for *Newsweek*. She sat in a chair a couple of feet from the table, wearing a short skirt and crossing her shapely legs. RIGHTS WATCH: AMALRIK WITH DISSENTERS IN MOSCOW, read the cutline.

Three weeks later, *Newsweek* accompanied a story of Ginzburg's arrest, Krimsky's expulsion, and the deepening rift over human rights with a photo of a Czech dissident lying naked on a tomb, a black square superimposed over his genitals.

On February 21, 1977, the crackdown made the cover of *Time.* "As if to test the U.S. resolve, the KGB arrested Dissident Alexander Ginzburg in a telephone booth," *Time* noted. The magazine also ran a drawing of two dark figures grabbing a bearded man inside the phone booth. KGB OFFICERS ARRESTING GINZBURG the cutline explained. There was also a drawing of a man in a trench coat bending over a toilet. According to *Time,* he was PLANTING FOREIGN CURRENCY.

"Why do the Soviets tolerate the dissidents to the extent that they do?" the magazine quoted Shcharansky's rhetorical question and his own answer. "To take more direct measures against us would be to return to the days of Stalin, and that they don't want. They are interested in Western opinion and in détente, and in good economic relations—and most of the present leaders are the very men who survived Stalin. World opinion is what keeps us going, what keeps us alive."

Even after Ginzburg and Orlov were carted off to prison, Shcharansky seemed to retain his belief in the power of Western influence on the Soviet leadership. *Time* writers had to tone down Shcharansky's hopeful exercise in behind-the-Iron-Curtain Kremlinology: "Mass terror was ended after Stalin's death, but no one doubts that if the dissident movement were ever to become a serious threat to Communist rule, the Kremlin would crack down with full force."

The Kremlin's crackdown, in fact, had begun six weeks earlier.

CHAPTER 22

JUST A JEW
TRYING TO LEAVE

On February 25, Dr. Sanya Lipavsky, the refuseniks' doctor and expert in arranging abortions and phone calls to the West, wrote a letter to Helsinki Commission Chairman Dante Fascell.

"My friends in the U.S. have told me that you have expressed interest toward me and my family as Jewish refuseniks senselessly refused by the Soviets in emigration to the state of Israel.

"My wife and I are doctors who have never worked in secret places. Nonetheless, the reason given for our refusal is access to state secrets. I am particularly pleased and honored that my fate is of interest to you, a major political figure who heads the American commission watching over compliance with the decisions of the Helsinki conference. Your interest in our fate gives us strength for further battles for emigration to the Motherland and gives us hope for speedy Exodus."

On March 5, another of Lipavsky's letters appeared in *Izvestia.*

"It was not easy for me to write this letter, but after thinking long and hard, I arrived at the conclusion that I must do this," he wrote. "Perhaps this open letter will open the eyes of those who are still deluded, who are still deceived by Western propaganda that shouts from the rooftops about the persecution of 'dissidents' in the USSR and which balloons the so-called questions of human rights."

This was followed by what was purported to be the inside look at the Soviet Jewish emigration movement. When he joined it in 1972, Lipavsky wrote, the movement was ruled by the triumvirate of "D. Azbel, A. Lerner and V. Rubin." The top men of the movement had connections amoung foreign reporters, diplomats, American intelligence operatives, and the emissaries of "anti-Soviet centers."

At first, this trio tried to grab worldwide attention by organizing international conferences independent of the Soviet scientific establishment. When that ploy failed, Lipavsky wrote, the leaders decided on another one: "Concerned by the prospect of a loss of interest from the foreign masters who gave them substantial material aid, they decided to unite with the so-called 'group of monitoring of implementation of the Helsinki agreements,' headed by the infamous Yu. Orlov. V. Rubin, and later, A. Shcharansky were brought into that group." Just before Lipavsky's "confession" appeared in *Izvestia,* he and Shcharansky had made arrangements to rent a room together.

It was Rubin who introduced Lipavsky to the CIA, the doctor claimed. His first contact was Melvyn Levitsky, a foreign-service officer who served as a liaison with the dissidents, he wrote. The first meeting took place at Rubin's apartment in 1974. A year later, the agency tried to get the doctor to get secrets from his friend, a defense scientist, Lipavsky wrote.

The accompanying story in the same issue of *Izvestia* contained more detail, including a bizarre set of instructions Lipavsky was said to have received from the CIA.

"We were made spritely by that which was contained in the bag and were glad to receive the film, which is closer to the information of interest to us," one of the alleged CIA instructions said. *Izvestia* clarified that the cryptic language wasn't a code, just bad Russian of the CIA "Russian specialists."

"Photographing is the most effective method of transferring such information and we wish for you to continue this method for addition to your answers to our questions and in all possible cases in the future," the alleged instruction continued. "Some 'names of work' to which 'K' has access (especially parts for guidance of powerful radars and development of communication equipment for submarines) interest us very much, and we ask you, try to acquire photographs of more detailed and current secret documents related to one or both these areas. . . .

"Adding, if the time and the circumstances allow, we need you to pass along more data about 'K' and the character of your relationship with him. Your detailed answers to these questions will help us very much to understand the situation."

Another alleged CIA instruction, called "Communications Plan," said, "We ask you to answer in detail to all our questions. These answers, along with any secret documents you have should be wrapped in the same type of waterproof material as last time. Put the wrapped material in a dirty cloth sack, as you did last time."

Izvestia's photo exhibits were also intriguing: a piece of cable stuffed with large bills and instructions, a photocopy of the actual instructions, and the diagram of the parking lot where Lipavsky was to lean his dirty cloth sack by the KEEP THIS PARKING LOT CLEAN sign.

The stories were conspicuously silent on what would be done with the Lipavsky case in the future. Was his "open letter" deemed sufficient by the authorities to absolve him of responsibility for having been in contact with the enemy and accepting cash for some form of service? Or was Lipavsky instructed by the KGB to infiltrate the dissident circles and demonstrate that it was possible to be recruited by the CIA using the dissidents' contacts in the U.S. Embassy?

A year later, President Carter, in an unprecedented move, acknowledged that the refuseniks' doctor had indeed contacted the Moscow station of the CIA as a "walk-in" and that he had been given assignments, but produced nothing. In the same statement the president said Shcharansky, then facing treason charges, was at no time connected with the CIA.

By admitting that Lipavsky had done work for the CIA, Carter was saying that the agency had abandoned its policy of not using Soviet dissident walk-ins. It was a policy that went back to the emergence of Soviet dissent in the 1960s. According to Donald Jameson, formerly a CIA Soviet specialist, recruitment of dissident walk-ins was considered an unsound strategy.

For one thing, it was obvious from the start that the dissident circles had been penetrated by the KGB, which meant any walk-in was likely to be a double agent, Jameson said. On top of that, involving dissidents in the CIA operations could harm the dissident movement. That would contradict U.S. interests.

"I suspect that someone [in the CIA] may have seen Lipavsky's offer as an opportunity to find an agent and did something foolish," Jameson, who retired from the agency in 1973, said in an interview. "I would hope at least that it taught them [the CIA] a lesson."

Yet the Lipavsky affair did not give the Soviets everything they were after. It did not implicate U.S. reporters in working with the CIA, either as recruiters or as spy runners. New evidence suggests that this was not for lack of trying on Lipavsky's part.

In May 1975, just weeks before he began supplying information to the CIA, Lipavsky called a friend, Yuri Tuvim. Lipavsky didn't want to talk on the phone. The matter was far too sensitive. He wanted to arrange a meeting. Tuvim drove out to Novo-Slobodskaya Street in the center of Moscow. Lipavsky was standing alongside his gray Volga. Tuvim parked behind him.

"Lipavsky said, 'I have some friends. They are engineers. Young guys. Russian patriots,'" Tuvim recalled later. "'They work at an electronics plant near Moscow. They hate the Soviet system and they would like to help America.'"

With these words, Lipavsky reached for a brown plywood suitcase. "'You know some correspondents, would you pass this along?'" Lipavsky asked.

Tuvim, a forty-five-year-old mechanical engineer, did indeed know several foreign reporters. He did not have news stories to push; he wasn't even a refusenik. For him, dealing with foreigners was socializing, not politics. Nonetheless, his anecdotes, all of them unattributed to protect his identity, were making their way into newspaper stories in the United States.

Lipavsky's request startled Tuvim. He had nothing to gain from becoming an accessory to espionage. Yet Lipavsky, a good friend, a man he considered a Jewish patriot, was asking a favor. Tuvim had met Lipavsky a year and a half earlier, and he had his own reasons to like the doctor. Lipavsky never had a bad word to say about anyone, an unusual trait in the politically charged atmosphere of the Jewish emigration movement.

Tuvim was not even suspicious of the fact that Lipavsky drove a Volga, an expensive car generally reserved for official use. The doctor explained that the car had been bought for him by wealthy American relatives. In fact, the relatives were so wealthy, Lipavsky said, that they had already bought the equipment for a radiotherapy office that Lipavsky would operate once he went to America.

Until that day the doctor had never asked Tuvim to use his connections with reporters. Finally, Tuvim's loyalty to Lipavsky overshadowed caution and fear. "If a friend asks you, you do it," Tuvim said. He put the suitcase in the car and drove about fifteen miles to the industrial town of Lyubertsy, to a garage where he kept his car in the winter. "On the way, I kept thinking, 'Why am I doing this? This is insane.'"

In the garage, he opened the suitcase. Inside were about two dozen manuals, each about half an inch thick. Tuvim started to leaf through the papers. There was a manual on welding aluminum. That was useless. Americans knew how to weld aluminum. There was a manual on determining the degree of blackness of a "black body," an object that, ideally, absorbs all radiation and emits none. The manual could have been of some interest to a physics professor, but hardly anything that could affect national security, Tuvim decided. Every manual in the suitcase was stamped SECRET or FOR OFFICIAL USE ONLY.

There wasn't a note in the suitcase, nothing to tell the CIA how to get in touch with the "Russian patriots." That meant that if Tuvim found a journalist who would pass the documents along, and if the CIA wanted to follow up, it would have to ask the journalist to pass word through Tuvim, who would have to contact Lipavsky, who would arrange the meeting.

Still, Tuvim did not suspect Lipavsky of being a double
agent. He just thought the doctor's plan was unwieldy and the
documents not worth the risk. "I don't know what I would have
done if there had been anything but trash in the suitcase,"
Tuvim said later.

The following day he arranged a meeting with Lipavsky. "I
said, 'Sanya, take your suitcase. I won't do it.' And here
Lipavsky lost his composure. He was upset. He started repeat-
ing, 'How can you do this? This is a matter of life and death.
These guys, they are risking their lives. These guys, these patriots . . . '"

"They shouldn't risk their lives over this trash," Tuvim said
to Lipavsky.

That was the last time Tuvim saw Lipavsky. In October
1975, Tuvim emigrated. While waiting for a U.S. visa in Rome,
he thought through the Lipavsky incident. With time, the suitcase incident seemed all the more shady. Lipavsky had seemed
to avoid him afterward. He didn't return Tuvim's calls; he didn't
reclaim an electric drill he had lent Tuvim earlier; he didn't even
come to Tuvim's going-away party. In January 1976, during a
routine interview at the U.S. Embassy in Rome, Tuvim told an
official that he suspected a Moscow acquaintance of his, Dr.
Sanya Lipavsky, of being a KGB agent provocateur.

At the embassy in Rome, such "leads" from Soviet émigrés
were commonplace. *Besides,* by then, it appears, the doctor had
already received pieces of cable stuffed with cash and illiterate
CIA instructions that included a request for higher-quality information.

In Israel, Helsinki-group member Vitaly Rubin was coming to
grips with the painful realization that his close friend Lipavsky
was less than a Jewish hero. The day Lipavsky's letter appeared
in *Izvestia,* Rubin, then professor of Chinese philosophy at
Hebrew University in Jerusalem, wrote in his diary:

"Today is the 24th anniversary of Stalin's death. In the
morning I heard the terrible news about *Izvestia* publishing
Lipavsky's letter in which he claims that a number of people,
aided by the U.S. Embassy, are involved in espionage. It could
be that my name is among those mentioned.

"So, the string is weaving no more. I often thought this could come to the most terrible end, and several times told Sasha [Lipavsky] that it would be a good idea to put an end to it all. He said nothing.

"After he passed something along to Mel [Levitsky], I thought that would be the end of it. But he decided to keep permanent contacts with them. I didn't think it possible to discuss the matter with him much because that could have seemed like cowardice.

"Had I been there, undoubtedly I would have been arrested. Now it's curious what they are going to make of it all. It could be they are preparing a show trial with many people in some way associated with Sasha. Yet that would give them no laurels, mostly because nobody would believe them, even if someone confesses. This could play the same role as the Leningrad trial [of a group of Jews who planned to hijack an airplane to escape from the USSR in 1970] because it will probably result in a sharp rise in anti-Semitism (with all sorts of excesses, perhaps even pogroms) which would trigger a mass of exit applications [from Soviet Jews]."

In the diary, the document where a man has nothing to hide, Rubin confirmed that he had introduced Lipavsky to U.S. Embassy official Levitsky, and he was aware of the doctor's connections with the CIA.

Now everything was coming apart at the seams, but Rubin thought something good could still come of it, perhaps even another spurt in the Jewish emigration movement. Five days later, on March 10, Rubin wrote: "Yesterday I gave that matter some thought and concluded that Sanya Lipavsky could not have written such a letter," he wrote. "My hypothesis was that he is in prison and doesn't even know about any of this. I was basing this conclusion on the fact that he hated treachery . . . [and] that he is a man of exceptional kindness (all the stories about the way he helped people, how he bore the persecution from his managers, and when I told him that he ought to complain somewhere, he said 'I can't even hurt a fly'). I also recalled how he behaved with great dignity. Therefore I think it's plausible that he doesn't know about the letter and is in prison. On the other hand, in the evening, Luntz [another former refusenik living in

Israel] told me that according to information from Moscow Lipavsky hadn't been arrested."

On March 13, Rubin had a telephone conversation with Shcharansky. Rubin described the conversation in his diary:

"Today I talked to Tolya and Aleksandr Yakovlevich [Lerner, another refusenik accused by Lipavsky]. They said there is no news. Tolya is still being followed by eight people. They are in a good mood—what good souls. I told Tolya about Natasha [Avital] and how she and Misha [her brother] will soon leave for the U.S., and that powerful forces are starting a campaign on their behalf in the U.S. When I told Tolya that I thought that with every day the odds of their arrest decreased, he replied, 'I think so, too. It's almost a pity—we are so well prepared.'

"'I see you haven't lost your sense of humor,' I said.

"'Of course not. We laugh all the time,' he replied.

"'That's what you call Jewish laughter,' I noted."

The call apparently filled Rubin with optimism about Shcharansky's and Lerner's fates. His "working hypothesis" that day was that the Soviets would let the two men out, after having squeezed all the "political capital" out of the Lipavsky story that linked Soviet Jews and dissidents with the CIA. "Perhaps Lipavsky will be the direct victim of this whole story," Rubin wrote. "I think that letter was written by the KGB on the basis of that testimony and that he knows nothing of the letter. Now he is being kept in isolation, but that can't continue long. Sooner or later he will reappear, and then his reaction will be either some form of denial (which could bring him a long prison term or death) or suicide. This must happen within a week. Either would become sensation No. 1. Within a month or two (or even sooner) anti-Semitism will escalate."

In Rubin's mind, Lipavsky had returned to his status of an authentic Jewish hero who would soon emerge to clear his good name—even if it meant giving his life for the cause of Jewish emigration.

On March 15, Rubin wrote, "Now it is clear that we have miraculously avoided a terrible fate. Had Lipavsky been uncovered a year earlier, he would have named me as his accomplice and I would have gotten at least 10 years. It's unlikely that I would have survived."

Now Lipavsky was no longer Rubin's hero, but the man who would have given him up as his accomplice in espionage. It was Rubin, after all, who introduced him to Levitsky. Now, Rubin wondered, why hadn't the KGB picked up other men named in Lipavsky's "open letter." "Their [the KGB] wavering regarding others is understandable," Rubin wrote. "After all, they know nothing, and the espionage charge is pure nonsense anyway.

"Why is it that everything is so clear in hindsight while predicting is so difficult? Now the progression of events connected with the Lipavsky accusations and the attempts to use him to compromise all activists seem completely natural; meanwhile the danger inherent in combining activism with espionage was not so obvious to me. (And not me alone: Mel Levitsky didn't understand it either when I consulted with him about it in the car on the way to his house in Washington.) What we could not have foreseen was their [the Soviets'] intention to use this to create an anti-Semitic psychosis inside the country. All of this is their response to Carter; it is within their style, but it was unforeseeable since Carter himself was unforeseeable."

On March 15, the Soviets unexpectedly announced the release of Mikhail Stern, a doctor from Vinnitsa in the Ukraine, jailed for bribery soon after applying for an exit visa to Israel.

Jewish groups in the West claimed Stern was railroaded into prison to discourage others from applying to leave. Later in March, a committee of fifty Nobel Prize winners, formed by French philosopher Jean-Paul Sartre, was scheduled to hold a two-day "tribunal" in Amsterdam to publicize the Stern case. Some said the persecution of the Vinnitsa doctor was the new Dreyfus case.

Baltimore Sun reporter Harold Piper and *Financial Times* reporter David Satter decided to use the Stern release as an excuse to stop by at Slepak's. "I hadn't seen Slepak in a while, so I decided to stop by," Piper recalled. "David wanted to come, too."

Shcharansky happened to be at Slepak's. He moved in after his arrangement to share a room with Lipavsky fell through. Slepak brought out some Armenian brandy and everyone had a shot.

"They may let some Jews out and then frighten others with a new trial," Shcharansky said to reporters. This prophetic remark appeared in the following day's *Sun*.

The Soviets could simply let out a celebrity inmate to earn some goodwill in the West, then use up that goodwill by cracking down on active dissidents. This was the KGB's method of damage control.

Piper and Satter asked Shcharansky what it was like to be followed so intensively. "I guess the cognac hit me in the head, so I said, 'Let's go. I'll show you,'" Shcharansky recalled.

Shcharansky, followed by the two reporters and Slepak, walked out of the apartment. Two KGB men waited on the staircase. Shcharansky pushed the elevator button, waiting and talking about the KGB. The elevator came, and the agents, Shcharansky, and the reporters squeezed in.

"First he gets out, then me, then the other one," Shcharansky started his demonstration of Soviet secret police in action.

More KGB men waited on the ground floor. As soon as Shcharansky and his escort stepped out of the elevator, the agents shoved the reporters aside, pushed Shcharansky from the back, then dragged him off into a waiting car.

This was an unexpectedly macabre ending of a macabre show-and-tell.

"Well, Tolya has been arrested," Rubin wrote in his diary the following day. "He is in Lefortovo."

Two weeks later on March 31, he added, "I guess there is a share of my fault in Tolya's arrest. The Lipavsky situation (about which I alone knew) created enormous danger for everyone, and I didn't realize it. Of course, Lipavsky's meeting with Mel couldn't have caused my disapproval since it's clear which side we are on in this war. But could I have stopped his follow-up meetings? I told him on several occasions that I thought his connections with the CIA were too dangerous and unnecessary, but I couldn't make him stop. It's curious that he confessed to Ina [Rubin's wife] that he had some financial interest in it."

Torn by his guilty conscience and straining to understand the high intrigue of the Lipavsky caper, Rubin decided to write an article about the events in Moscow. He was certain on one issue:

"Now the Shcharansky matter poses the question of the relationship between the Jewish and the democratic movements in mid-70s. What can I write about now? About the actual relationship between the Jewish and the democratic movement and the true character of our collaboration. Here I would have to decide whether I should concentrate on Tolya or write in broad terms. . . . What would my main thesis be? That at this time the Jewish question cannot be separated from the dissident movement; that these questions are intertwined not only in the perception of Soviet authorities, but in reality? The point of such an article would be to discredit the idiotic position that participation in the democratic movement in fact undermines the Jewish positions. In fact, it is important to realize that there is now a united front of the Jewish and democratic movements since their goal is one and the same."

He, Orlov, and Shcharansky were at the heart of uniting the two movements. In the Moscow Helsinki group, Rubin, Shcharansky, and later Slepak were free to pursue their agenda—emigration. But that agenda wasn't judged to be any more special than those of the Pentecostals, the Crimean Tatars, or ethnic Russians.

Now, with Orlov and Shcharansky under arrest, Rubin saw that it was up to him to fight the ethnocentric view that the Jewish question was somehow different from all others. That was a delicate situation for Rubin since the position he considered "idiotic" was publicly espoused by the State of Israel, a number of Jewish organizations worldwide—and Shcharansky's wife, Avital.

During her many subsequent world tours, Avital stressed that Shcharansky was just a Jew trying to emigrate to Israel.

CHAPTER 23

THE COURTROOMS

On February 22, as her plane landed in Vienna, Alexeyeva found herself face-to-face with the unknown. She was fifty, she didn't speak English, and her profession—historian and Russian editor—wasn't in great demand in the West. Her final destination was the United States, where, an American friend who admired her cooking once told her, she would probably do well as a caterer.

It was only after arriving in Vienna that Alexeyeva began to give some thought to her future. It didn't look bright, she concluded, comparing her past as a fighter for justice with her future in catering. On her second day in Vienna, Alexeyeva discovered that she fell into panic whenever she was left alone. Once, while waiting for her husband, she leaned against a building, fighting dizziness, her mind racing. Sometimes, even when she was accompanied by Williams, her son Michael, or others, she caught herself listening to her own speech, as if she had lost control over whatever she was saying.

Her mind, as it did its involuntary twists and turns, usually returned to Orlov, to their farewell in the tiny foyer of her Moscow apartment. She wondered who else in the world would be interested in helping Orlov. Ginzburg, another Helsinki-group prisoner, had a powerful ally, Solzhenitsyn. Shcharansky, whose arrest now seemed imminent, would undoubtedly become a *cause célèbre* among Jews in the West. But what about the physicist who had been ripped out of their farewell embrace by the KGB a month earlier? She decided to find Orlov an attorney in the West.

On March 7, Alexeyeva arrived at Heathrow Airport, half an hour late for her meeting at the House of Commons. She addressed the Tories, then the Labour party, then the Liberal party, the sponsor of her London tour. After a couple of days in London, she bought a set of postcards of the House of Commons and sent them to her mother, inscribing one with "I go to this building every day, as if I work here."

She had dinner with Jeremy Thorpe, the Liberal party's foreign-affairs specialist. "How far can one really push the Soviets?" Thorpe asked her through a translator.

"Till you push them down," she said. She also asked Thorpe if he had a barrister to recommend.

"Just a minute," said Thorpe and picked up the phone. The attorney he called, a Liberal-party activist named John Macdonald, agreed to take the case.

"It was as if he had been expecting that call all his life," Alexeyeva recalled. Later that week, Macdonald picked up Alexeyeva and a translator to take them to dinner at his house in Wimbledon. As they drove through London, Macdonald told Alexeyeva that the Orlov case was something he couldn't pass up. Macdonald, who was in his forties, invoked the memory of British premier Neville Chamberlain and his promise of "peace in our time" through accommodation with Hitler. No man can afford to be a Chamberlain, Macdonald said. When fascism rears its head, it must be fought by every free man in every nation. Now, Macdonald said, he saw something all too similar to fascism in the USSR, and it was up to him, John Macdonald, QC, to stand up to injustice.

Alexeyeva liked the analogy with fascism. It reminded her of Orlov's 1973 letter to Brezhnev and of her friend Malva Landa's dream of the Bolsheviks answering for their crimes at a second

Nuremberg tribunal. She also enjoyed the tone of Macdonald's speech, which she attributed to his proper British upbringing and Oxford education. He was precisely what she pictured an Englishman to be: He had a longish face, was terribly refined, a bit stiff, yet sensitive enough to talk about an individual's responsibility to fight the evil of fascism. Macdonald appeared to be a good listener. So good, in fact, that he kept missing turns trying to keep up with the translator's renditions of Alexeyeva's fast speech.

Of course, Macdonald said, he realized that the objective of the Orlov defense would be to galvanize world opinion, conducting the trial in newspapers. He would also have to apply for a Soviet visa to meet with his client and, if allowed, argue for his acquittal before a Soviet court. That presented several problems. For one thing, Macdonald said, he had no experience in such cases. On top of that he spoke no Russian and knew nothing about Soviet law and procedure. That meant that even if the Soviets were to allow him to speak in court and even if he engaged a translator, he would still be at a disadvantage.

"What if the Soviets satisfy my requests and allow me in the country?" Alexeyeva remembers Macdonald's horrified question.

"You have nothing to worry about," she assured the barrister. "They won't let you in."

On June 15, the Helsinki Final Act signatories were to meet in Belgrade to review one another's performance under the agreement. The word was that the U.S. delegates were preparing a verbal pummeling of the Soviets over human rights.

At least according to the conventional wisdom of Soviet dissidents, it seemed logical for the Soviets to let out at least one of the three best-known Helsinki-group prisoners. It would be a gesture of goodwill and a way to make the West soften its verbal attack.

That is, if the Soviets still feared verbal raids.

"I represent Aleksandr Ginzburg, a brave, heroic young fighter for freedom inside the Soviet Union, whom I have never had the honor or the privilege to meet and it appears that there are those who are not in any hurry to see me get that honor or privilege," said Edward Bennett Williams, taking the witness stand at the Commission for Security and Cooperation in Europe June 3. It was his first speech as Ginzburg's defender.

It was Aleksandr Solzhenitsyn who had recruited Williams to defend Ginzburg. Williams's clients had included Joe McCarthy, Jimmy Hoffa, Frank Costello, Robert Vesco, and *The Washington Post*. He was the kind of man whose phone calls would always get through, even to the Oval Office or the office of Soviet Ambassador Anatoly Dobrynin. The Soviet government, in fact, had hired Williams twice, in 1960 and in 1968, when he successfully defended Soviet citizens accused of espionage in the United States.

"Legal counseling in Ginzburg's case will open up a new world even to a lawyer with your vast experience and world prestige," Solzhenitsyn promised, following up his phone call with a letter to Williams. Solzhenitsyn, a millionaire, was prepared to pay for Williams's services. "I couldn't take money from a man who has done so much for mankind," Williams said to Solzhenitsyn at a meeting at Solzhenitsyn's estate in Cavendish, Vermont.

Williams was one of the best-connected men in Washington, but Ginzburg wasn't to be tried in Washington. From the beginning, Williams publicly acknowledged that he doubted that the Soviets would let him meet with his client, that they would let him into the court of law, or that they would even allow him inside the country.

To give Ginzburg a vigorous defense, Williams had to become a lobbyist and a publicist.

Shortly after Williams agreed to take the case, the Solzhenitsyns—using unofficial channels—instructed Ginzburg's wife to dial Williams's private number and confirm that she would like Williams to represent her husband. Without consent from the defendant or his close relative, an American attorney cannot take a case.

The dissident's wife and the Washington lawyer talked for ten minutes. They could hear each other for eight of those minutes. Through unofficial channels, Williams asked Arina to spread the word that the firm was accepting letters in Ginzburg's defense, and dozens of testimonials from his friends—including a petition with 325 signatures—were smuggled out of Russia.

Williams and Connolly, Williams's firm, organized the Committee to Free Aleksandr Ginzburg. Williams also asked Natalya Solzhenitsyn to grant interviews to journalists and to write. She had written at least two articles, which were translated into English. One recipient, *Time,* attempted to add some drama to her epistle. "Late last week a brown Volvo rolled through the snowy streets of a Vermont ski village and stopped in front of a restaurant, where *Time* correspondent Marlin Levin was waiting. A hazel-eyed woman got out and greeted Levin with a manuscript," a one-paragraph foreword to Natalya Solzhenitsyn's short essay ("the manuscript") read.

On the less-publicized side, Williams's firm compiled a list of political prisoners worldwide. The list, which eventually included over forty names of Communists and other leftists in jails in rightist countries around the globe, was to be passed along to the State Department and the National Security Council, to aid the Carter administration in arranging a multicountry prisoner swap that would include Ginzburg. In December 1976, in a deal arranged by the Ford administration, the Soviets had agreed to free imprisoned dissident Vladimir Bukovsky in a swap for Brazilian Communist Luis Corvalan.

"You do not have to be Sherlock Holmes to deduce why Aleksandr Ginzburg was arrested," thundered Williams, addressing the Helsinki Commission as if it were a jury. "He was arrested because he embraced the cause of human freedom, because he believed in the right of free expression, because he believed in political expression, because he believed in the right of political assembly, and because he was presumptuous enough to believe that the Soviet regime meant it when they signed the Helsinki Accord on August 1, 1975. That is why Aleksandr Ginzburg was arrested."

Actually, Ginzburg was not naïve enough to believe that the Soviets meant to fulfill their Helsinki promises. Indeed, had Ginzburg believed in his government's good faith, he would have seen no need to monitor the Soviets by joining Orlov's group. It is also unlikely that Williams actually believed Ginzburg to be "presumptuous enough" to believe in his country's good intentions.

But the attorney had a case to build: Ginzburg, believing in his country's good faith, runs the charitable fund and joins the

Helsinki group. Meanwhile, the country has no intention of carrying out its promises. So the big bad state puts Ginzburg in prison.

Ludicrously, this account of the events implied that Yuri Orlov's group, a nationwide umbrella organization of a broad cross-section of the disaffected factions in the USSR, started out as a result of a misunderstanding of the Soviet government's true intentions rather than as a daring attempt to catch the Soviets in a lie.

"My involvement in this matter came about this way, members of the Commission," Williams continued. "After a call and a letter, I visited Mr. Aleksandr Solzhenitsyn in Cavendish, Vermont, and I spent one day with him. And I must tell you that I became a convert to a belief that I think all of you have. I am a dedicated convert to it now. I know now the Soviets understand and respect strength, and they have contempt for vacillation and ambiguity. I believe that as long as we keep the searchlight of world opinion on their treatment of dissidents, the cause of freedom will benefit to the maximum in the Soviet Union. . . .

"I applied for a visa. I talked to the Soviet ambassador, the Honorable Anatoly Dobrynin," Williams continued at the Helsinki Commission hearing. "I asked for the right to see him. He would not see me, but he talked to me on the telephone and he told me that my request was 'unprecedented, presumptuous, and arrogant,' but that I should reduce it to writing, and it would be submitted to Moscow. I did do that. I complied. I wrote a long, formal request for a visa and I waited in respectful silence for an answer.

"I believed that because the Soviets had embraced the spirit and letter of freedom in the Helsinki Accord, I would get it." Now it was Edward Bennett Williams who was betrayed, because, just like his client, Aleksandr Ginzburg, he was naïve enough to believe in the sincerity of the Soviet government.

"I belong to an old-fashioned school—I believe one good turn deserves another, and so I was naïve enough to think that when I called Mr. Dobrynin he would say, 'Of course, you can go visit Mrs. Ginzburg. Of course, you can go counsel with her. Of course, you can go help her select counsel.' But I was peremptorily denied that right. I asked for reconsideration, and I thought naïvely that perhaps when I made the case again, they would understand. But this week, once again, I was peremptorily denied the right to travel to the Soviet Union." The Soviets owed Williams a favor; two favors—one for each of their accused spies he got off. They weren't returning the favors, and Ed Williams was mad.

He was stopping just short of accusing the Soviets of breach of Helsinki contract.

On June 12, Alan Dershowitz stood up to plead the Shcharansky case before an even more unorthodox audience: the viewers of an NBC News broadcast of a live ninety-minute debate on human rights between three Soviets and three Americans.

"Following the signing of the Helsinki Accord, several prominent Soviet citizens established what's known as the Public Group to Promote Observance of the Helsinki Agreement in the USSR," said Dershowitz, who was on the U.S. team. "They have issued dozens of well-documented reports, none of which is available in the Soviet Union, which paint a sorry picture of the state of freedom throughout that country.

"The Soviet response has been swift and dramatic. Eight of the most prominent members of the Helsinki group have been arrested. The sudden arrest of the leadership of the Helsinki monitoring group constitutes a direct challenge to the Helsinki Accord, to Soviet-American relationships, and to President Carter. It is as if former president Nixon had ordered the arrest of the entire board of directors of the American Civil Liberties Union and *The Washington Post* in response to the Watergate allegations.

"One of those arrested was a twenty-nine-year-old Jew named Anatoly Shcharansky, who had applied to rejoin his wife in Israel. His wife is currently in the United States."

More specifically, Shcharansky's wife was in the audience. Pointing her out and asking her to stand up would probably have stirred applause from the fans of the home team, but the political atmosphere of the debate was hot enough even without such a gesture. A day earlier, an instruction from Moscow directed the Soviet team to pull out unless debate rules were changed to prohibit cross-examination by the Americans. The Soviet demands were accommodated.

During the debate, Dershowitz didn't disclose that he was acting as Shcharansky's attorney in the United States.

"American concern about the human rights of Soviet citizens like Shcharansky, particularly those who want to leave, does not constitute interference with the internal affairs of another country. . . . Indeed, the Soviet Union has always and continues to concern itself, perhaps more than any country in the world, with the rights of citizens of other countries. One dramatic example will suffice to illustrate the double standard employed by the Soviet Union in the area of human rights: When Angela Davis, the black Marxist professor from California, was charged with conspiracy to murder a judge, fourteen prominent Soviet citizens called President Nixon urging him to safeguard her life. The Soviets said that it was 'their duty to safeguard the rights of the individual to fight for progress, even in another country.'

"Now, instead of responding that this was an undue interference in American domestic affairs, President Nixon immediately issued an invitation to the Soviet citizens to attend the Davis trial as official observers in order to assure themselves that she would receive a fair trial. After Davis's acquittal, the Soviet Union invited her to the USSR, where she was awarded the Lenin Medal. She is now back in the United States, speaking freely.

"Ironically, Professor Henry McGee, a black American lawyer and chairman of the Law Professors Committee to Assist in the Angela Davis Defense, went to the Soviet Union and attempted to attend the trial of a young Jewish woman charged with distributing some Hebrew books, which constitutes anti-Soviet propaganda. He was excluded from the trial, and, eventually, he was expelled from that country.

"I invite you to explain this double standard to the audience watching this debate today."

Professor Samuel Zivs, senior researcher of the Institute of State and Law, took the microphone. "As my colleague from Harvard, Professor Dershowitz, mentioned mainly one particular case, I would like to explain the situation with the harassment of eight members of the Helsinki group, as he called this group, this well-known group of dissidents in my country.

"Of course, Shcharansky and others are people who are making some noise under the cover of different labels of different organizations and groups during, I guess, some years, some five or six years. And, of course, it is not the question of so-called Helsinki defense activity, but the very definite charges that were brought against Shcharansky.

"What is important under these conditions, you see, Shcharansky is charged with a specific crime under a specific article of the criminal code. Now preliminary investigation has only started and is going on.

"As a lawyer, I guess, you will agree with me that no kind of interference in this stage of criminal procedure would be acceptable and would be fair, on any level, including any official statement by the Administration or whatever governmental body, statements in this stage, when all evidence is not collected, when presumption of innocence is staying. . . ."

DERSHOWITZ: "Right. Two very brief responses. I commend you that there should be no statements by any official organs of your government while the case is under investigation. But surely you read the *Izvestia* articles that appeared on March 16, 1977, where Shcharansky was declared guilty of treason by the newspapers.

"Moreover, although the trial may be far off, and we hope may never occur, I would like to put you a specific question: If there is a trial, may I attend as his legal observer? I want to invite you to attend any trial in the United States that you would like to attend as a legal observer, but I want you to answer the question directly: May I . . . attend Shcharansky's trial if there is an investigation leading to a trial?

ZIVS: "All trials of such kind are public. . . ."

He couldn't finish the sentence. "It's a lie!" shouted a woman from the audience.

"Please," implored NBC News correspondent Edwin Newman, the moderator. Zivs was indeed lying through his teeth. As for the woman whose outburst he provoked, she was more than a casual observer.

She was Avital Shcharansky.

"All trials of such kind are public," Zivs started over. "And it is up to the presiding judge to so rule these questions."

The exchange sounded like a game Soviet dissidents liked to play with the guards charged to keep them away from trials of other dissidents. "Is the trial open?" dissidents generally asked.

"Yes, the trial is open."

"So let us in."

"No."

"But you said the trial is open."

"Yes, it's open."

"Well, let us in."

"No."

This could go on for hours, and usually did.

Dershowitz did more than score debating points. Shortly after taking the Shcharansky case, he went to see Stuart Eizenstat, his former student who had become Carter's chief domestic adviser, and Robert L. Lipshutz, the president's counsel. Dershowitz had a little request: a statement by President Carter categorically denying that Shcharansky was in any way connected with U.S. intelligence-gathering services.

Dershowitz followed up the conversation with a memo. He received no response from the White House, but on June 13, a day after the debate, the president said that he had "inquired deeply within the State Department and within the CIA, as to whether or not Mr. Shcharansky has ever had any known relationship in a subversive way, or otherwise, with the CIA. The answer is 'No.'"

President Carter's declarations notwithstanding, it was up to every observer, up to every reader, to determine the matter of Shcharansky's innocence. By associating with Lipavsky, Shcharansky became, at least tangentially, part of a murky story involving the KGB and the CIA. Peter Osnos, who had met both Shcharansky and Lipavsky during his Moscow stint, appeared to be among the skeptics. In the March 10, 1978, issue of *The Washington Post,* Osnos wrote:

American officials—eventually including President Carter—have repeatedly denied that Shcharansky "had any known relationship in a subversive way or otherwise with the CIA."

Thus with President Carter's credibility on the line, an obscure young technician—who only wanted to leave the Soviet Union as tens of thousands of other Jews had done before—has become a consequential figure in superpower politics.

Unlike Andrei Sakharov, the great physicist, or Alexander Solzhenitsyn, the great writer, Shcharansky is a very ordinary person.

So, we thought, was Lipavsky.

THE TRIAL OF TERROR read the headline in London's *Daily Mail* June 14. "The terror merchants of the Kremlin and the KGB stood accused before the world in an extraordinary show trial staged in London yesterday," the story began. Staring off the page was the picture of Yuri Orlov, looking grim, bushy-haired, in black-rimmed glasses. PRISONER read the caption.

The tribunal was called by John Macdonald. After reading translations of Soviet law and after conferring with former Soviet attorneys, Macdonald determined that Orlov would most likely be charged with anti-Soviet propaganda under Article 70 or of slandering the state under Article 190-1 of the Russian Republic's Criminal Code. To convict him under either of the articles, the prosecution had to prove that he deliberately and knowingly spread lies about the Soviet system. The best defense was to argue that Orlov and his Helsinki Watch group never told a lie.

Politically, June 1977 may have been the optimal time to strike. Judicially it wasn't. Soviet authorities were still months away from completing their investigation and officially charging Orlov. Also, it was clear that Macdonald wouldn't be allowed to plead the case before a Soviet court.

Finding a solution, Macdonald held a "court proceeding" June 13, calling fifteen witnesses to "testify" in the elegant blue-ceilinged room at Britain's Institute of Physics. The witnesses, all of them Soviet émigrés, including Amalrik, Alexeyeva, and Voronina, swore that the facts in documents issued by Orlov's group were true. At the end, the transcripts were sent to Investigator Tikhonov, the man in charge of the Orlov case at the

Procurator General's office in Moscow. Macdonald was asking the KGB to consider the testimony of people who had emigrated after spending many years on the agency's black list.

If the Soviets were concerned about being verbally lashed at Helsinki Commission hearings, on NBC Sunday-morning programs, and at a moot-court hearing in London, they did a fine job of hiding it.

CHAPTER 24

THE NEW RULES

O n Saturday, June 11, 1977, Robert Toth walked out of his Moscow apartment carrying an empty glass jar. He had to pick up some sour cream to go with the caviar he had bought to celebrate his elder daughter's graduation from eighth grade.

That wasn't the only errand Toth had to run that day. Just as he was walking out the door, Toth got a call from Valery Petukhov, a dissident scientist with an interest in extrasensory perception. Petukhov said he was in the neighborhood and wanted to meet immediately.

Toth crossed the wide Garden Ring Road to meet Petukhov by the Obraztsov Puppet Theater. Few would harbor dark suspicions while carrying empty jars to meetings with parapsychologists in front of puppet theaters on the days their daughters clear eighth grade.

"We talked about a mutual friend who had since emigrated," Toth wrote later that day in a How-I-Got-Detained article for the Sunday edition of the *Times*. After the chat, Petukhov, a

balding and nervous man in his mid-thirties, opened his briefcase and pulled out twenty sheets with text and graphs, which
Toth presumed to be Petukhov's paper on parapsychology. As
Toth turned to walk back, a Soviet-made Fiat drove up to the
curb. A plainclothesman opened the door and pulled the reporter inside. The car took off, a man on each side pinioning
Toth's arms at the wrists. One of the men allowed Toth to put
the empty jar on his lap. A half block down the street, Toth saw
a black Volga pull up to parapsychologist Petukhov, with
plainclothesmen grabbing him.

At the police station where Toth was taken, he demanded to
call the U.S. Embassy. The inspector declined, instead calling
the Soviet Academy of Sciences. Within a half hour, a man
identifying himself as an Academy official, pronounced the
documents secret. The Academy official's evaluation read: "The
article, beginning Petukhov, Valery G., from the words 'micro-
organism self-radiation . . .' to the words 'by means of vacuum
particles in space,' states that within the content of living cells
are particles . . . and these particles are grounds for discussing
the fundamental problems of biology in the context of biology
and parapsychology. There is also information about the uses of
such particles. This material is secret and shows the kind of
work done in some scientific institutes of our state."

The day's events left Toth pondering some weighty matters.
It seemed that he had been set up. Why would Petukhov have
insisted on seeing him right away, and why did the KGB let
Toth observe the scientist's arrest? It seemed like a play, a mys-
tery. Why did the Soviets choose to frame him? After all, his
three-year stint at the bureau was to end in one week.

There were broader questions. Why did the Soviets choose
to detain a U.S. reporter just four days before the preliminary
meetings of the Helsinki Final Act performance-review conference in Belgrade? Would that not be a sure way to anger Americans, to trigger international outrage?

On Tuesday morning Toth got a call from U.S. Embassy official
Ted McNamara, who wanted the reporter to come to the embassy.

"Serious?" asked Toth.

"Serious."

Earlier that morning, the embassy had received an official note that read:

> The Ministry of Foreign Affairs is authorized to state the following to the American Embassy:
>
> Competent organs have at their disposal information that the correspondent of the newspaper *Los Angeles Times* accredited to the Soviet Union, the American citizen Robert Charles Toth, born in 1929, during a specific period of time has been engaged in activities incompatible with the status of a foreign journalist accredited to the USSR, that is, with the collection of secret information of a political and military character.
>
> On the 11th of June of this year Robert Charles Toth was apprehended at the moment of meeting with a Soviet citizen, Petukhov, Valeriy Georgiyevich, which took place under suspicious circumstances. When apprehended, the American journalist was found to have materials given to him by Petukhov containing secret data. The Ministry of Foreign Affairs states its protest in connection with the impermissible activity of the American correspondent Robert Toth consisting of collection of information of a secret character, and expects that the American side will take necessary measures for the prevention in the future of similar actions on the part of American correspondents accredited to the Soviet Union.
>
> At the same time the Ministry of Foreign Affairs informs the American Embassy in Moscow that in conformity with established procedure, Toth will be summoned for interrogation by the investigatory organs, in connection with which his departure from Moscow until the end of the investigation is not desired.

This was the most potent blow the KGB had struck in its attempts to smash the reporters' dissident connection. There had been accusations of espionage, even the expulsion of a reporter. But now the KGB was trying something new: detaining a U.S. reporter and threatening to charge him with espionage.

In a meeting, McNamara and two other mid-level officials

told Toth the embassy recommended that he submit to KGB questioning. The conversation was held in one of the regular embassy offices rather than in the "tank" safe room which, nearly a decade later, was used by the CIA in talking to *U.S. News & World Report* correspondent Nicholas Daniloff.

Toth recalls that one of the officials described the entrance area to the Lefortovo prison where Toth was to be interrogated. From the start Toth realized that the questioning would undoubtedly turn to his connection with Shcharansky. But all his conversations with the refusenik were on the record, and typically were held on Moscow streets in daylight. To "prove" that Shcharansky had been a source on many of Toth's stories, the KGB had to do little more than go through back issues of the *Los Angeles Times.*

Refusing to answer questions would accomplish nothing, Toth decided. He resolved to answer the investigator's questions regarding all sources he quoted by name in his stories and not mention sources he didn't quote by name. This behavior could even benefit Shcharansky by demonstrating that the refusenik's relationship with reporters had no element of secrecy, so no espionage could have been committed.

Embassy officials advised Toth to answer at least some of the questions. "Playing games," he was told, could prompt the Soviets to jail him for up to two years. Within a couple of hours, Toth, his translator, and embassy Vice Consul Larry Napper entered 3A Energeticheskaya Ulitsa, the Lefortovo prison. In the lobby, Napper and Toth's wife, Paula, were told they could go no farther and Toth went in alone. Later Toth wrote:

"The messenger ushered me up a flight of stairs . . . pea-green walls up to shoulder height, dirty blue-gray above, and through another door that he opened by pressing a button. It seemed to take us into another building. Up another flight of stairs—these had wire screens the entire length, stair to ceiling, to prevent anyone from leaping over railings—through another door. This one required several buttons to be pressed in a coded sequence. And then down a very long dingy brown linoleum-floored corridor to Maj. Dobrovolski."

Toth was seated in a straight-backed chair at a child-sized desk. It was hot inside. Dobrovolski, a dark-haired man in his late thirties, had opened the window but closed it after Toth was seated. "Not a pleasant view," he said.

"Do you know why you are here?"

"I assume it is in connection with Saturday's incident," said Toth through a translator who introduced himself as Smirnov. He was the same translator who had been present at Toth's first interrogation at the militia station Saturday.

"Precisely," Dobrovolski said, then started to inform Toth of his rights and responsibilities under Soviet law. Toth took out his pen and started taking notes.

"This is not a press conference, Mr. Toth. Put down your pen," another interrogator interrupted Toth's note-taking. "According to our law," the major said, "you may be questioned about everything of interest to this organization, and your statements should be real and should show the whole picture of the situation, and even more, ought to answer the whole question about the whole situation. You are warned not to give unreal statements and not to refuse to answer, according to our law, Articles 108, 109 of the Criminal Code. As a witness, you may read the protocol [official account of the questioning], make statements, or give new statements in addition."

"I may not refuse to answer then?" asked Toth. "Under our law . . ."

"You are under Soviet law. You have no diplomatic immunity," the major interrupted before Toth got a chance to tell him about the American right to remain silent or have an attorney present.

Dobrovolsky wrote down Toth's biography, then asked who had introduced him to Petukhov. Toth said it was Eduard Trifonov, a refusenik who had by then emigrated, who first brought them together a few months earlier.

"Maj. Dobrovolsky then asked how, in general, I gather information," Toth recalled in a news story later. "I described three kinds of information—officially released in the Soviet press, travel around the country and observation, and unofficial information about Jewish emigration, harassment, Marxist reformers here and the like. And our first argument began:

"'I said unofficial information, not illegal,' I emphasized. 'Does that distinction come through in the Russian?'

"He just smiled and shrugged to indicate there was no difference to him."

At 6:00 P.M., after some haggling over details, Toth signed the official record of the interrogation, adding a disclaimer: "This protocol has been translated for me, and with its essence I have no major objections."

"You are finished for today," the KGB officer said. "*Do zavtra*. Until tomorrow. You are required to return at ten tomorrow morning."

That evening, at a party, Toth learned that a Soviet journalist at the UN had said that Toth was likely to stand trial on espionage charges and that the White House and State Department had issued strongly worded statements protesting his detention.

The next day, at Lefortovo, Toth decided to go on the offensive, forcing the Soviets to say why he was being interrogated.

"Why am I here?" he asked his interrogators, who introduced themselves as Major Vladimir Chernish and Colonel of Justice Volodin. "Why can't the American consul be present? What am I charged with? What's the purpose of this investigation? Who is accused? Of what?"

"The consul cannot be here because you are interrogated as a witness, not an accused person," the Colonel of Justice answered the first question. "It does not make any difference to you who is accused and what is the charge."

Then the colonel got to the point: "You know Shcharansky. Tell us how you got to know him, everything about it. He said he gave a lot of information to you. What kind?"

Toth told the interrogators that he had met Shcharansky shortly after arriving in the USSR, that the two had met regularly, usually taking walks in the vicinity of Toth's apartment at Sadovo-Samotechnaya. Shcharansky had also served as Toth's translator at dissident press conferences. The Soviets could no doubt get that information from their clandestinely taken photographs, bugged telephone conversations, tapes of press conferences, and testimony by the likes of refusenik doctor Sanya

Lipavsky. Some information could be obtained from the *Los Angeles Times,* where Shcharansky was quoted by name.

"Is this your article?" Volodin asked, picking up the *International Herald Tribune* with a reprint of Toth's *Los Angeles Times* piece RUSSIA INDIRECTLY REVEALS SECRET WORK CENTERS.

The piece probably represented the most creative jockeying of information provided by dissidents. For years, Moscow Jewish activists had kept lists of applicants refused exit visas on secrecy grounds. Versions of the lists, which included hundreds of names, were held by the Israelis and American Jewish activists, who used it to channel financial assistance and letters to refuseniks.

The existence of the list was no secret in the USSR and in the West. Many of the list's entries were made by Jewish activists stationed outside the doors of OVIR, the visa office, conducting an "exit poll" by asking every Semitic-looking person to emerge from OVIR if he had been refused exit. In the West, the list was the subject of open controversy, as the Union of Councils for Soviet Jews and London-based Jewish activist Michael Sherbourne unceasingly accused the Israelis of not sharing their version of the list with grass-roots activist groups.

One of the first people to suggest that Toth make use of the list was Alexander Goldfarb, Shcharansky's predecessor as a translator for the refuseniks who emigrated in 1974. Toth toyed with the idea for at least two years, then came up with a stinging piece listing some of the "secret" plants and research institutes where some of the refuseniks worked and finding that some of those places had pending applications at the U.S. Department of Commerce for the purchase of IBM 360 and IBM 370 mainframe computers.

The Toth story asked two questions: Was the U.S. helping build up Soviet "secret"—which presumably means military-related—enterprises? Or was the secrecy label widely misused by the authorities?

Toth asked the interrogators if he could see the story before answering questions about it. While he was reading, the phone rang. Toth was unable to understand who was calling or what the call was about, but as soon as Volodin hung up, he turned to the reporter and said: "We understand you are invited to lunch with the American ambassador at one o'clock today. It is now eleven-thirty, we will let you go at twelve-twenty and you will return at three-thirty. We will begin writing the protocol now."

After fifty minutes of haggling over details of the minutes of the interrogation, Toth was allowed to leave, signing nothing. Over lunch, served at his residence, Ambassador Malcolm Toon asked Toth about the interrogation, then said: "You are in a difficult situation. Don't be clever."

Later that day, back in Lefortovo, Toth and the interrogators plowed through a stack of newspapers, with Toth confirming that it was Shcharansky and other refuseniks who had provided him with lists for the "secrets" story. That, too, was not an earthshaking revelation since Shcharansky was named in the piece.

As the interrogation continued, Toth was asked to verify that he had talked with the people he quoted in his stories. He also confirmed that he had talked to people whom he didn't quote, but who had since emigrated. Then once again the haggling over minutes began, with the text being translated in writing into English, at Toth's insistence.

"Will you want me to come back tomorrow?" Toth asked after signing the minutes.

"We'll see," said Volodin.

Later that night Toth was told his testimony was no longer needed and he was free to leave the USSR.

The decision to submit to the KGB interrogation made Toth a controversial figure among American Soviet Jewry activists and Soviet expatriates. Shortly after returning to the United States, Toth got a letter from Aleksandr Luntz, former Moscow refusenik at whose *press-konferentsiya* Toth had met Shcharansky. "I know that you are a brave and a clever man, Bob, but you were tricked by the KGB," Luntz wrote from Israel. Luntz said the KGB would doctor the interrogation minutes, adding whatever testimony it wanted over Toth's signature.

Another view frequently expressed by émigrés was that Toth had got in over his head. "He is a reporter. His forte is writing news stories; ours is dealing with the KGB," said Alexeyeva before Shcharansky's release. "I can't blame him for talking. And I am sure Tolya doesn't blame him for talking." Still, for nearly a decade, in Soviet émigré circles, one could hear references to

Toth's "betrayal" of Shcharansky and about his "weakness" in submitting to signing the interrogation protocol, and the "guilt" with which he was said to be coping.

"In retrospect, we'd all do things differently," Toth said. "But I made my calls at the time on what I felt Tolya wanted me to do. He'd reminded me at our last meeting that everything we did was in the open."

Three days after having been freed in a U.S.-Soviet prisoner swap, Shcharansky told Toth in Israel that he had read the transcripts of Toth's interrogations and they were "one hundred percent accurate." The testimony was neither damaging nor helpful to his case, Shcharansky said.

But what amazed Shcharansky most was that the reporter was interrogated at all. "The fact that an American correspondent was interrogated was so unprecedented . . . Something very serious had changed in the outer world," Shcharansky said.

CHAPTER 25

"THERE IS NO SAFETY, MISS PAULEY. THAT'S THE TERRIBLE TRUTH."

I n November 1977, the *Columbia Journalism Review* attempted to examine what it called a "burst of coverage" of Soviet dissent by American journalists.

"During the first third of 1977, readers of *The New York Times, The Washington Post*, and the *Los Angeles Times* could have been forgiven for thinking that not much was happening in the Soviet Union beyond the controversies over dissidents," wrote Fergus M. Bordewich, a journalism teacher and free-lance writer.

"Coverage of dissidents earlier this year reflected a confluence of the publicity for the issue created by the president, available news sources, and the natural sympathy of journalists brought up under the First Amendment (and of publishers and editors for dramatic stories that conform with their prejudices)."

According to Bordewich's figures, in January 1977, *The New York Times* ran thirty-one stories about dissent in the USSR, out of the total of thirty-eight stories on Soviet politics in general. The same month, the *Los Angeles Times* carried nine dissent stories and *The Washington Post* ran thirteen. The following month, *The New York Times* did fifty-four stories, the *Los Angeles Times,* twenty, and *The Washington Post,* thirty-six. In March the score was: *The New York Times*—fifty-eight; the *Los Angeles Times*—twenty-nine; and *The Washington Post*—twenty-eight.

"This burst of coverage matched . . . President Carter's vigorous offensive for human rights abroad, particularly within the USSR," Borewich concluded. "How could it happen that, after more than two decades of hard lessons in the dangers of fronting for American policy, American newspapers lined up so promptly?"

Actually, the coverage matched a burst of news: The Soviets were cracking down on their dissidents, thereby challenging the new U.S. president. Was Borewich suggesting that the press should have ignored this crucial issue in superpower relations? There was also a question of what constitutes a "burst of coverage." Most of the stories Borewich counted up were small items buried in the back pages of the papers.

In the same package of stories, in the *Columbia Journalism Review*, Peter Osnos, who had just returned from a three-year Moscow tour to become *The Washington Post's* foreign editor, lambasted his colleagues for blowing the dissident story out of proportion. "The correspondent wants to know Russia and get a good story. Dissidents offer both. The dissidents want to tell the world what they think. They also believe that if their names are recognized abroad, authorities will treat them less harshly—a belief for which there is probably some validity. The result of this mutual usefulness, as well as the relatively easy access of news about dissidents compared with other kinds, is what seems at times to be a disproportionate emphasis on them. . . .

> Take the case of Yuri Orlov. . . . In the spring of 1976 he organized a group to monitor Soviet compliance with the Helsinki Accord's human-rights provisions. . . . The Helsinki group, as it came to be called, held press conferences almost weekly to issue reports on subjects as diverse as official interference in telephone and mail to harassment

of the religious. Offshoot committees were established in Georgia, the Ukraine, and Lithuania. The authorities lent credibility to the effort by seizing Orlov on the street and warning him that his activities were illegal. Reporters came to refer to Orlov as "a leading dissident." Committee findings, as carried in the press, were analyzed by foreign ministries in Western Europe. Additional data were forwarded to a special U.S. Congressional-executive panel keeping track of compliance with the Helsinki document. . . .

Thus, a small number of little-known private citizens in the world's most powerful totalitarian state had an influence on opinion in the West. Only Western reporters in Moscow could have brought them so prominently to the public eye and kept them there.

Relying on dissidents, Osnos wrote, "is rather like viewing the United States from the perspective of our most disenchanted and most persecuted citizens. Dissidents in the Soviet Union say what most Americans want—and expect—to hear about the evils of communism. Excessive dependence on them, however, creates a picture of that complex country as oversimplified in a way as Soviet reports about the United States being a land of little more than poverty, violence, corruption and racism. The Soviet press may not be able to do a better job. But we can."

When Orlov formed his Helsinki group, the story fell through the cracks of Western journalism. Most journalists, including Osnos, considered the story unusable. What coverage there was was broadcast on shortwave radio stations to the USSR but, for the most part, wasn't considered important enough to make newspapers in the United States. Those stories that made it were buried in the back pages.

Thus, unbeknownst even to well-informed Americans, Yuri Orlov brought Soviet dissent to its highest form. He accomplished this by focusing the demands of groups so diverse that they had never sat down together, groups Orlov hadn't even heard about when he started the group.

There was no shortage of signs that Orlov's endeavor was different from anything that had ever been tried by Soviet dissidents. For one thing, the original group of eleven included people who had never before met under the same roof. Then groups sprang up in the Ukraine, Lithuania, Georgia. A similar committee sprang up in the U.S. Congress. Helsinki-group documents, albeit dry, began to reflect some exotic subjects, including the separate problems of Lithuanian Catholics, Nakhodka Pentecostals, Ukrainian Baptists, and Jewish activists. Remarkably, all of them were working through the same umbrella group.

Reporters weren't so far away that they couldn't see it. They ate at the same tables with dissidents. They drank vodka out of the same cups, they helped smuggle group documents out of the country, yet not until the crackdown did anyone attempt a comprehensive story about the group.

In his *Columbia Journalism Review* story, Osnos was in effect explaining his decision to virtually ignore the Helsinki-group story before the crackdown, and Bordewich was supplying hack commentary. With this lack of understanding of what the Helsinki group actually was, the stage was set for a media brouhaha.

There were cover stories on Soviet dissent in *Time* and *Newsweek,* there were appearances of dissidents' friends and relatives on the *MacNeil-Lehrer Report* and the *Today* show. There was even an Art Buchwald column, a mock "Dear Comrade" letter to the editor of *Izvestia.* "I don't wish to criticize your system, but I would suggest that if you permitted your dissidents to speak freely as much as we permit ours to, you wouldn't get so upset about them and have to put them on trial," wrote Buchwald, identifying himself as an American Jewish dissident "who, despite what he says about his government, can't get arrested to save his life."

On April 13, 1977, Jane Pauley, in an attempt to make her viewers relate to Soviet dissent in human terms, asked Avital Shcharansky if she would consider going back to the USSR if she were allowed to live with her husband. "It is a very strange question because asking me that is like asking me whether I would go back to prison," said Avital. Having interpreted Avital's answer as an emphatic no, Pauley turned to her other guest, Representative Millicent Fenwick. "Really, the only weapons we have to protect those dissidents, the only enforcement in the Helsinki Agreement, is essentially shock and outrage; is it not?"

"Yes, it is," said Fenwick. "There is no safety, Miss Pauley, that's the terrible truth. But it does seem to work to some extent if the government in Russia, in the Soviet Union, is aware that people are watching."

The threat of an outburst of anti-Semitism in the USSR did not galvanize the Jewish groups in the West. The released Soviet refuseniks dispatched on U.S. lecture tours by Israel's Soviet Jewry office were warned to stay away from Irene Manekofsky, a leader of the "grass-roots" Union of Councils. "Irene, they told me you were a dangerous person," one refusenik who disregarded the Israeli officials' instructions told Manekofsky. "They say you support the dissidents."

Shortly after Manekofsky organized the Capitol Hill briefing attended by Andrew Young, she received a protest from Richard Krieger, executive director of the Jewish Federation of North New Jersey, an "establishment" group. Krieger wrote that he objected to Manekofsky's having contacted a New Jersey congressman.

"I am sure that your contact with him was made with the best of intentions," he wrote. "But there is a format and a process we use when dealing with congressional representatives to avoid duplicity [*sic*] and the seeming internecine [*sic*] political infighting that apparently might exist within certain aspects of the Jewish community." In the future, Krieger wrote, Manekofsky would have to work through the Jewish Federation that represents the home base of the congressmen or the senators she contacts.

Nothing about the official Israeli reaction was put in writing, but information compiled by "grass-roots" activists seems to point to an Israeli reluctance to make much of the Shcharansky case. "Shcharansky was a naughty boy," a British Jewish establishment figure was reported saying. "He shouldn't have got mixed up with the Helsinki group." In Paris, an Israeli official was reported as saying, "We must not forget that the Soviets, after all, do have a case against Shcharansky."

At a closed briefing at the Israeli Embassy in Washington, an Israeli official was quoted to the effect that the arrest points to the danger inherent in Jewish activists' association with dissidents. There were reports that in December 1979, a Knesset member about to fly to Moscow at the invitation of a peace organization inquired of Israel's Soviet Jewry office whether it would be prudent to raise the Shcharansky case. "Shcharansky is not an Israeli case," the parliamentarian was told. On her U.S. tours, Avital often found herself booked for two events at the same time. One event was planned by the "grass-roots," and another by the "establishment." On at least one occasion, the Israeli embassy called Avital, who was staying at Manekofsky's house, to ask her to show up at an "establishment" event.

"It's horrible," Avital said to the *Northern California Jewish Bulletin* a year after the campaign to free her husband was launched. "Sometimes I don't know whether to laugh or cry. All the time I would like to shout to all these people: 'What are you doing! You are hurting the movement, hurting the people who are the most involved! . . . I would like to believe that these people [who head the two groups] want to help Soviet Jews. But everyone has his own way and the conflict starts there. I hope it's not just a prestige war because that is very low and very dirty. . . . Sometimes I need their help and yet I have to help them patch up their differences. I don't feel used because I don't let people use me easily, but it's still horrible to watch. [The fighting] takes 90 percent away from our efforts to help my husband. That doesn't mean they would have released him right away, but more harmony would have shown the world that there *is* a Jewish pride and that the Soviet Jewry fight is a just fight."

Increasingly, Avital was taking the campaign into her own hands. At her many appearances, she portrayed Shcharansky as a Jew trying to leave rather than as a member of a dissident group. This line of defense led to Avital's disagreement with Alexeyeva, who argued that playing down Shcharansky's role in the human-rights movement would cut him off from the support of non-Jews in the West. In response, Avital asked Alexeyeva to make no statements about Shcharansky without coordinating them with her.

So well known did Avital become that in mid-July 1978, Union of Councils president Manekofsky found herself fighting off requests by *Washington Post* reporter Sally Quinn to interview the refusenik's wife. Manekofsky, who was arranging Avital's schedule, was no fan of Quinn's high-gloss personality profiles. There was no way of telling what kind of a spin Quinn would put on the Avital story. "Before the trial I had to like jump through hoops to get publicity for her," Manekofsky lamented over the phone, trying to stonewall Quinn. "Now they [the press] are tearing me apart. You have no idea what they are doing to her. She collapsed on me once when she was here before."

Quinn persisted, finally getting an interview. On July 20, *The Washington Post*'s Style section ran Quinn's story headlined AVITAL SHCHARANSKY AND THE POLITICS OF SORROW. Avital, Quinn noted, looked like an Israeli Audrey Hepburn, was affiliated with radical Zionist groups, and carried a Gucci bag. The story Avital told Quinn—as well as to hordes of other reporters—was as simple as they come: She had met Anatoly Shcharansky outside the Moscow synagogue, they studied Hebrew together, then moved in together. On July 4, 1973, they were married in a religious ceremony, and since then, he had not been allowed to join her in Israel. Avital was a natural media event. She was beautiful, she was photogenic, and her story, which was simple enough for anyone to understand, avoided the complexities of her husband's life. Not least of these complexities was his membership in a dissident group that in effect demanded that the Soviet Union become a free society.

Her book, *Next Year in Jerusalem,* mentioned Yuri Orlov only once, in a footnote. Now it was Avital, not Anatoly, who was setting the agenda in the West, and largely because of her efforts, Shcharansky's name remained a household word long after the end of his celebrated trial. Meanwhile, Orlov got forgotten by everyone except a relatively small number of concerned scientists and human-rights cognoscenti.

CHAPTER 26

PRISONERS AND EXILES

On May 17, 1978, Orlov stood up to address the court: "You can sentence me to seven years. You can sentence me to five. You can shoot me, but I remain convinced that such trials do nothing to alleviate the troubles and shortcomings to which the Helsinki-group documents have attested."

Judge Valentina Lubentsova found him guilty of anti-Soviet propaganda under Article 70 and sentenced him to seven years in the "strict regimen" camp followed by five in internal exile.

Less than two months later, on July 10, in the nearby town of Kaluga, Judge A. Sidorkov began examining the defendant: "Your name?"

"Ginzburg."

"Year of birth?"

"1936"

"Nationality?"

"*Zek.*"

"Previous sentences served?"

"Five years in prison, five in the 'special regimen' camps, and five in internal exile."

"When did you receive this sentence?"

"I will receive it here, at this trial."

On July 13, Ginzburg was found guilty of anti-Soviet propaganda and sentenced to eight years in the camps. The following day, in Moscow, Shcharansky said to the court:

"Five years ago I applied to emigrate to Israel. Today I am further from that dream than ever before. It would seem that I would regret what has happened, but it is not so. I am happy.

"I am happy that I have lived honestly, at peace with my conscience, staying true to my soul even under the threat of death. I am happy that I have helped people. I am happy that I have met and worked with such honest and brave people as Sakharov, Orlov, Ginzburg, the carriers of the traditions of the Russian intelligentsia. I am happy that I have witnessed the revival of the Jewish people in the USSR. I hope that the absurd accusation leveled against me and the entire Jewish emigration movement will not hinder the liberation of my people.

"My friends and those close to me know how much I would like to have traded my role of an activist in the emigration movement for a quiet life with my wife in Israel.

"For over two thousand years my people have been in the diaspora, but wherever they were, they repeated, 'Next year in Jerusalem!' This minute, as I am further than ever from my people, from my Avital, and as I face many difficult years of imprisonment, I say to my people, to my Avital, 'Next year in Jerusalem.'

"As for this court, which must merely confirm the sentence that has already been passed, to this court I have nothing to say."

Shcharansky was found guilty of treason and anti-Soviet propaganda and sentenced to three years in prison followed by ten in the camps. Outside, Ida Milgrom, his seventy-year-old mother, watched the prison van take her son to the Gulag. "Shame on you! Shame on you!" she cried to the guards who did not allow her to attend the trial. "Why wouldn't you let me see him?"

Sakharov, who was comforting Milgrom, joined her cry of

frustration. "You are not people," he shouted. "Fascists! Fascists!"

In 1978, statements by defendants somehow said more than a sober analysis of what was happening. Theirs were clear-cut cases of good versus evil, might versus right, and individual versus the state. Reflecting, the actors in the Helsinki-group drama asked themselves how—and why—the KGB had allowed so many people to have so much freedom for so long. Had the Soviet Union's mechanism of oppression malfunctioned? Had the KGB failed?

The secret police knew about the Helsinki group from the start. They knew enough to have tried to issue a warning to Orlov before he announced the group's formation. KGB moles, including Lipavsky and Petrov-Agatov, had to be filing regular reports. The listening devices planted in dissidents' apartments had to be yielding intelligence.

Yet the agency stood by as Western reporters and Soviet *khodoki* entered the apartments of Helsinki-group members. They stood by as dissidents staged pack-journalism events and courted reporters individually. Still, from May 1976 to January 1977, Orlov's group was left untouched. Reporters were becoming fearless, too.

Looking back, Robert Toth wonders how he could have been so cheerful when he walked out to meet a parapsychologist, a practitioner of a discipline the Soviets considered secret. George Krimsky, too, marvels at his backfired plan to write a story about the life-style of a Soviet GI. "It seemed reasonable at the time. The old taboos were breaking down," he said.

Sakharov, the Soviet Union's most prominent dissident, seemed to have lost all fear. He started to make appearances at the foreigners' compound and, after an explosion on the Moscow metro, called the press with a factually unsupported view that the blast could have been set by the KGB in order to blame it on dissidents later.

Ginzburg was receiving foreign funds for the running of an underground welfare agency. Millicent Fenwick, on her trip to Moscow, visited refuseniks and dissidents, as did other Western dignitaries. *The Washington Post*'s Peter Osnos introduced little-known Jewish activist Anatoly Shcharansky to Robert L. Bernstein, president of Random House and a human-rights activist in the United States. American Jewish activists spent hours conferring with Soviet Jews, sometimes on the phone, and sometimes in person. There was so much to say—and so many people attempting to say it—that Vladimir Slepak once asked Irene Manekofsky not to send so many people to see him.

These people-to-people East-West relations were certainly in the spirit of the Helsinki Final Act. But how long could they continue in a totalitarian state?

Thanks to Orlov and his Helsinki monitors, Soviet dissent had reached its highest point. The best-known dissidents and their key allies were united on a single platform: insistence on Soviet implementation of the human-rights provisions of the Helsinki Final Act. It could have been a powerful movement, one that united Moscow human-rights activists, Russian nationalists, Ukrainians, Lithuanians, Georgians, Armenians. On the other side of the Atlantic, the same effort, for the first time, united Congress and the administration. In January 1977, when the Soviets cracked down on their leading dissidents, they also struck at the Western perception that the USSR was vulnerable to pressure from the West.

Peter Reddaway of the London School of Economics noted in a 1984 paper that "despite the well publicized arrests and heavy sentencing of figures like Yuri Orlov and Anatoly Shcharansky, the total number of known arrests [of dissidents] in 1977 was a mere 82 . . . the lowest figure since 1965, and this rose only to 94 in 1978." Meanwhile, Jewish emigration kept increasing. In 1977, 16,736 people left the country. The number of émigrés was up to 28,864 the following year.

In 1977, when Andropov's KGB cracked down on dissent, it targeted the leaders. By arresting Orlov, Andropov told his countrymen not to start unofficial groups. By arresting Ginzburg, he pointed to the consequences of becoming a career dissident and channeling money from the West to help the families of political prisoners. Shcharansky's arrest was to demonstrate that dealing with Jewish groups in the West and foreign reporters in Moscow could have grave consequences for a Soviet citizen.

The KGB's apparent goal was to defuse the situation, without starting a bloodbath. Had it been otherwise, Amalrik, one of the pioneers of Soviet dissent, would not have been forced to leave the country. Alexeyeva and Grigorenko, too, would have been dispatched to Siberia rather than the West.

In 1979, the Soviets made the last attempt to revive détente. That spring, ten political prisoners, including Ginzburg, were released in a trade with the United States. In the summer, Carter and Brezhnev signed the SALT II agreement. Emigration that year jumped to 51,320, a record. But by the fall of 1979, the ratification of SALT II was running into trouble in Congress, and there were no signs of U.S. reconsideration of its stance on tying trade and emigration.

According to Reddaway's 1984 assessment, in November 1979, the Soviets appeared to have decided to abandon their pursuit of détente. They stepped up arrests on political charges, clamped down on emigration, then, in December, invaded Afghanistan. That year, 144 dissidents were arrested. The following year, the number of arrests reached what appears to be the post–Stalin-era record of 268. In 1980, emigration was down to 21,471; in 1981 it was at 9,447. Emigration kept declining, eventually petering out at about 1,000 a year after 1982.

The Moscow group stopped its work on September 6, 1982. "The Moscow Helsinki group has been put into condition where further work is impossible," the group's three remaining members announced. "Under these conditions the group . . . has to cease its work." Earlier that day, group member Sofya Kallistratova, then seventy-five, was charged under Article 190-1. After the group was dissolved, the case was dropped. Over the years, more than one hundred people passed through the Helsinki groups and their affiliates, and at this writing fifteen are in prisons, five have died in the camps, two have died under suspicious circumstances, and thirty-four have emigrated.

Those who remained gave a new meaning to the old dissident toast "To those who aren't with us." It used to refer to political prisoners. Now it refers also to prisoners and exiles.

Ludmilla Alexeyeva and her husband, **Nikolai Williams,** live in Northern Virginia. Shortly after Alexeyeva arrived in the United States, a publisher asked her to write a book explaining her road to dissent. She gave the book a good try, then gave up, realizing that her road to dissent was too personal and too much rooted in the Soviet environment to be explained to the American reader. Instead she wrote *Soviet Dissent* (Wesleyan University Press, 1985), an encyclopedic description of eighteen of the Soviet Union's dissident movements, from Russian nationalism to Meskhetian separatism.

Andrei Amalrik was killed in a 1980 automobile accident in Spain.

Vyacheslav Bakhmin, head of the commission on abuses of psychiatry, was arrested in 1980 and has served three years for "slandering the Soviet state." He lives in the town of Kalinin, outside Moscow.

Mikhail Bernshtam emigrated in the summer 1976. He is a demographics professor at Stanford University's Hoover Institution on War, Revolution, and Peace. He says he has taken Orlov's advice to stay out of politics. "It was the best advice I ever got," he said in an interview.

Aleksandr Ginzburg served a year and three months of his eleven-year sentence. He was released in a prisoner swap April 27, 1979. Since his release, Ginzburg has had several clashes with Alexeyeva. Their rift emerged almost immediately after his release when, in an apparent attempt to establish that he is a Russian patriot, Ginzburg said on U.S. television that he would rather have remained in a Russian prison than live in exile in America.

Alexeyeva, who had previously vouched to U.S. officials that Ginzburg, Orlov, and other imprisoned Helsinki monitors would indeed agree to leave the USSR, saw this statement as undermining her reputation. But most of all, she feared that after such a remark by Ginzburg, the United States would stop trying to secure Orlov's and Shcharansky's releases.

Ginzburg and Alexeyeva continue to disagree on virtually everything, especially Ginzburg's support for a group of former Soviet dissidents who say the United States should get out of the Helsinki Final Act because it is being ignored by the Soviets.

Ginzburg and his wife, **Arina Zholkovskaya,** live in Paris.

Nikolai Goretoy, the Pentecostal leader, after the arrests of Ginzburg, Orlov, and Shcharansky, wrote an open letter to Christians of the world.

"These people will be tried for having placed their lives on the altar of Good and Justice," he wrote in March 1977. "On March 27, 1977, thousands of our brothers and sisters—men, women, children, and the elderly—will fast and bow their heads in prayer for Yuri Orlov, Aleksandr Ginzburg, and Anatoly Shcharansky."

Goretoy was arrested in December 1979, found guilty of anti-Soviet propaganda under Article 70 of the RSFSR Criminal Code and of "attempted violation of individuality and rights of citizens under the guise of carrying out religious rituals," Article 227. He was sentenced to seven years in the camps and five in internal exile. He was freed in 1987, as part of Mikhail Gorbachev's limited amnesty.

Petr Grigorenko in November 1977 was granted a six-month travel visa to the United States to get medical care. In March 1978, he was informed that a decree of the Supreme Soviet had stripped him of Soviet citizenship "for behavior damaging the prestige of the Soviet Union" and "actions irreconcilable with citizenship of the Soviet Union."

Subsequently, Grigorenko wrote an eight hundred-page memoir that, among other things, gave the serial number of a rifle he was issued in 1922 (No. 232684) and included a picture of Grigorenko, looking tough as nails, in front of the Golden Gate Bridge. He died in 1987.

Malva Landa, following a December 1976 fire in her apartment, was convicted for "negligent destruction or damaging of state property and personal property." Landa, who claimed the fire was set by the KGB, served eight months of her term and was released in an amnesty in honor of the sixtieth anniversary of the October Revolution. She lives outside Moscow.

Sanya Lipavsky appeared as a witness for the prosecution at the Shcharansky trial. In 1979, a Soviet prosecutor who had emigrated to Israel said that Lipavsky had become a KGB informer in 1962 to save his father, who had been arrested for economic crimes and was threatened with execution. Lipavsky's whereabouts are unknown.

Anatoly Marchenko was released from internal exile in 1979 and rearrested two years later, after persistently ignoring KGB threats that unless he emigrated he would be arrested. He was convicted of "anti-Soviet propaganda" and, as a repeat offender, was given an especially harsh sentence: ten years in strict-regimen camps and five in internal exile. In August 1986, Marchenko went on a hunger strike, demanding freedom for political prisoners, resumption of visitation rights for his wife, and an official inquiry into a 1983 incident in which camp guards beat his head against the cement floor. He died of a cerebral hemorrhage on December 8, 1986, after having spent twenty of his forty-eight years in the Soviet penal system.

Mark Morozov, the mathematician who befriended a KGB captain, committed suicide in the Christopol prison in 1986. He was to be released in October 1993.

Viktor Orekhov, the KGB captain who, through Mark Morozov, warned Orlov about his impending arrest, was himself arrested in the summer of 1978, charged with communication of information on ongoing KGB operations, and sentenced to twelve years in the camps.

Yuri Orlov served nine years of his twelve-year term.

In 1983, while Orlov was serving the sixth year of his sentence in a Siberian camp, the U.S. Helsinki Watch Committee, a New York human-rights group, published a poster with his picture.

FORGOTTEN MAN OF THE YEAR the poster said.

Orlov was released in a complicated U.S.-Soviet deal that also freed U.S. reporter Nicholas Daniloff. On October 5, 1986, when Orlov arrived at New York's Kennedy Airport, his first words to friends and the press were: "I have no hatred toward anyone."

He is a senior scientist at Cornell University's Physics Department. **Irina Orlova** returned to the USSR after a few months in the West.

Vladimir Pavlov, the worker who went out on Gorky Street and asked passersby if they could direct him to Orlov or Sakharov and who was later featured in a Helsinki-group document, was allowed to leave the USSR in 1977. He is living in Australia.

Viktoras Petkus, the Lithuanian group founder, was arrested in August 1977, sentenced to ten years of "special regimen" and five in internal exile. At this writing he is serving the internal-exile term.

Vitaly Rubin taught Chinese philosophy at Hebrew University in Jerusalem. He died in an auto accident in 1981.

Mykola Rudenko was arrested in February 1977 and sentenced to seven years in the camps and five in internal exile. His wife, **Raisa,** was sentenced to five years in the camps and five in internal exile for sending his prison poetry to the West. Both were freed during Gorbachev's limited amnesty in 1987, and have left the USSR.

Andrei Sakharov was arrested in Moscow in January 1980 and sent to the closed industrial city of Gorky, 240 miles east of the capital. He was not convicted of any crime. His wife, **Yelena Bonner,** in 1984 was convicted under Article 190-1 and sentenced to internal exile in Gorky. In December 1986, in a telephone conversation, Soviet leader Gorbachev invited Sakharov to "return to patriotic work" in Moscow. Soon thereafter Bonner was pardoned.

Fyodor Sidenko, a Pentecostal-emigration activist who first met Ginzburg in the Snakepit, was arrested in October 1979, served a three-year term for anti-Soviet propaganda, then was committed to a mental institution. He was released in 1986.

Vladimir Slepak and his wife, **Maria,** on July 1, 1979, after more than nine years of fighting for an exit visa, walked out on the balcony of their Moscow apartment and unfurled banners saying LET US GO TO OUR SON IN ISRAEL. The banners attracted a crowd on Gorky Street below, and later that day the Slepaks were arrested. The two were found guilty of hooliganism. Vladimir was sentenced to five years in internal exile and Maria to three years' probation and three years under surveillance. In the fall of 1987, more than seventeen years after they first applied, the Slepaks were allowed to emigrate.

Nina Strokata, a member of the Ukrainian group, and her husband, **Svyatoslav Karavansky,** left the USSR in 1979. They live in Denton, Maryland.

Vladimir Shelkov, the Adventist leader who printed the Helsinki-group stationery at his True Witness publishing house, was hiding out in Soviet central Asia when he heard about Ginzburg's and Orlov's arrests. The news moved the octogenarian to write a letter to President Carter:

"In the name of the Lord, in the name of Jesus Christ, the martyr of the Golgotha, in the name of His fairness and His justice, I beseech you, dear Mr. President, as a Christian, to raise your authoritative, powerful voice in defense of A. I. Ginzburg, Yu. F. Orlov, A. D. Sakharov, and others. . . . I beseech you, as a Christian, in the name of the Word of the Lord: 'Rescue those who are being taken away to death; hold back those who are stumbling to the slaughter. (Proverbs 24:11)'"

On March 14, 1978, a year and three weeks after Shelkov wrote the letter to Carter, the KGB burst into his hideout in Central Asia. A year later, the eighty-four-year-old Shelkov was found guilty of religious and anti-Soviet propaganda, sentenced to five years' imprisonment, and sent to a labor camp in Yakutia. He died on January 27, 1980, after a year and a half in the camps. When Shelkov's family asked if they could transport his body back home, the camp administrator said Shelkov still had three years to serve. "Come back in three years," the administrator said. Shelkov's True Witness publishing house continues its work.

Oleksa Tikhy was arrested in February 1977, sentenced to ten years in a "special regimen" camp and five in internal exile. He died in the camp in 1984.

Valentin Turchin, Orlov's graduate-school friend and one of the founders of the unofficial USSR chapter of Amnesty International, is teaching computer science at New York University.

Tomas Venclova was allowed to lecture in the United States in January 1977. Six months later, his Soviet citizenship was revoked. Since then he has published five books and finished a Ph.D. He is professor of Slavic literature and the Lithuanian language at Yale University.

Lydia Voronina, after earning a doctorate in philosophy at Boston University, took a job with the Voice of America. She and her American-born daughter Svetlana live in Arlington, Virginia.

EPILOGUE

Afer the KGB strangled all forms of open dissent in the USSR, the monitoring of Soviet performance under the Helsinki Final Act was carried out almost exclusively in the West.

In the U.S. Congress, the Commission on Security and Co-operation in Europe published the findings of all Soviet Helsinki monitoring groups. It gave countless briefings—and heard testimony from Washington insiders, released Soviet prisoners of conscience, former refuseniks, and American businessmen interested in trade with the USSR.

Most Americans have never heard of the commission. Yet, despite its obscurity, it is a place where U.S. officials can get reliable information on what it is Soviet dissidents want. The commission's staff has briefed delegates to Helsinki review conferences in Belgrade, Madrid, and Vienna. At those conferences, whenever the Soviets attempt to defend their human-rights record, the West has been able to provide evidence to the contrary. Much of this evidence is kept in the commission's filing cabinets in House Annex 2. There are files on Ukrainian poets, Lithuanian separatists, Russian priests, Leningrad trade unionists, Ilynka Jews, Uzbek mullahs, Moscow Hare Krishnas. There are files on the persecuted peaceniks, environmentalists, and fans of heavy-metal music. There are also files on Orlov, Ginzburg, Shcharansky, Bonner, Sakharov, Landa, Rudenko, Nekipelov, Marchenko.

The commission is not alone in monitoring the Final Act. In 1978, a Helsinki Committee was formed in Norway. In essence, it was a loose affiliation of civil libertarians, quite similar in spirit to Amnesty International or the American Civil Liberties Union. Like the Orlov group, the West's Helsinki monitors represent the intellectual elites.

In 1979, the U.S. Helsinki Watch Committee was formed in New York. In 1982, at a conference in Bellagio, Italy, an umbrella organization—the International Helsinki Federation for Human Rights—was created. The association, based in Vienna, has ten member groups in Western Europe and North America.

Over the past decade, the West has been relentless in demanding that the Soviets improve their performance on human rights. The Soviets, too, were relentless in stating and restating their position that monitoring constitutes interference in the Soviet Union's internal affairs. This standoff lasted until the Soviets realized that any meaningful summit with the West where the issue of human rights is not addressed is simply unthinkable.

On January 16, 1987, Yuri Kashlev, head of the Soviet delegation at a Helsinki Final Act review conference in Vienna, announced the impending release of about two hundred people convicted on the charges of "anti-Soviet propaganda" and "slandering the Soviet government."

"These people, in the past, have made us uncomfortable and strained our relations with other countries," Kashlev said. That was nothing less than the first admission of the existence of political prisoners. In 1987, the Soviets freed about five hundred prisoners of conscience.

A group of released prisoners has formed a Moscow-based

club, *Glasnost,* named after a dissident slogan adopted by Gorbachev. The club has spun off a seminar on human rights, which promptly joined the International Helsinki Federation for Human Rights. The "seminar" is also in contact with the New York-based Helsinki Watch Committee and the congressional Helsinki Commission.

In 1987, the Helsinki Watch Committee and the staff of the Commission on Security and Cooperation in Europe were allowed to visit the USSR. That constituted a reversal of a decade-old Soviet policy of decrying all Western efforts to monitor Soviet performance under the Final Act.

All this still leaves a lot of room for improvement, but any one of these recent developments can be called a breakthrough. Together, they demonstrate that in 1987 the Soviet Union has acknowledged political reality.

It was Yuri Orlov who shaped that reality.

SOURCES

INTERVIEWS

Michael Alexeev
Ludmilla Alexeyeva
Eduard Arutyunyan
Mikhail Bernshtam
Yevgeny Bressenden
Catherine Cosman
Millicent Fenwick
Catherine A. Fitzpatrick
Dorothy Fosdick
Alfred Friendly, Jr.
Martin Garbus
Aleksandr Ginzburg
Jerry Hough
Donald Jameson
Irina Korsunskaya
Aleksandr Korsunsky

George Krimsky
Yefrosinya Kulabukhova
Irene Manekofsky
Warren L. Miller
Yuri Orlov
Peter Osnos
Harold Piper
Louis Rosenblum
Anatoly Shcharansky
Nina Strokata
Robert C. Toth
Valentin and Tatiana Turchin
Yuri Tuvim
Tomas Venclova
Lydia Voronina
Nikolai Williams
Christopher S. Wren

PRIVATE PAPER COLLECTIONS AND ARCHIVES

Ludmilla Alexeyeva, private archive.
Alfred Friendly, Jr., private archive.
Commission on Security and Cooperation in Europe, U.S. Congress, archives.
Helsinki Watch Committee archives.
Henry M. Jackson Foundation archives.
Vitaly Rubin's diary in unedited and unpublished form. It is being prepared for publication in Russian: Vitaly Rubin.
Dnevniki, pisma. Jerusalem: Biblioteka Aliya.
Radio Free Europe/Radio Liberty Bulletins. Munich.
George Krimsky, private archive.
Irene Manekofsky, private archive.
Anatoly Marchenko, *Zhivi kak vse,* a manuscript being prepared for publication.
Lydia Voronina, private archive.

BOOK LIST

Throughout this book, I did not use English translations of many Russian-language materials. This is by no means a reflection on the quality of translations. (In fact, glancing at some I found them smoother than the originals.) Nonetheless, translators and editors frequently leave out details they consider tangential, unclear, or impossible to relay to a Western reader.

The list includes Russian-language sources and all the translations I am aware of, though in most cases I have not consulted the translations. In chapter source notes I do not refer to translations. Newspaper and magazine stories are cited in the source notes only when their dates of publication are not mentioned in the text.

Albright, Madeleine K., and Alfred Friendly, Jr., "Helsinki and Human Rights," in *The President, the Congress and Foreign Policy,* Edmund S. Muskie, Kenneth Rush, Kenneth W. Thompson, editors. Lanham, Md.: University Press of America, 1986.
Alexeyeva, Ludmilla. *Istoriya inakomysliya v SSSR.* Benson,

Vt.: Khronika Press, 1984. [Translation: *Soviet Dissent: Contemporary Movements for National, Religious and Human Rights.* Middletown, Ct.: Wesleyan University Press, 1985.]

Alexeyeva, Ludmilla. "Yuri Orlov—rukovoditel' Moskovskoy Helsinkskoy gruppy," *Kontinent,* Nos. 21, 22. Paris: 1978.

Alexeyeva, Ludmilla, editor. *Delo Orlova.* New York: Khronika Press, 1980.

Alexeyeva, Ludmilla, editor. *Sbornik dokumentov obshchestvennoy gruppy sodeystviya vypolneniyu Helsinskikh soglasheniy,* Vols. 1 through 8. New York: Khronika Press, 1977. [English language compilation: Commission on Security and Cooperation in Europe. *Documents of the Helsinki Monitoring Groups in the USSR and Lithuania (1976–1986.* Washington: U.S. Government Printing Office, 1986.]

Amalrik, Andrei. *Prosushchestvuyet li Sovetskiy Soyuz do 1984 goda?* Amsterdam: Fond Gerzena, 1969. [Translation: *Will the Soviet Union Survive Until 1984?* New York: Harper & Row, 1984.]

Amalrik, Andrei. *SSSR i Zapad v odnoy lodke.* London: Overseas Publications Interchange, 1978.

Amalrik, Andrei. *Statyi i pisma, 1967–1970.* Amsterdam: Fond Gerzena, 1971.

Amalrik, Andrei. *Zapiski dissidenta.* Ann Arbor, Mich.: Ardis, 1982. [Translation: *Notes of a Revolutionary.* New York: Knopf, 1982.]

Arzhak, Nikolai (Yuli Daniel). *Govorit Moskva.* New York: Inter-Language Literary Associates, 1966. [Translation: *This Is Moscow Speaking.* London: Collins; Harvill P., 1968.]

Berdyayev, Nikolai. *Samopoznaniye: opyt filosofskoy avtobiografii.* Paris: YMCA Press, 1949.

Brzezinski, Zbigniew. *Power and Principle: Memoirs of the National Security Adviser 1977–1981.* New York: Farrar, Straus, Giroux, 1983.

Carter, Jimmy. *A Government as Good as Its People.* New York: Simon and Schuster, 1977.

Commission on Security and Cooperation in Europe. *Profiles: The Helsinki Monitors.* Washington: U.S. Government Printing Office, 1979.

Dershowitz, Alan M. *The Best Defense*. New York: Vintage Books, 1983.

Doder, Dusko. *Shadows and Whispers: Power Politics Inside the Kremlin from Brezhnev to Gorbachev*. New York: Random House, 1986.

Fitzpatrick, Catherine. *The Moscow Helsinki Monitors: Their Vision, Their Achievement, the Price They Paid*. New York: Helsinki Watch Committee, 1986.

Fosdick, Dorothy, editor. *Staying the Course: Henry M. Jackson and National Security*. Seattle: University of Washington Press, 1987

Garbus, Martin. *Traitors and Heroes: A Lawyer's Memoir*. New York: Atheneum, 1987.

Ginzburg, Aleksandr. *Istoriya odnoy golodovki, May–Iyn 1969 g*. Frankfurt: Possev, 1971.

Grigorenko, Petro. *V podpolye mozhno vstretit tolko krys*. New York: Detinets, 1981. [Translation: *Memoirs: Petro G. Grigorenko*. New York: Norton, 1982.]

The Jerusalem Post. Anatoly and Avital Shcharansky: The Journey Home. San Diego: Harcourt Brace Jovanovich, 1986.

Kaminskaya, Dina. *Zapiski advokata*. Benson, Vt: Khronika Press. 1984. [Translation: *Final Judgment: My Life as a Soviet Defense Attorney*. New York: Simon and Schuster, 1982.]

Litvinov, P., M. Meyerson-Aksenov, and B. Shragin. *Samosoznaniye: sbornik statey*. New York: Khronika Press, 1976.

Marchenko, Anatoly. *Moi pokazaniya*. Paris: La Presse Libre, 1969. [Translation: *My Testimony*. New York: E. P. Dutton, 1969.]

Orbach, William W. *The American Movement to Aid Soviet Jews*. Amherst: University of Massachusetts Press, 1979.

Rudenko, Mykola. *Prozrinnya*. Baltimore: V. Symonenko Smoloskyp Publishers, 1978.

Sakharov, Andrei. *O strane i mire*. New York: Khronika, 1976. [Translation: *My Country and the World*. New York: Knopf, 1975.]

Sakharov, Andrei. *Trevoga i nadezhda*. New York: Khronika, 1978. [Translation: *Alarm and Hope*. New York: Alfred A. Knopf, 1978.]

Scammell, Michael. *Solzhenitsyn: A Biography.* New York: W. W. Norton & Co., 1984.

Shcharansky, Avital, with Ilana Ben Joseph. Stefani Hoffman, translator. *Next Year in Jerusalem.* New York: William Morrow and Co., Inc., 1979.

Vance, Cyrus. *Hard Choices: Critical Years in America's Foreign Policy.* New York: Simon and Schuster, 1983.

CHAPTER 1

Reconstructing the events leading to the start of the group, I relied primarily on Alexeyeva's *Yuri Orlov—rukovoditel' Moskovskoy Helsinkskoy gruppy* (*Kontinent,* Nos. 21, 22. Paris, 1978), which was written only months after she emigrated from the USSR; numerous interviews with Alexeyeva, Ginzburg, Bernshtam, Toth, Krimsky, Orlov, Shcharansky.

The history of the Jackson-Vanik Amendment is from the Fosdick and Manekofsky interviews; William W. Orbach, *The American Movement to Aid Soviet Jews* (Amherst: University of Massachusetts Press, 1979); and Dorothy Fosdick, editor, *Staying the Course: Henry M. Jackson and National Security* (Seattle: University of Washington Press, 1987).

The description of the American Jewish movement is from Manekofsky interviews; *The Vigil: Information from the Washington Committee for Soviet Jewry,* Issues 1 through 50, November 1973 to May 1979; Orbach; and Alan Dershowitz, *The Best Defense* (New York: Vintage Books, 1983).

Sources on the reaction to the signing of the 1975 Final Act of the Conference on Security and Cooperation in Europe: Alexeyeva, Fenwick, Fosdick, Ginzburg, Krimsky, Orlov, and Toth interviews; and Madeleine K. Albright and Alfred Friendly, Jr., "Helsinki and Human Rights," in *The President, the Congress and Foreign Policy,* Edmund S. Muskie, Kenneth Rush, Kenneth W. Thompson, editors (Lanham, Md.: University Press of America, 1986); "Showtime in Helsinki," *Time,* Aug. 4, 1975.

CHAPTER 2

Biographical information on Orlov is from Orlov, Alexeyeva, Ginzburg, and Turchin interviews; Orlov's letters from the camps to his wife, Irina; Alexeyeva's compilation of documents in Orlov's biography, *Delo Orlova* (New York: Khronika Press, 1980); and Amalrik, *Zapiski dissidenta* (Ann Arbor, Mich.: Ardis, 1982).

Descriptions of the southwest Moscow area where Orlov, Alexeyeva, Ginzburg, and the Turchins lived are based on interviews with Orlov, Alexeyeva, Ginzburg, the Turchins, Fenwick, Krimsky, and Toth. Details of Ginzburg's biography are from Ginzburg interviews; Ginzburg's *Istoriya odnoy golodovki;* and Michael Scammell, *Solzhenitsyn: A Biography* (New York: W. W. Norton & Co., 1984). Sources on the workings of the Russian Social Fund: Ginzburg and Alexeyeva interviews; Scammell.

Yevtushenko's account of his conversation with Robert F. Kennedy is in *Time,* Feb. 9, 1987. Donald Jameson's story disputing Yevtushenko's version of the events is in *The New Republic,* June 22, 1987.

The history of the Soviet human-rights movement is based on Alexeyeva, Ginzburg, Orlov, and Korsunskaya interviews; the diary of Vitaly Rubin; Andrei Sakharov, *O strane i mire* (New York: Khronika, 1976); Andrei Sakharov, *Trevoga i nadezhda* (New York: Khronika, 1978); Nikolai Arzhak (Yuli Daniel), *Govorit Moskva* (New York: Inter-Language Literary Associates, 1966); Amalrik; Anatoly Marchenko, *Moi pokazaniya* (Paris: La Presse Libre, 1969) and *Zhivi kak vse,* a manuscript being prepared for publication; Dina Kaminskaya, *Zapiski advokata* (Benson, Vt: Khronika Press, 1984); and *Khronika tekushchikh sobytiy,* Nos. 1–15 (Amsterdam: Fond Imeni Gertsena, 1979).

The petitions that followed the crackdown on the intelligentsia after the fall of Khrushchev were being named after the number of people who signed them: the Letter of 170, the Letter of 80, the Letter of 24. Among the signatories was Andrei Sakharov, one of the creators of the Soviet hydrogen bomb, who at the time began to express concern about the disastrous effects of nuclear testing. Many of those who signed the open letters lost their jobs and foreign-travel privileges. Among those fired was Alexeyeva, who signed the Letter of 80. Sources on the Soviet human-rights movement's relationship with the Jewish movement: Alexeyeva, Ginzburg, Orlov, Shcharansky, and Manekofsky interviews; and the Rubin diaries. The text of Orlov's letter to Brezhnev is in Alexeyeva's *Delo Orlova*. Information about the period following Orlov's firing from IZMIRAN—and the KGB warning against starting dissident groups—is from Orlov interviews. The article "Is Nontotalitarian Socialism Possible?" is in *Samosoznaniye: sbornik statey* (New York: Khronika, 1976).

CHAPTER 3

Sources on Shcharansky's pre–Helsinki group work: Voronina, Toth, Krimsky, and Manekofsky interviews; Dershowitz; the Rubin diaries; and *The Jerusalem Post, Anatoly and Avital Shcharansky: The Journey Home* (San Diego: Harcourt Brace Jovanovich, 1986).

The description of Rubin is based on the Rubin diaries and interviews with Alexeyeva, Ginzburg, Orlov, Manekofsky, and Toth. In his autobiography, Amalrik writes that it was Rubin who suggested the title for his famous work *Will the Soviet Union Survive Until 1984?* Amalrik writes that he had not read Orwell's *1984*, which is banned in the USSR. The description of Amalrik is based on interviews with Alexeyeva, Nikolai Williams, and Ginzburg.

The description of Shcharansky's idea which led to the formation of the Moscow Helsinki group—and the idea's evolution—is from interviews with Shcharansky and Orlov. In an interview, Shcharansky said that he suspects that his name was not included in the original letter announcing the formation of the Moscow group because the group had too many Jewish members. Orlov said he did not include Shcharansky's name because he was unable to reach the young refusenik and get his final consent to join the group.

For nearly a decade, Alexeyeva has maintained that the names of all eleven members of the Moscow group were present in the document announcing its formation. After Orlov's release, it turned out that two members, Shcharansky and Malva Landa, were added to the list after the group's formation was announced. Also, it appears that the group was announced just after midnight—early on the morning of May 13. The Reuters story—as well as a one-paragraph Associated Press story—confirm that though the group's documents are dated May 12, the group was formed the following day. The Reuters and AP stories also indicate that the group had nine, not eleven, members.

The anatomy of Ginzburg's decision to join the Helsinki group is from Ginzburg interviews. Bernshtam's background, ideas, and decision to join the group are from Bernshtam interviews. The description of Landa is from interviews with Orlov and Alexeyeva. The description of Marchenko is based on interviews with Alexeyeva and Orlov; and the Marchenko books.

Grigorenko's decision to join the group is from his memoir, *V podpolye mozhno vstretit tolko krys* (New York: Detinets, 1981). When I began work on this book, Grigorenko was seriously ill, which made interviews impossible. Judging by the statements the general had made shortly after foreign radio stations announced that he was among the members of the Moscow Helsinki group, it appears that he was not fully aware of what the group would do. His memoir, in the original Russian, conveys the impression that Grigorenko had not been given a chance to think the matter through.

CHAPTER 4

Sources on Sakharov's background and relationship with other dissidents: *O strane i mire;* and the Alexeyeva, Orlov, and Shcharansky interviews. In an interview shortly after his release from exile in Gorky, Sakharov said, "Because of my psychological makeup and aspirations, I am not and cannot be leader of any movement." The remarks were published in *The Washington Post,* Dec. 28, 1986. In his memoirs, Amalrik made Sakharov's decision not to sign a number of dissident documents more controversial than it actually was. In fact, Sakharov has always made it clear that he did not like to sign group letters and take part in dissident groups.

The events of May 12 are from Orlov and Bernshtam interviews. I have gone back to both sources several times to make sure that their recollections coincide. The announcement of the group is in *Sbornik dokumentov obshchestvennoy gruppy sodeystviya vypolneniyu Helsinkskikh soglasheniy* (New York: Khronika Press, 1977). Henceforth, no references will be made to *Sbornik dokumentov*. Unless they appear elsewhere, all documents will be referred to by title or number.

Sources on Orlov's negotiations with Sakharov and Bonner: Orlov and Bernshtam interviews. Bonner, speaking through an interpreter, describes her decision to join the group in the May 12, 1986, conference: "I have to say, in the beginning, I think I joined the group only formally. I even said right at the outset that I wouldn't do any work. But I gave my name, so that people would not think that Sakharov was against the group." The transcript was published in *The New York Review of Books,* June 26, 1986.

Sadly, it will be impossible to answer some of the questions I had while comparing Grigorenko's written recollections of the group's formation with those of other group members. For instance, describing Orlov's telephone call, Grigorenko quotes this exchange:

Orlov: "'Petr Grigorievich, I want to announce the group. And I am counting on you.'

"'Yura, why do you need me, with my diseases? It's unlikely that I can be of any use to you now.'

"'We need your name.'

"'Well, if it's really so valuable, then let's continue this conversation tomorrow.'

"'No, it's impossible. I am calling from Andrei Dmitrievich's apartment. Foreign correspondents are already here. If I don't announce it today, then it seems I'll never announce it. For a week I have been followed by "our best friends."'

"'Well, then go ahead and include me.'"

Note that Grigorenko quotes Orlov's reference to "foreign correspondents," when in fact only one correspondent, from Reuters, showed up. Was this the case of Grigorenko making a slight error in his memoir? Or was it a case of Orlov using the plural in the hope that more reporters would show up? I am afraid this will never be known.

The text of Natalya Solzhenitsyn's note was reconstructed by Ginzburg in an interview.

CHAPTER 5

Grigorenko's second thoughts about the group are from interviews with Alexeyeva, Ginzburg, and Orlov. Reaction to the group is from *The New York Times,* May 14; *Los Angeles Times,* May 14; AP dispatch, May 14. "It's Meatless Thursday in Moscow Cafes," is from *Los Angeles Times,* May 14. Sources on Malva Landa's reluctance to join the group: Orlov, Alexeyeva, and Bernshtam interviews.

The description of Orlov's detention is from Orlov and Bernshtam interviews; Alexeyeva subsequently reconstructed the events for British attorney John Macdonald, who included it in a legal brief. Malva Landa's letter is in *Gruppa sodeystviya vypolneniyu Helsinkskikh soglasheniy v SSSR,* Nos. 25–26 (Frankfurt: Volnoye Slovo/Possev, 1977). This compilation contains a number of letters not included in the Khronika compilation.

The reconstructed conversation between Orlov and the KGB was taken from the Macdonald brief and confirmed by Orlov in an interview. The Tass story, "Warning to Provocateur," was most likely given to dissidents by a Western reporter. It was subsequently included in *Delo Orlova.*

The story about the KGB warning to Orlov is from *The New York Times,* May 16, 1976.

The Helsinki groups May 15 meeting is reconstructed by Bernshtam and confirmed by Alexeyeva. Details on Sakharov's and Bonner's trip to the Dzhemiliev trial are from an AP story that appears as "Sakharovs Ask Trial to 'Air Injustice,'" *Los Angeles Times,* April 17, 1976. The story said: "Sakharov . . . told Western correspondents that he hit a uniformed policeman in the face while being dragged from a court hallway in the Siberian city of Omsk. . . . Yelena, his 53-year-old wife, said she struck two policemen in the same struggle that ensued when the authorities refused to let the couple into the courtroom. . . . 'I cannot deny that it happened,' Sakharov told reporters. . . . But, he added, 'In my opinion, the militiaman should have

stood on the side of the law and not on the side of the law violators.'"
The rationale for choosing the Dzhemiliev conviction for Document 1 is from an Alexeyeva interview.
The diplomats' reaction to the group is from Orlov interviews.

CHAPTER 6

Millicent Fenwick's remarks are from the *Congressional Record*, May 17, 1976. The history of the Commission on Security and Cooperation in Europe is from the Fenwick interview; and Albright and Friendly. Details of Fenwick's trip to the USSR are from Fenwick, Orlov, and Turchin interviews. Orlov's letter to Fenwick and Dante Fascell's reply to Orlov are from the archives of the Commission on Security and Cooperation in Europe.

CHAPTER 7

The reporters' initial reaction to the formation of the Moscow Group of Assistance to Implementation of Helsinki Agreements in the USSR is from Toth, Osnos, Krimsky, Piper, Friendly, and Orlov interviews. Amalrik's personal dislike for Osnos is from interviews with sources who asked not to be identified; and Amalrik's strong disagreement with Osnos's views of dissent is from his *SSSR i Zapad v odnoy lodke*.
Sources on the history of the relationship between dissidents and reporters: Alexeyeva and Ginzburg interviews; Amalrik in *Zapiski dissidenta*, and *Statiy i pisma*. Toth's and Krimsky's biographies, their strategies in treatment of the dissident story, their perception of their editors' interest in dissent, and their personal contacts with dissidents are from interviews with the two reporters. Toth's story about Voronina, "Her Mother Won't Let Her Emigrate," is in the *Los Angeles Times*, March 26, 1976.
Patrick J. Leahy's statement about bringing a letter to Shcharansky is in the transcript of the June 6, 1978, hearing of

the Commission on Security and Cooperation in Europe. (Transcript in *Implementation of the Helsinki Accords,* Vol. IV [Washington: U.S. Government Printing Office, 1978].) Leahy said: "I met Mr. Shcharansky in 1975 in Moscow. I had the pleasure of bringing him a couple of letters from his wife. . . . She gave me letters in a sealed condition here in Washington and I carried them in my jacket to Moscow and handed them over to him in the hotel room at the Hotel Rossiya. . . ."

Sources on Krimsky's "Soviet GI" story and the espionage accusations leveled by the Soviet newspapers against U.S. reporters: Friendly, Toth, and Krimsky interviews; Krimsky's notebooks; "Popravka Ts.R.U. . . ," *Literaturnaya gazeta,* May 27, 1976; "Vot tak-to, dzhentlmeny," *Literaturnaya gazeta,* June 23, 1976; Tsypin's letter is in *Vechernyaya Moskva,* May 17, 1977.

CHAPTER 8

Sources on Bernshtam's disagreement with the group and his subsequent departure: Bernshtam, Alexeyeva, Orlov, Ginzburg, Shcharansky, and Krimsky interviews.

A copy of Bernshtam's letter to "Yevrei v SSSR" is from Krimsky's archives. Bonner's outrage at the letter, as well as Sakharov's reaction, were described by Orlov and Alexeyeva. Ginzburg's conversation with Bernshtam, in which he relays Sakharov's and Bonner's reactions, is pieced together from interviews with Bernshtam and Ginzburg.

CHAPTER 9

The conversation preceding the May 27 press conference is from Rubin's diaries. Rubin's high regard for Sanya Lipavsky and the details of Rubin's departure are from his diary. Rubin's intent to recommend Lipavsky as his replacement in the Helsinki group is from a Shcharansky interview. Orlov's opinion of Lipavsky is from an Orlov interview.

CHAPTER 10

The descriptions of Rudenko, Petkus, Gamsakhurdia, and Shagen Arutyunyan are from *Profiles: The Helsinki Monitors* (prepared by the staff of the Commission on Security and Cooperation in Europe [Washington: U.S. Government Printing Office, 1979]); Alexeyeva, Orlov, Ginzburg, Arutyunyan, Venclova, and Strokata interviews. The histories of the Ukrainian, Armenian, Volga German, Meskhetian, Crimean Tatar, Baptist, and Seventh-day Adventist dissent are from *Istoriya inakomysliya*. Also consulted was *List of Political Prisoners in the USSR* (Munich: USSR News Brief, 1983).

Source on the Yefimenko story and the Moscow intelligentsia's reaction to the group: Alexeyeva interview.

Sources on Camp 17a and its inmates: Ginzburg, Bressenden, and Alexeyeva interviews; *List of Political Prisoners; Khronika,* Nos. 1–15; *Istoriya odnoy golodovki.* Sources on Pentecostal history and theology: Bressenden, Voronina, and Ginzburg interviews; *Istoriya inakomysliya.* Sources on the events immediately following Ginzburg's release from the camps, including his and Solzhenitsyn's attempts to aid the families of political prisoners: Ginzburg interview; Scammell in *Solzhenitsyn.*

Ginzburg, Alexeyeva, and Orlov learned "Vasya's" true identity after his arrest, when his photo was passed along to the West. But since "Vasya" was never charged with having served as a courier to the Moscow Helsinki group, and since he remains in the USSR, his name must remain secret. In an interview, Ginzburg said he was surprised to see the "Public Group of Assistance to Implementation of Helsinki Agreements in the USSR" stationery when Vasya delivered it to him. Orlov said he was not surprised. In fact, the Adventists had come to Orlov earlier and given him a chance to select the typeface for the stationery.

CHAPTER 11

Sources on Vladimir Pavlov: Helsinki group Document 9, Alexeyeva interview; Alexeyeva in *Kontinent.*

The story of the Ukrainian Baptist woman is in Document 5. Sources on the Ilynka Jews: Shcharansky, Toth, and Alexeyeva interviews; Toth story, "Soviet Jews Survive in 'Lost Place,'" *Los Angeles Times,* June 27, 1976. The most detailed account of Tarasov's testimony appears in the unofficial transcript of the trial of Tatiana Osipova, held March 31 through April 2, 1981. The transcript was compiled by her husband, Ivan Kovalev, and is held at Radio Liberty/Radio Free Europe Samizdat Archive.

Other *khodoki* stories are from Alexeyeva, Orlov, and Ginzburg interviews. The Nikolai Vilyams (Williams) story is in the *Los Angeles Times,* Oct. 18, 1976.

CHAPTER 12

Sources on Rudenko: Alexeyeva, Orlov, and Strokata interviews; *Istoriya inakomysliya; Profiles: The Helsinki Monitors;* the CSCE archives. The poem "The King of Tasmania" is in Mykola Rudenko's *Prozrinnya* (Baltimore: V. Symonenko Smoloskyp Publishers, 1978).

Sources on the connections between the Ukrainian dissidents and the Moscow human-rights activists: Strokata and Alexeyeva interviews. The first three of the Ukrainian-group documents are in *Sbornik dokumentov.*

CHAPTER 13

Sources on the Lithuanian group, its formation and its members: Venclova, Alexeyeva, Nikolai Williams, and Michael Alexeev interviews; *Profiles: The Helsinki Monitors; Istoriya inakomysliya.* The passage from *The Inspector General* is from *Collected Tales and Plays of Nikolai Gogol.* Constance Garnett, tr., Leonard J. Kent, ed. (New York: Pantheon Books, 1964). Venclova's and Alexeyeva's conversation with the Lithuanian education officials was reconstructed by Alexeyeva immediately after returning from Vilnius. It appears in *Khronika,* No. 43. The initial documents of the Lithuanian group are in *Sbornik dokumentov.* The scene at the press conference announcing the Lithuanian group was reconstructed by Alexeyeva and confirmed by Venclova. The report of the Petkus trial is in *Khronika*, No. 50.

CHAPTER 14

Sources on Voronina's biography: Voronina, Alexeyeva, Toth, and Krimsky interviews. The presentation at a seminar on Jewish culture was reconstructed by Voronina in an interview. The Pentecostals' arrival in Moscow and appearance before reporters is from an Alexeyeva interview. Background information on the Pentecostals in the USSR is from Yevgeny Bressenden, Nina Bressenden, and Yefrosinya Kulabukhova interviews and *Istoriya inakomysliya*. Sources on Voronina's trip to the northern Caucasus and Nakhodka: Voronina interviews; Voronina's report on the trip is in *Sbornik dokumentov*. Toth's story, "Pentecostals Seek to Leave Russia," is in *Los Angeles Times*, Jan. 1. 1977.

CHAPTER 15

Orlov described his search at a press conference, a report from which made the Jan. 24, 1977, issue of *Newsweek:* "When his doorbell gave a long, insistent ring, Yuri Orlov knew something was wrong. 'Only provincials and police use a long ring,' the 52-year-old Moscow physicist explained last week. Orlov refused to open up, but police broke the door in and turned the apartment upside down. After a lengthy search, they carted off documents Orlov had collected on Soviet mistreatment of political prisoners, religious groups and ethnic minorities." Orlov did not tell reporters why he refused to open the door. In an interview after his release from the USSR he said that while the police were demanding to come in, he was destroying documents.

Sources on the Ginzburg search: *Sbornik dokumentov;* Ginzburg and Krimsky interviews. Sources on Alexeyeva's search: *Sbornik dokumentov;* Alexeyeva, Alexeev, Williams, Krimsky, and Voronina interviews. The quotations from Alexander Zinoviev's *The Yawning Heights* are translated by Jordon Clough. The Victor Nekipelov poem is from *Kontinent*, No. 12,

1977. Sources on Voronina's search: Voronina's exchange with the investigator is from *Sbornik dokumentov;* Voronina interview. Krimsky's story about the searches is from the printout off the AP Teletype kept in Krimsky's records.

CHAPTER 16

Sources on Orlov's conduct after the search, his letter about a "war," and his apprehension by the KGB: Orlov, Alexeyeva, Ginzburg, and Voronina interviews; Alexeyeva in *Kontinent;* Krimsky archive; UPI, "Russ Dissident Arrested on Way to News Conference," *Los Angeles Times,* Jan. 6, 1977.

The description of Ginzburg's press conference is from *Sbornik dokumentov;* Ginzburg, Alexeyeva, and Krimsky interviews. Sakharov's and Bonner's reluctance to sign Orlov's letter is from an Alexeyeva interview. The documents of the Initiative Group on Abuses of Psychiatry are in *Sbornik dokumentov;* Irina Kaplun's reaction to the reporters' insistence on talking about the searches is from Alexeyeva's interview. The circumstances of Voronina's permission to emigrate are from a Voronina interview. Orlov's letter to Fascell and Friendly's note that accompanied the letter when it was handed to the congressman are from the archives of the Commission on Security and Cooperation in Europe.

Orlov's repeated suggestions that Alexeyeva emigrate are from Alexeyeva interviews. Details of the interrogations are from Orlov, Ginzburg, and Alexeyeva interviews. Statements about the Moscow metro explosion are compiled in Sakharov's *Trevoga i nadezhda; Sbornik dokumentov;* David K. Willis, "Soviet Dissent Resisted. . . ," *Christian Science Monitor,* Jan 18, 1977; "Moscow Subway Blast Laid to Terrorist Bomb," *Los Angeles Times,* Jan. 11, 1977; "Small Explosion Could Grow," *The Washington Post,* Jan. 12, 1977; Paul Wohl, "Dissidents Differ on Subway Blast," *Christian Science Monitor,* Feb. 24, 1977.

In "Dissident Sakharov Accused of Making Slanderous Charges. . . ," *Los Angeles Times,* Jan. 29, 1977, Toth pointed out that Sakharov was out on a limb claiming that the KGB might have set the explosion: "Few people here believe the authorities would deliberately set off a lethal blast . . . just to blame dissidents and set them up for repression. Lesser excuses would serve the purpose." The story also quoted Sakharov's second statement about the blast and, putting the matter in perspective, said that in April 1976, Sakharov had "slapped a policeman who refused to let him into a trial in Omsk." Sakharov's original claim that the explosion might have been set by the KGB was reconstructed by Krimsky in an interview.

CHAPTER 17

Fascell's note to Vance is from Friendly's archive. The Carter speeches are from *A Government as Good as Its People* (New York: Simon and Schuster, 1977). The Dershowitz speech and the telephone conversation were taped by the Union of Councils for Soviet Jews. The tape is from Manekofsky's archives. The description of the JDL case and other work for Soviet Jewry is from Dershowitz's *The Best Defense*.

CHAPTER 18

The description of Orlov's party is from Orlov, Alexeyeva, Williams, and Voronina interviews; Alexeyeva in *Kontinent*. The fortune-telling is reconstructed in conversation with Williams using Agnes M. Miall, *The Book of Fortune-Telling* (London: Hamlyn, 1972). The telephone conversation with the United States was taped by the Union of Councils for Soviet Jews and obtained from Manekofsky. For sources on the metro explosion, see notes to Chapter 16.

The details of the press conference are from an interview with Alexeyeva. The events leading up to Sakharov's letter to Carter are from an interview with Garbus and his book *Traitors and Heroes: A Lawyer's Memoir* (New York: Atheneum, 1987).

CHAPTER 19

The Kendall CSCE testimony is from Jan. 13, 1977, Commission on Security and Cooperation in Europe hearings

("Basket II, Helsinki Final Act: East-West Economic Cooperation"). The description of *Traders of Souls* is from Manekofsky's
archives. The events leading up to Krimsky's expulsion and the
circumstances of the explosion are from Krimsky interviews and
archives.

CHAPTER 20

Sources on Ginzburg's arrest: Aleksandr Petrov-Agatov,
"Liars and Pharisees," *Literaturnaya gazeta*, Feb. 2, 1977;
Ginzburg interview. The atmosphere at the press conference at
Ginzburg's apartment was described by Alexeyeva. Sources on
Captain Orekhov and his warning to Orlov: Alexeyeva and Orlov interviews. Until Orlov's release from the USSR Alexeyeva
believed that Orlov was hiding in the village where he had spent
his childhood. Actually, Orlov said in an interview, he was hiding elsewhere. Irina Orlova's accusation to an American reporter is from Alexeyeva in *Kontinent* and an Alexeyeva
interview.

The phone calls to the Krimskys are from notes kept by
Paula Krimsky. The conversation with Ambassador Toon is
from Krimsky's interview. Toon's promise that a Soviet reporter
who was not a spy would be expelled from Washington was apparently not kept. Vladimir Alexeyev, the reporter, is believed
to have worked for the KGB. The connection came out at the
espionage trial of USIA employee Ronald L. Humphrey.
Sources: Christopher Dickey, "Suspect Reported Spy Bid, Trial
Told," *The Washington Post*, March 22, 1978; interview with
Warren L. Miller, Humphrey's attorney.

CHAPTER 21

The circumstances of Orlov's arrest are from Alexeyeva, Or-
lov, Alekseev, and Williams interviews; Alexeyeva in *Kontinent*.
The events leading up to Sakharov's letter to Carter are from
an interview with Garbus and his book *Traitors and Heroes*. The
Carter administration's decision to write to Sakharov is from the
Garbus book and interview; Zbigniew Brzezinski's *Power and*

Principle: Memoirs of the National Security Adviser 1977–1981 (New York: Farrar, Straus, Giroux, 1983) and Cyrus Vance's *Hard Choices: Critical Years in America's Foreign Policy* (New York: Simon and Schuster, 1983). The Carter inaugural address is from *A Government as Good as Its People*. Bonner's remark that she and Sakharov were surprised to see the letter to Carter released to the press is from a Friendly interview.

CHAPTER 22

Lipavsky's Feb. 25, 1977, letter to Dante Fascell is from Manekofsky's archives. Rubin's reaction to Lipavsky's allegations is from his diaries. The circumstances of Shcharansky's arrest are from interviews with Shcharansky and Piper, and Harold Piper, "Jewish Dissident Freed as Soviets Arrest Another," *The Baltimore Sun*, March 16, 1977.

CHAPTER 23

Alexeyeva's arrival in the West, the account of her dinner with Jeremy Thorpe and her meeting with John Macdonald is from Alexeyeva interviews and from Macdonald's brief for Orlov's defense.

Edward Bennett Williams's testimony is in *Hearings Before the Commission on Security and Cooperation in Europe*, Vol. IV, "Soviet Helsinki Watch, Reports on Repression," June 3, 1977. Information on the Williams and Connolly defense of Ginzburg is from the firm's archives.

The NBC June 12 debate is from the transcript. The transcript notes that a person from the audience stands up and causes a disturbance. In his book, *The Best Defense*, Dershowitz identifies that person as Avital Shcharansky. Details on Dershowitz's lobbying the White House on Shcharansky's behalf are from the book. My repeated attempts to ask Dershowitz why he didn't mention at the debate that he represented Shcharansky were unsuccessful.

CHAPTER 24

Toth's detention and interrogation is from Toth interviews and his stories in the *Los Angeles Times:* "Times Correspondent in Russia 'Detained' by KGB," June 12, 1977; "Toth's Story: From the Chilling to the Ludicrous," June 19, 1977; "Shcharansky, Newsman Recall Arrest," Feb. 15, 1986.

CHAPTER 25

The Jane Pauley interview with Avital Shcharansky and Millicent Fenwick is from a tape-recording of the broadcast.

The details on the Israeli reaction to the Shcharansky case and the rift in the Jewish movement is from the Manekofsky interviews and archives. The letter from Richard Krieger to Manekofsky is from the Manekofsky archives. The "grass-roots" groups' concerns and dissatisfaction with the Israelis were stated at a meeting of Soviet Jewry activists in Israel April 4, 1978. At the meeting, Nechemiah Levanon, head of Israel's Soviet Jewry office, said that Israel would distribute its lists of refuseniks on a "need-to-know" basis and would deal only with "establishment" groups. Levanon also expressed disappointment with the fact that more than half of the Soviet Jews were going to the United States. The meeting was recorded, and the tape is from Manekofsky's archive.

The Israeli and the "establishment's" initial reaction to Shcharansky's arrest is detailed by Michael Sherbourne at the same meeting. The account of a statement of an Israeli official at the embassy in Washington is from a Toth interview. The account of the Knesset member's discussion with the Soviet Jewry office in Israel is from Robert A. Toth, "Soviet Dissidents Isolated by West's Official Silence," *Los Angeles Times,* March 4, 1979. Avital Shcharansky's remarks about battles in the Jewish movement in the West are from Phil Bronstein, "Internal Battles Hurt Soviet Jewry," *Northern California Jewish Bulletin,* July 28, 1978.

CHAPTER 26

Orlov's final statement to the court is from *Delo Orlova*. Ginzburg's exchange with the judge is from an unofficial transcript from the Helsinki Commission archive. Shcharansky's last word is from *Khronika*, No. 50.

Arrest figures are from Reddaway's paper, *Soviet Policies on Dissent and Emigration: The Radical Change of Course Since 1979*, Occasional Paper No. 192, presented August 28, 1984, at Kennan Institute for Advanced Russian Studies. Information about arrests in the USSR sometimes takes years to reach the West, and, Reddaway said in 1987, new information has arrived since he completed the paper. Reddaway said, however, his conclusions about the overall trend in levels of arrest from year to year remain valid. Emigration figures are from the National Conference on Soviet Jewry.

Biographical notes are from *Delo Orlova, V podpolye mozhno vstretit tolko krys, Zhivi kak vse, The Moscow Helsinki Monitors, List of Political Prisoners in the USSR;* Paul Goldberg, "Marchenko Died in Battle," *The Washington Post,* Dec. 14, 1986; Alexeyeva, Ginzburg, Orlov, Strokata, and Venclova interviews and Helsinki Watch and Helsinki Commission archives.

INDEX